MORE STORIES FROM LANGLEY

MORE STORIES FROM LANGLEY

Another Glimpse inside the CIA

Edited and with an introduction by Edward Mickolus

Potomac Books

An imprint of the University of Nebraska Press

An earlier version of chapter 11 first appeared as "Spy versus Spy: A Hoosiers Tale of Espionage and Basketball during the Cold War," *Indiana Alumni Magazine* 38 (May/June 2008): 34–38. An earlier version of chapter 20 first appeared as "Developing a Better Understanding of the Personal Dimensions of Working at the Central Intelligence Agency," *Journal of Strategic Security* 8, no. 5 (2015): 1–14, http://scholarcommons.usf.edu/jss/vol8/iss5/1/. Updated and reprinted with permission.

Earlier versions of chapters 24 and 25 first appeared on https://www.ingloriousamateurs.com /blogs/cables/the-cia-book-of-honor and https://www.ingloriousamateurs.com/blogs/cables /camp-chapman-anniversary and are reprinted with permission.

Chapter 28 first appeared in *CIRA Quarterly* (Fall 2016) and is reprinted with permission.

This book has been reviewed by the CIA's Publications Review Board. This does not constitute an official release of CIA information. All statements of fact, opinion, or analysis expressed are those of the authors and do not reflect the official positions or views of the Central Intelligence Agency (CIA) or any other U.S. Government agency. Nothing in the contents should be construed as asserting or implying U.S. Government authentication of information or CIA endorsement of the authors' views. This material has been reviewed solely for classification.

Library of Congress Cataloging-in-Publication Data
Names: Mickolus, Edward F., editor of compilation.
Title: More stories from Langley: another glimpse inside the CIA / edited and with an introduction by Edward Mickolus.
Description: Lincoln: Potomac Books, an imprint of the University of Nebraska Press, 2020. | Includes bibliographical references and index.
Identifiers: LCCN 2020000750
ISBN 9781640123694 (paperback)
ISBN 9781640123755 (epub)
ISBN 9781640123762 (mobi)
ISBN 9781640123779 (pdf)
Subjects: LCSH: United States. Central Intelligence Agency—Officials and employees— Biography—Anecdotes. | United States. Central Intelligence Agency—History—Anecdotes. | Intelligence officers—United States—Biography—Anecdotes. | Spies—United States— Biography—Anecdotes. | Intelligence service—United States—Anecdotes.
Classification: LCC JK468.I6 S754 2020 | DDC 327.12730092/2—dc23
LC record available at https://lccn.loc.gov/2020000750

Set in Lyon Text by Mikala R. Kolander.

To those 133 officers, named and unnamed, who are recognized on the CIA's Memorial Wall. They include:

Douglas S. Mackiernan
Jerome P. Ginley
Norman A. Schwartz
Robert C. Snoddy
Wilburn S. Rose
William P. Boteler
Franck G. Grace, Jr.
Howard Carey
James J. McGrath
Chiyoki Ikeda
Stephen Kasarda, Jr.
Leo F. Baker
Wade C. Gray
Thomas W. Ray
Riley W. Shamburger, Jr.
Nels L. Benson
John G. Merriman
Barbara A. Robbins
Buster E. Edens
John W. Waltz
Edward Johnson
Michael Deuel
Michael A. Maloney

Louis A. O'Jibway
Walter L. Ray
Billy Jack Johnson
Jack W. Weeks
Wayne J. McNulty
Richard M. Sisk
Paul C. Davis
David L. Konzelman
Wilbur Murray Greene
Raymond L. Seaborg
John Peterson
John W. Kearns
Raymond C. Rayner
William E. Bennett
Richard S. Welch
James A. Rawlings
Tucker Gougelmann
Robert C. Ames
Phyliss Nancy Faraci
Kenneth E. Haas
Deborah M. Hixon
Frank J. Johnston
James F. Lewis
Monique N. Lewis
Scott J. Van Lieshout
Curtis R. Wood
William F. Buckley
Richard D. Krobock
Matthew K. Gannon
Robert W. Woods
Barry S. Castiglione
Lawrence N. Freedman
Lansing H. Bennett, MD
Frank A. Darling
Freddie R. Woodruff

Jacqueline K. Van Landingham
James M. Lewek
John A. Celli
Leslianne Shedd
Thomas M. Jennings, Jr.
Molly H. Hardy
Johnny Micheal Spann
Helge P. Boes
Gregg David Wenzel
William Francis Carlson
Christopher Glenn Mueller
Gregory R. Wright, Jr.
Rachael A. Dean
Jeffrey R. Patneau
Jennifer L. Matthews
Harold E. Brown
Elizabeth C. Hanson
Darren J. LaBonte
Scott Michael Roberson
Dane Clark Paresi
Jeremy Jason Wise
Dario N. Lorenzetti
Marcell Rene Gough
Bill Wyrozemski
Pete McCarthy, Jr.
Charles Mayer
Mark S. Rausenberger
David Bevan
Darrell Eubanks
John Lewis

CONTENTS

After the publication of *Stories from Langley*, the contributing authors' families and friends inundated them with notes about how much they enjoyed having a published author/spy in their Rolodexes. The most entertaining anecdote came from contributor Hugh Pettis:

> Hi Ed! I hope this tale brightens your holidays! "Stories from Langley" has made a hit in the Shenandoah Valley—as follows.
>
> This past Monday afternoon (12/15/14) I was being prepped for an emergency esophageal procedure, lying flat on my back on the table while a surgical team bustled around the theater getting stuff ready—a young LPN equipment technician ("Ryan" by name), an RN surgical nurse, and one other RN and the anesthesiologist were setting up for the operation. Making conversation, he asked where I had worked for the USG before embarking on my academic post-retirement life.
>
> When I replied "CIA," Ryan almost flew to the ceiling like an over-excited Jack Russell terrier. "Oh wow!" he exclaimed. "I am the BIGGEST CIA buff—I have almost five hundred books on or about the CIA and its mission. What did you do?"
>
> I replied (of necessity) "I can't tell you. BUT, a book 'Stories from Langley' has just been published, and it will tell you what my work involved." (Mind you, Ed, I was half-groggy and about to go under the anesthetic.) Ryan whipped out an iPad, tapped on it, and called out to the crew, "I have it right here." A few more

taps and he declared, "And here is Hugh Pettis!" Much astonishment all around. They gathered around the table and Ryan read aloud your neat bio on me as one of the contributors to the book's firsthand accounts. The gastroenterologist came in. They took in Ryan's reading and shared his excitement.

"When did you start with the CIA?" Ryan then asked. "Early on," I managed to say, "incorporated by its OSS gang in 1949." Someone else (the surgical nurse perhaps) offered, "You must have a lot of secrets to share."

"I do," I replied, and turning to the anesthesiologist who was about to pump in my Happy-Land juice, I added, "Be careful. If that stuff is sodium pentothal [truth serum], you all may end up in mortal danger."

Ed—it was a great hit. I don't think Ryan has fully recovered yet from having a veteran CIA officer in sight, on hand, and talking—one embedded in one of his five hundred books about the agency.

Just thought you'd like to know your book flies with excitement in Virginia's Shenandoah Valley.

—Hugh

Always good to know that someone's reading your books!

This volume opens the discussion to all of the agency's directorates—the major organizational units within the agency. The contributors worked in the agency from the 1950s through the 2010s, when there were usually four directorates. Some had careers that spanned several decades, some became senior executives, some still serve, some toiled in one or several of the directorates. During most of that period, the directorates were as follows:

- Directorate of Intelligence (housing all-source analysts; called for a few years the National Foreign Assessment Center; now called the Directorate of Analysis)
- Directorate of Science and Technology (whose scientists and engineers built tiny gadgets, giant rockets that delivered satellite collection systems, and anything in between)

- Directorate of Administration (sometimes called Directorate of Support; sometimes divided into mission support groups, handling the day-to-day operation of a large organization)
- Directorate of Operations (sometimes called the National Clandestine Service, which housed those who collect intelligence, conduct counterintelligence operations, and run covert action programs)

Under then director John Brennan, a fifth directorate, the Directorate for Digital Innovation, was added in 2015 to reflect a change in the operational/analytical environment facing intelligence.

This book is designed to give those considering a career in the agency an idea of the spread of opportunities available. Watching movies or television shows and reading spy-fi novels would never lead one to think "I'm a librarian. I could work for the CIA." Yet two of the memoirs in this volume are from professional librarians who made the agency their life's work. Two public affairs officers also explain their contributions. Still others describe their roles as scientists, presidential briefers, managers, trainers, targeters, innovators, accountants, auditors, and logistics wizards. Others provide insights into life serving overseas, including some of the unexpected pressures. One chapter presents the results of numerous interviews about agency culture, conducted by an academic researcher with agency officers.

More Stories is also for the reader who wonders if all of those movies, TV shows, and novels are accurate. In these pages you will get a better idea of what actually takes place in the halls of headquarters and in overseas postings, and how a wide range of specialties contribute to making Americans safer and help policymakers make better-informed decisions.

More Stories salutes the lives of those who gave their lives in service to their country, as evidenced by the litany of stars on the CIA's Memorial Wall on the dedication page. Virtually every agency officer knows at least one of these brave officers. Not all of these heroes can be named; even in death, their covers must be protected to safeguard the lives of their families and their assets, some of whom still provide assistance in understanding the inner workings of their governments and organizations.

I've also included a list of books written by agency officers; a bibliography of scholarly journal pieces, newspaper op-eds, website postings, etc., would fill hundreds of pages. The readings here should guide readers to other stories told by those who served.

Finally, *More Stories* might just inspire one or two of you to think, "I wonder what I could do with my specialty?" and give a recruiter a call.

Ed Mickolus

Somewhere in northeastern Florida

MORE STORIES FROM LANGLEY

ONE

The Directorate of Intelligence

Do Your Brother a Favor

Apply to the CIA

ELIZABETH ARENS

The images of the CIA that you see in movies and read about in novels are of spies running through foreign capitals, chasing bad guys, and using high-tech gear to barely escape with their lives. Hollywood doesn't depict the other CIA, the one that consists of ordinary people—analysts, editors, graphics designers, and countless others who pack their lunches in Tupperware containers, sit in traffic, and vie for the best parking spaces. After a hard day's work, they pick up their kids at day care and go home to cook dinner, do the laundry, and pay the bills. This kind of life may not be as exciting as spying, but it is equally valuable to our country. And it does have its memorable moments. How do I know this? Because I recently concluded a career working for the U.S. intelligence community: for nearly twenty-five years, I was one of the U.S. government's ordinary people.

I first set foot on the CIA's campus in Langley, Virginia, sometime in the 1970s. I was attending high school in Vienna, Virginia, when a student came up with an innovative idea: for three days the students would take over the school and arrange classes in every subject imaginable—from basket weaving to astrology—and cool field trips to out-of-the-way places. The three-day extravaganza was called Free School, and in the spirit of the times, the principal agreed to the idea. For one of my activities I chose a field trip to the CIA. Looking back, I think one of the organizing kid's moms or dads must have worked there because the facility was—and remains—off-limits to the public. In any event, I boarded a school bus and soon found myself in the CIA's Bubble—its auditorium—watching a slideshow about the agency. "Interesting," I thought to myself, with no inkling that I would spend the bulk of my career working there.

Fast forward to 1985. I was working as a ghostwriter for a U.S. senator. I occasionally got to do some foreign travel, serving as an administrative assistant. One time I traveled around the world on Air Force One. Nice work if you can get it. Back in the United States, op-ed pieces that I drafted were appearing under the senator's name in newspapers such as the *Wall Street Journal*, the *New York Times*, the *Christian Science Monitor*, and others. I had an interesting, though stressful, job on Capitol Hill, but I wondered, "What next?" A former intern who had worked in our office one summer came to have lunch with me. She was attending Syracuse University and studying communications. I got interested in Syracuse's master's degree program in public communications, applied, won a scholarship, and traded my professional wardrobe in for jeans. I especially wanted to learn how to write scripts for radio and TV. I went to Syracuse intending to apply at Voice of America after I got my master's.

While at Syracuse, my brother, who was working for the Defense Intelligence Agency, suggested I apply to the CIA and mailed me an application. I didn't think I wanted to work for the CIA. After all, I was a creative type; I wasn't really into foreign affairs. I filled out the application only because I didn't want to hurt my brother's feelings.

When I was close to finishing my master's degree, I got a call from a manager at CIA. He said he would like to interview me for a scriptwriting position. So off I went for the interview at a building in the Navy Yard in Washington DC. It was an incredibly hot day and I had to park a long way from the CIA building. My makeup was melting off my face by the time I reached the door. The building had no windows and it was kind of spooky inside, but the job sounded interesting and I left hoping to be selected. I was. My security investigation was completed in a record three months because the agency very much wanted my scriptwriting skills.

I began writing scripts for CIA intelligence videos and later became a branch chief. One video that my team and I produced required that we fly on the agency's private jet to a secret location called The Farm. I felt a little like James (or Jane) Bond boarding the plane.

After a couple of years, again I wondered, "What next?" I picked up my secure phone line and called the CIA's Office of Public Affairs to see whether it had any openings. They were looking for a speechwriter for the director of central intelligence, then Judge William Webster, and his deputy, Dick Kerr. After applying and submitting several writing samples, I was hired.

Judge Webster left the CIA after my first year. Working for his successor, Bob Gates, in the early 1990s was an awesome experience. The Berlin Wall had just come down, and it was a new era for the intelligence community: threats had become more diffuse, and as Gates used to say, there were more mysteries and fewer secrets. One of my most poignant memories of my speechwriting days is of attending a ceremony for the dedication of a small part of the Berlin Wall, which was put on display outside CIA headquarters. It bears these words: "And the wind cries democracy, freedom. Tear down the wall." I could hardly believe that only a few years before, in 1986, as one of my last official duties as a U.S. Senate staffer, I had traveled to West Berlin and gone through Checkpoint Charlie into East Berlin. I had seen the soldiers doing their goose steps and gotten glimpses of residents trapped behind the wall. I could not have imagined then that the wall would come down in my lifetime. Yet here it was, a testament to the desire in every human heart for freedom—and to those who had died for that freedom.

After my two-year speechwriting tour was up, it was time again for me to ask myself, "What next?" I knew that my prospects would be dim if I returned to my home office, so I decided to look elsewhere. I had undergone foot surgery, was walking on crutches, and had a huge cast. The only clothing that would fit over my cast was a pair of wide-legged, army green corduroy shorts. Wearing those shorts—looking like an out-of-style hiker—I put my resume in my backpack and hobbled through CIA headquarters knocking on doors. A colleague had suggested that I apply to the National Intelligence Council (NIC). The NIC is the intelligence community's think tank, housed at CIA headquarters. The director of the NIC's Analysis and Production Staff (APS), whose name was Phil, interviewed me. The "interview" consisted mostly of Phil telling me long, fascinating stories about his adventures overseas. I must have been a good listener because the NIC/APS hired me.

As a senior analyst for NIC/APS, my job was to do analytic and editorial reviews of National Intelligence Estimates and other reports produced by the NIC. National Intelligence Estimates are the intelligence community's premier reports; they outline the views of all intelligence agencies on strategic issues for the president of the United States and senior policymakers. At first I thought to myself: Am I really qualified to do this job? What do I know about these issues? I soon realized that my relative ignorance was a strength: I was not expected to be an expert on subject X; rather, I was to read the reports as an intelligent generalist reader and raise questions.

Like patients coming into the emergency room, the reports that crossed my desk for review suffered from a variety of conditions: some needed only a good antiseptic and a few carefully placed band aids; others needed major surgery and some new body parts. During my years at the NIC, I did everything from copy editing to reorganizing and sometimes totally revamping reports. I had the most fun with the ones that needed the most work. I was like a kid in a sandbox, rebuilding a castle that someone else had made: too many turrets here . . . let's get rid of the seven doors to the castle—you only need one . . . and how about that statue by the pond—a bit ornate, isn't it? I'm sure that at times I was a thorn in writers' sides: I questioned the logic of their analysis, pressed them to define their terms, and picked, picked, picked at their language. I wanted every report I worked on to be the best that it could be.

I worked on reports on every national security topic imaginable, from humanitarian emergencies and climate change to terrorism and WMD. I have the dubious distinction of having served as the editor of the now-infamous 2002 National Intelligence Estimate on Iraq's WMD program. Working in the intelligence community gives you an insider's perspective that you can never, ever replicate "out there"—wherever "there" might be. I know the ins and outs of how the National Intelligence Estimate on Iraq's WMD was put together because I was there. I sat side by side with the analysts at the coordination meetings for that report and many others. At coordination meetings, the intelligence community's experts on a given subject discuss drafts line by line. I was blown away by the analysts' detailed knowledge. Sometimes coordination meetings would last for several days, sometimes they were contentious, and always they were fascinating. I got a free education that one could not get in any other venue. I know how the agency heads thought about critical issues because I was there—as a notetaker at National Intelligence Board meetings (the meetings where agency heads review and approve National Intelligence Estimates for publication). I listened to their discussions, aware that the reports being discussed would be read carefully by the president of the United States and senior policymakers.

Of course, not every moment of my career was filled with knock-your-socks off excitement. I spent many hours toiling in my cubicle: plunk, plunk, plunk went my fingers on the keyboard as the years melted away, almost twenty of them at the NIC. Even on the tedious days, though, I felt that I was a valued member of the team and enjoyed bantering with my colleagues. Toward the latter part of my NIC career, as the new century dawned, I began to ask myself again, "What next?" This time the answer came not from inside the CIA's hallowed halls, but from my own heart: I had been called to adopt a baby. I proceeded to do the paperwork and to prepare myself to walk the tightrope of single parenthood. Meanwhile, big changes were afoot in the intelligence community. The Office of the Director of National Intelligence opened on April 21, 2005. The same day, my daughter was born halfway around the world. Because the NIC is an IC organization—not exclusively a CIA entity—I was asked to convert to the Office of the Director of National Intelligence. I did so. In June 2006 I boarded a plane at Dulles Airport to bring my daughter home. My colleagues—and my boss—were incredibly supportive. I took six months off without pay to bond with my daughter.

When I returned, I changed to a part-time schedule, and six years later, in 2012, I retired. Today I work a few hours per week for the NIC as a contractor. I am an editorial "firefighter," one who is called upon to serve as needed. Occasionally, an unclassified project comes my way and I can work at home. My new life is full of American Girl dolls, play dates, and school projects. The other day, after dropping my daughter off at school, I sat down with a cup of tea, planning to spend the day tackling the laundry. The phone rang. A report had just arrived at NIC/APS that needed some work, and the inboxes of the full-timers were overflowing. Could I come in? I quickly changed from my grungy-looking outfit, threw on some professional clothes and makeup, and headed to my car. On that day, my country needed me, and I was happy to answer the call.

Reflections from an Analytical Change Agent

Twenty-Seven Years and Counting

A CURRENTLY SERVING DA OFFICER

Twenty-seven years. I can't believe it's been that long since I first stood on the agency seal and pledged to uphold the Constitution. It was 1990, and one year before that moment I was a senior and president of the student government at Simmons College—a women's college in Boston—ready to take on the world. I remember the day of my interview. One of our political science professors was adamantly against recruitment on campus by the agency. I walked around picketers, pledging my support for my fellow students for taking a stand for what they believed in. After all, I was their president. Nine months later, after spending some time in Europe traveling around with my college roommate (literally chipping away pieces of the Berlin Wall to take home), I was standing on the seal and taking the oath.

You might ask, and many have, how I could have spent the last twenty-five years at the same job, the same agency—and why CIA? I would argue, as many have before me, that each job I've held at the agency has been a dramatically different experience, so it isn't actually accurate to say I've been at the same job. In addition, the agency itself has changed substantially over the years, both in its mission and in the general environment, so I'm also not sure it's accurate to say it's the same agency.

Why CIA in the first place takes a little more explanation. I originally came to the agency because I got the travel bug during my junior year abroad in England and wanted to continue to travel. More importantly, however, I wanted to do something that had profound meaning. Too many of my friends at the time were going

9

off to work in industries whose sole purpose was to make money. My college roommate and I both pledged that we were going to do something more meaningful, to give back. I had graduated as a political science/finance major, was a near-miss for the Harry S. Truman Scholarship (a highly competitive program for political science majors granting full tuition for two years of undergraduate work and two for graduate school to those planning to be change agents in government, nonprofit, or educational institutions), and had spent a summer on Capitol Hill as an intern for then senator John Kerry during his first term. I had also worked on the Joe Kennedy (Robert's son, who won his uncle's seat in the eighth congressional district) campaign in Boston. Ever since my parents first took me to DC at the age of thirteen I knew I wanted to live in Washington. I always thought that it would be as a senator focused on domestic issues. However, that summer working on the Hill cured me of the dream to serve in public office. I didn't feel like the Hill would be the place where I could have the most profound impact since all I had seen were wheels spinning and spinning. I'd like to tell you that I then spent weeks researching executive branch jobs and discovered after careful consideration of a number of viable options that the agency was for me, but I'd be lying if I did. The agency happened to come to my campus during my senior year, and I happened to interview with them. At the time it seemed like a good fit. "I'll try this for a few years," I thought to myself, "and then move back to Boston." A few years turned into a few more, and before I knew it I was standing in front of a room of my peers collecting my twenty-five-year pin.

Back to the beginning of my career story. After my first two years in the agency's Office of Financial Management, I said to my division chief at the time, "I'd like to do something a little more analytical." She had spent time with Directorate of Intelligence (DI) people overseas, so she referred me to someone there, and after a few informational interviews I found myself working as a DI economic analyst. In the early 1990s Eastern Europe was finally opening up to the rest of the world after betting on the wrong horse during the Cold War. What an exciting time it was to be there! I vividly remember, one morning during my first month on the account (the agency term for the topics on which one works), the amazing feeling I had when I walked up to the folks editing the President's Daily Brief with my first "snowflake"—a short but surprisingly difficult piece to write on a large mob riot over agricultural policies. What a rush it was to wake up the next day as a twenty-four-year-old knowing the piece I had written the day before was going to be read by the president of the United States! You never forget that feeling. I still keep that piece in a binder in my office, and I carry it with me from job to job.

A few years later I was given the opportunity to brief President George H. W. Bush in Texas after he had left office. I remember arriving in Houston and going into a small office where the former president greeted me with a kind smile and changed his suit jacket to a cardigan sweater (like Mr. Rogers, I thought to myself). He spent the first few minutes showing me photos of his children and grandchildren that he had in a photo album on his desk. He also showed me around his office, where he kept trinkets from the state trips he took as president. He didn't have his presidential library yet, so all those amazing items were stored around him in his private office. He had a story to tell for each one, and he was gracious and endearing as he relayed each story to me. After at least a half-hour of what felt like visiting an old friend, we made our way over to the couch and I went through my briefing. He asked insightful questions, was so engaged, and had a great grasp of the material. After the briefing I quietly asked my boss, who had come to Houston with me, if it would be okay to ask the former president for a photo. The president overheard and pulled out his own Polaroid camera, which he happened to keep in his desk, and asked my boss to take a photo of us. We had another one taken with my camera, which I framed. It's hanging in my home with a handwritten note the former president sent me a few weeks later that says, "Thanks for getting me smarter on South Asia." I keep the Polaroid on my desk.

I later applied and was accepted for the U.S. Department of Agriculture's Women's Executive Leadership Program. This was like an executive MBA program for government employees; it involved shadowing assignments, senior interviews, and one- to two-month internships. The program was flexible, allowing each participant to design their own program. I chose to work in two private companies that year—one specializing in international consulting and the other a large multinational. I did my third internship in the Clinton White House working for the special assistant to the president for economics, covering such things as China's accession to the World Trade Organization, the North Atlantic Free Trade Agreement, other trade and labor negotiations, and the president's trip to the Asia-Pacific Economic Cooperation meeting. Many times the White House was short-staffed, so I represented the White House at key meetings at the U.S. Trade Representative and the U.S. Department of the Treasury, among other places. Although the agency had an economics Presidential Daily Brief, we didn't have someone at the National Economic Council until I was assigned. I felt my presence there often prompted the economic principals to ask what I thought CIA's position was on this or that issue. It was great to have a voice at the table as things were transpiring. I was there just before President Clinton's second term, and I extended my internship to see the transition through.

The year 2001 was monumental for all of us. Each of us at the agency (and the United States in general) remembers exactly where we were when we heard about the second plane hitting the World Trade Center Twin Towers on September 11 and realized it was a terrorist attack. That day, and in the days that followed, all we all wanted to do was help out with the war on terror. Two days later, on September 13, I received my opportunity. My boss called me in and asked me to join a start-up unit at the agency called the Red Cell. It was originally established by Director George Tenet to do devil's advocate analysis and think about creative options for determining how the next terrorist attack might occur and preventing it. The few of us who were asked to be part of this unit were chosen because we were creative, and none of us had any experience analyzing terrorism. The whole point was to have a fresh perspective. We were a fantastic and creative team, often writing and editing pieces on potential terrorist attacks against the United States and its interests at home and abroad and inventing new types of analytical assessments as we went along. There was no hierarchy in the group. We had an open office arrangement—like a newsroom—and brainstormed everything as a group. It was an amazing and scary time for all of us. Many of our pieces fed directly into meetings of the Principals Committee (executive branch senior leaders) and discussions in the Oval Office. Director Tenet had told us on the first day that he wasn't sure the unit would last through the week. Every day we'd come in thinking we'd be disbanded. But nearly fifteen years later, the Red Cell is still churning out alternative analysis.

Throughout my career I've been part of a number of other startups at the agency too, including the DI Women's Council, which brought flextime to the DI, and a strategic futures analytic center, which did some of the agency's best scenario and gaming work. I've worked closely with hundreds of our nation's experts both inside and outside government to ensure that the agency continually seeks fresh perspectives, and I've helped run an innovation center focused on working collaboratively and creatively on the agency's hardest problems. When I introduce myself either in a classroom (I now run executive leadership programs) or to new staff (I've been a manager for more than eleven years), I start by saying that I'm a change agent and that many of the units I've been a part of don't exist anymore because they've challenged the status quo and pushed the envelope on analysis, innovation, organizational development, and leadership. Once their ideas or practices became mainstream throughout the agency, they closed up shop. I believe all the units and projects I've been associated with at the agency, in one way or another, have pushed the organization to be just a little bit better or move the creative ball just a little bit further. I look back and am both proud and grateful to have been a part of all of those amazing teams.

Twenty-seven years ago I stood on the seal and thought, "I'll stay for a few years and move back to Boston." I'm so glad I decided to ride it out and stay a while. I don't know what's in store for me over the next ten years, but I know it will almost certainly be interesting.

What's a Librarian Do at the CIA?

PEGGY TUTEN

I grew up in Edgewood, Maryland, and always thought I'd be a teacher. I was stuck in the mindset of the 1960s: women could only be teachers, nurses, librarians, or airline stewardesses. I always loved school, and my father encouraged me to be a teacher. But I started to have doubts about that choice when I was in high school. My father was a disabled veteran, and his status qualified me for veterans' benefits for college. To receive the funding, I had to see a counselor at the Veterans Administration and do some career testing. Librarian came up at the top of the possible career choices for me, and I decided to pursue this path. Financially, I was limited to state schools, and fortunately I found that the University of Maryland offered a program in library science education. I completed the program but realized that I didn't want to be a school librarian, so I decided to go to graduate school to get a master of library science degree to increase my qualifications for other librarian positions. I attended Emory University, and when I graduated in 1976, I really wanted to be a reference librarian in an academic library: I loved the challenge of a difficult reference question. But the economy was bad, and I was happy to get any job. It took me six months to find my first professional position, at a small organization in Washington DC. I knew almost from the start that it wasn't a place where I wanted to stay for long, so I enrolled part-time at George Washington University with plans to get a second master's, this one in Russian area studies. Many university librarians have a second master's degree, and I hoped this would make me more competitive for a university position.

I began my career at the CIA as a GS-9 reference librarian at the National Photographic Interpretation Center (NPIC) in 1979. I didn't especially want to work at CIA, but I wanted a government job because the salaries were higher. I met Eric, the man who would later be my boss and mentor at NPIC, at a library conference, and he was recruiting for a librarian. Having gone to Emory was a plus; Eric had hired another Emory graduate the year before, and she was on her way to a very successful career. And studying Russian helped me to stand out. Years later, as a recruiter, I felt a bit guilty about my ambivalence because I met so many students whose life ambition was to work at CIA. But once I started there, I never wanted to leave. The people were friendly and professional, and the mission was fascinating, which more than made up for NPIC's location at the Washington Navy Yard—very close to the present Nationals Park in an area that was depressed until the extension of the Washington Metro Green Line into that part of southeast DC.

NPIC's job was to analyze U2 and satellite imagery. It was NPIC that first identified the Soviet Union's missiles in Cuba in 1962, leading to the Cuban Missile Crisis. President Jimmy Carter had recently declassified the existence of satellite reconnaissance, so the role of NPIC was new and exciting to me. We librarians provided collateral information—including classified analytical reporting—to imagery analysts to help them understand what they were seeing on the ground and put it into context. We found reports in the RECON database that CIA indexers maintained of intelligence community reports. We also did traditional library research using books and journal articles and the few open-source databases that were available—Dialog and the New York Times Information Bank—via dial-up modem. To write up our reports and memos, we used IBM Selectric typewriters. Each librarian was assigned a group of analysts and had to review all incoming materials and forward new items of interests to their group.

I recall providing direct support during several crises, including the Soviet invasion of Afghanistan and Iran hostage crisis in 1979 and the Chernobyl disaster in 1986.

The man who would become my husband was an imagery analyst at NPIC in 1982. It was nice to be in a relationship with someone else at the CIA so we could talk about our jobs with each other, although at one time or another we were both involved with programs that we couldn't talk about. We married the same year as at least two other couples who'd met at NPIC.

After a few years, I became a section chief for the reference librarians and then a branch chief. The CIA does a terrific job of training in both substantive skill and personal skill development. Unlike my colleagues in other government agencies who had to pay to attend professional library conferences, we usually had a large enough training budget to send most of the librarians to a conference each year. I received substantive training from NPIC and management training from both NPIC and the CIA so that I understood the work of an imagery analyst as well as military terminology. The CIA's Directorate of Science and Technology (DS&T) offered a three-month career development course that included an extensive look at the CIA and the other components of the intelligence community. It included trips to visit several military sites—I remember touring a submarine in Norfolk and seeing both the Hubble Telescope and last KH-9 satellites in California. I also participated in an Outward Bound course with other NPIC managers—a memorable and very personally rewarding experience. Sleeping in a tent and overcoming several physically difficult challenges was great for team building and helped to boost my confidence.

I was selected to be a DS&T representative to CIA's chapter of the Federally Employed Women program, which helped to bring a daycare center to CIA. I also served as a guinea pig for a new women's leadership program. We spent a week being treated like U.S. Marine recruits, led by a marine gunny. Since most CIA managers, especially at the senior levels, were male and ex-military, this gave us a look at how men lead and act in teams. Men learn to work in teams through participation in sports and serving in the military. It doesn't matter much whether they like their coworkers or not. Women look for social relationships at work and find it more difficult to work with people they don't like. If a man goes out of his way to help you and says "you owe me one," you'd better reciprocate when he asks for your support.

I'm most proud of my work participating in Vice President Gore's Environmental Task Force, which was established in 1992. I was a member of the Classification Review Task Force. The task force reviewed all national-level imagery and recommended to President Clinton which images from CORONA (KH-1 to KH-4), the first satellite imagery reconnaissance systems, should be declassified. I attended Vice President Gore's press conference announcing the executive order to release this imagery. I was responsible for identifying repositories of the original imagery along with indexes and finding aids to the individual imagery frames, and for arranging for their storage and access at the National Archives in College Park, Maryland. The release of this imagery has been a tremendous resource for environmental study, establishing a baseline in the 1960s for assessing environmental changes. Historians and archaeologists are also finding the imagery useful. Its declassification led the way to commercial imagery, including the Google satellite imagery we take for granted today. I was honored to receive the National Intelligence Certificate of Distinction award for my role in this project.

After Operation Desert Storm in 1991, the Department of Defense criticized the intelligence community for its use and dissemination of imagery intelligence to the field. There were calls for imagery analysis to be moved under the control of the Department of Defense. After much debate, the move finally happened in 1996 with the establishment the National Imagery and Mapping Agency (NIMA), now called the National Geospatial Intelligence Agency. NPIC was merged with the Defense Mapping Agency, a much larger organization, along with a few other organizations responsible for imagery collection and intelligence. The change was stressful and traumatic for all employees involved. Many NPIC employees did not want to work for the Department of Defense and found jobs in other parts of CIA. I did too after several years.

By this time I had been chief of the NPIC library and then acting division chief, responsible for the library, map library, film archive, and handheld photography collections. I was deeply involved in planning the merger of libraries for NIMA, including serving on a task force to develop support services for NIMA. I procured funding for a new automated library system that would eventually tie the libraries together, standardizing practices across the former NPIC and Defense Mapping Agency libraries. Eventually I became head of the library in one of the defense mapping buildings. I soon ran into a major clash of cultures—from a highly rank-conscious organization to one with unionized civilian employees. Of the fifty or so employees I managed, only one had a professional librarian's degree. By the time I left, NIMA required new librarians to have a master's degree in library science. After three years at NIMA, a librarian in the CIA Library alerted me that the chief librarian position was open. I decided it was time for me to go back to the mothership and accepted the position when it was offered. I was happy to have had the experience at NIMA, but it made me appreciate working at the CIA even more. I thought at the time that the formation of NIMA from several other organizations would make for a fascinating business school case study. Trying to merge the organizations was a difficult and stressful process.

I became chief of the CIA Library in 1999. I had never worked at CIA headquarters before, and I loved it, despite my longer commute. I enjoyed all of the services and amenities of working in a very large building—Starbucks coffee in the cafeteria, two gyms, a full-service credit union, and an employee store. I also saw many of my former NPIC colleagues, and a few worked for me in the library again. The library had a reputation for being the best in the intelligence community. The library staff were among the agency's first internet users in the mid-1990s; other employees were just getting access in 1999. We often mulled over who should be able to use the internet, and this spawned many security discussions. Some senior managers thought that everything would be free on the internet and that there would no longer be a need for libraries or librarians. I fought that battle quite a few times and was gratified that by the end of my career, many offices, domestic and overseas, wanted their own librarian to provide tailored research.

In 2001 I dealt with another major reorganization and management challenge. The CIA Library had been in the Directorate of Intelligence (DI), home of all-source intelligence analysts, since the creation of CIA. The library was part of a larger support organization within the DI that was being split up. After lots of debate and several false starts, the library was moved to the Foreign Broadcast Information Service (FBIS) in the DS&T. This did not go over very well with most of the staff. FBIS primarily translated foreign media and was just beginning to analyze open-source information. FBIS suffered many budget cuts during the 1990s, and library staff were concerned that more would follow. However, in retrospect, this was probably one of the best things that could have happened to the library and the careers of librarians.

Everyone remembers what he or she was doing on 9/11. I was interviewing for new librarians, and every time I finished an interview and checked the television outside of my office, there was more bad news. It quickly became evident that the attacks were made by terrorists. By late morning, we were given orders to go home (at that time, the fourth plane was still in the air; if the Pentagon had been hit, CIA headquarters could be next). I still remember that no one wanted to leave—we knew the analysts would need our research assistance. The next day, everything changed. Many analysts were reassigned to terrorist accounts but had no previous experience or specialized knowledge of this issue. The staff was busy pulling together information for these analysts to quickly get up to speed on their new accounts. We were also assigned a project—to document the nationality of everyone killed in the attacks. President Bush needed this information to appeal to countries who had lost citizens in the attacks to join us in the war on terror.

The CIA experienced heavy downsizing and budget cuts after the end of the Cold War. In contrast, after 9/11, the CIA began to hire in large numbers. But the headquarters compound was becoming overcrowded and there was no space to train the new employees. Some senior managers wanted to move the library out of the building to make space for new recruits.

I knew that we couldn't maintain the status quo and was willing to give up some space in exchange for funding for a total renovation. Fortunately, my new manager in FBIS had just come off an assignment on Director of Central Intelligence (DCI) George Tenet's staff and was very politically savvy. He and I put together a task force of representatives across the agency to provide input into a plan for the library of the future. Many DI analysts came to our rescue—they still needed access to library staff and resources onsite to help them with priority taskings (urgent requests). And they still needed print material to review; they sometimes searched through the indexes of books to find the information that they needed. They weren't willing to wait a day or more for material to come from offsite storage. Senior management approved the task force recommendations and the DI provided much of the necessary funding for a renovation; they were the primary beneficiaries of the space vacated by the library. Thus began a period of major disruption for the staff. There was no swing space for us to move into, so the renovation was done floor by floor with the staff—and customers—dealing with the noise, fumes, and so on.

During this time FBIS also faced major changes. FBIS was the major open-source resource in the intelligence community. The vast majority of their reporting was unclassified and could be widely used and shared. The unclassified reports were part of the U.S. government's Federal Depository Library Program and can be found in many government document collections. Both the 9/11 Commission and WMD Commission noted that open-source information was undervalued and underused by the intelligence community. In 2005 Congress established the Director of National Intelligence's Open Source Center (OSC), and FBIS became its heart.

After many years of defending budgets and the need for libraries and librarians, it was wonderful to finally see open-source information being recognized for its value—after all, librarians have been experts at exploiting this information since the days of papyrus scrolls!

Moving to FBIS/OSC opened up a new career opportunity for me. I had never been in a career service that offered overseas positions and had only had a few opportunities for work-related overseas travel. I decided to apply for a job as a manager at one of FBIS's overseas bureaus. I didn't succeed the first time, but I tried again in a few years. By this time senior FBIS managers had gotten to know me and, I assumed, thought highly of my managerial skills. They asked me to apply for a position in the Middle East.

My heart was set on an assignment in Europe, but after some research and talking to people who had served there, I agreed to the position in the Middle East. Fortunately, my husband had retired several years earlier, so it was fairly easy for us to pick up and move. In 2006 I became manager of a bureau with staff hired to translate the media for the region. Our bureau was located on the outskirts of the city, and I was able to walk to work—a joy after my one- to two-hour commutes. I visited the embassy several times a week and had a seat at the table for the ambassador's country team meetings. I worked closely with State Department officers, learning much about the scope of their responsibilities while I marketed OSC's products. I loved living overseas and all that comes with it. The cultural and travel opportunities were tremendous, and living within walking distance of the Mediterranean Sea was wonderful. This was a two-year assignment with an option to extend it for one year, which I did. At the end of three years, I came back to Washington, wondering what was next.

OSC was continuing to expand its role in the intelligence community and was placing liaison officers in various organizations. I accepted a position at the Drug Enforcement Administration (DEA) headquarters, where I was responsible for drafting a plan for how the DEA could incorporate the use of open-source information in their analysis and for promoting use of open-source information by DEA analysts. I again experienced quite a culture shock. Communication was sparse and meetings to discuss programs and projects were infrequent, so it was difficult for me to suggest specific open sources to support programs. I completed this assignment and was happy to return to CIA.

As chief of the NPIC and CIA libraries, I had always enjoyed recruiting librarians, and I applied for a position as a regional recruiter in CIA's Recruitment and Retention Center. I was selected for this position and became responsible for managing recruiting events at colleges and universities in the Southeast. Recruiting was fun but exhausting, involving lots of travel, long days, and many hours standing. I registered the CIA for recruitment fairs and arranged for space for CIA information sessions and interviews. I participated in events sponsored by college and university career centers, including mock interviews, résumé reviews, and career panels. I really enjoyed meeting students and helping them prepare to compete for careers at the CIA. When I visited a university that had a graduate library science program, I planned meetings with library school faculty and students to promote the CIA as a career. I also encouraged fellow recruiters to consider librarians for jobs outside the library. Librarians have specialized research skills that are easily transferable, and they were being hired to other positions within the agency.

Finally, it was time to consider retirement. When I started at the CIA as a GS-9 reference librarian, I never envisioned the path that my career would take. By the time I'd become a GS-15 manager, I had a fascinating career with many different work experiences, training and travel experiences, and the opportunity to work with many wonderful, talented, and committed people.

Based on my experience at the recruitment center, I'd like to share a few tips for those interested in pursuing a career with CIA. Regularly review CIA's website, CIA.gov, for career information. See what jobs interest you and check the requirements. Ask your college career center if CIA recruiters regularly visit campus. If they do, go meet them—even during your freshman year. Study foreign languages. Try to do a study abroad program or foreign internship to get some overseas living experience. Pursue experiences that will help you hone your problem-solving and teamwork skills. Keep up your GPA—you should have at least a 3.0. And if you don't succeed the first time, keep trying; perhaps go to graduate school or get some relevant work experience before you try again.

I'm now retired, living in a small town in southeast Georgia. I had a hard time giving up work completely, so I've been working as an on-call reference librarian at Florida State College in Jacksonville. I usually work a day or two a week when I'm in town, but my husband and I travel frequently, so the on-call schedule suits me fine. We love traveling to Europe, but we recently bought an Airstream trailer and are looking forward to more travels in the United States and Canada.

4

More of What a Librarian Does at the CIA

KIM CONDAS

When I joined the CIA in 1984, online resources were very new and very limited. One day a patron needed an article from an old *Playboy* magazine. In the 1960s and 1970s, journalists were writing articles about the CIA in magazines such as *Soldier of Fortune, Mother Jones,* and *Playboy.* The CIA Library kept many years of these publications so that we could provide copies of articles from them as needed. I used the venerable *Reader's Guide to Periodical Literature* in its bound red volumes to look up the article the patron had requested, found the citation, and went to the files, which were housed in a vault with desks for individual reading and research. The article was not in the cited issue, so I pulled out the six issues before and after that issue and started paging through them to see if I could find it. After a few minutes, I felt someone standing behind me. I looked over my shoulder to see a middle-aged man looking at the issue of *Playboy* that was open in front of me. "I'll bet you like looking at the pictures, don't you?" he said, with a lascivious wink. I bristled. "I'm a librarian here, and I'm locating articles about the CIA in these old issues!" "Oh, I'm sure you are, my dear, I'm sure you are," he said, and, chuckling, he walked away. I was mortified, but it made me wonder how many library patrons knew we stored years' worth of *Playboy* in the study vault. And how many perused them during work hours? It certainly explained why the copies were always out of order.

For many years I was a member of the Special Libraries Association, and my name and work address were listed in its yearly member directory. A patron had come in with a question about something that appeared to be a zoo in the background of some photographs of a drug dealer's homestead, and he asked me if there was a way to find out if there was a zoo in that town. I looked up "zoological parks" in a directory of professional organizations and found a national organization that focused on zoos. I called the number listed for its library. "Hi, I'm Kim Condas from the CIA Library, and I have a question about how to locate particular zoos around the world. Can you help me?" Dead silence. Then, "Did . . . did you just say that this is the CIA?" "Yes," I answered patiently. "I am a librarian here, and I'm doing some research on zoos for a patron. I'm hoping you can help me." She said that she could not, but she'd leave a message for the librarian to call me back. An hour or so later I got a return phone call. "Hi," she said. "Is Kim there?" When I told her that I was Kim, she said, "I received the oddest message from our secretary that you had called from the CIA with a question. You're not really from the CIA, are you?" "Yep," I told her, "I am." Before I could explain my question, she said, "I'm sorry, but for all I know, you're blowing smoke. How do I know you're really a librarian at the CIA?" I replied, "Do you have a copy of the Special Libraries Association's directory? I'm listed in there." "Really? I'm a member as well. Let me look you up." Of course I was in there. The librarian then believed I was legit, and she answered my question: there was no zoo listed in that city in that country. "I think I'm going to frame our secretary's note about your phone call," she told me. "It's not every day we get a call from the CIA."

The upfront approach sometimes backfired, however. Another time when I was doing research I again called a professional organization that I thought might assist me. When I did my usual introduction, the woman at the other end of the line said hesitantly that she didn't know anything about the organization or country in question. I said, "You're listed as the expert in this area of knowledge; are you sure you can't help me?" Her voice trembled as she said, "I'm just a housewife—I don't know anything that the CIA would want know!" "I beg your pardon," I said. "This isn't the XYZ Institution?" "No, this is Mary Jones and you've called me at my home." I apologized profusely and hung up. I told this story to a friend who had worked at the CIA for many years, and she still teases me about calling up random citizens to ask them to answer questions for the CIA.

The CIA's Office of Public Affairs fields many, many calls from the public, and some of those calls are from cranks who are angry with the CIA. Sometimes those callers would be given the library's direct line—gee, thanks!—and we'd have to deal with their odd questions. One man called to ask, "How does the CIA define the word 'plant?'" I asked him to tell me a bit more about what he was looking for, but he just insisted that he wanted "your" definition of "plant." I retrieved a dictionary of espionage terms and read him the definition of "plant." He asked, "But is this how the CIA defines the concept?" I said, "Sir, you've reached the CIA Library. And this is a dictionary on our shelves with the definition. I can't say if it's how the CIA defines it, but the CIA Library depends on standard reference sources, and this is how the CIA Library is defining it." He hung up. I've always wondered how he would have reacted had I read from a horticultural dictionary instead.

5

Getting to Do What I Was Meant to Do

ROBERT KRESGE

I made my way into the CIA via military service. My journalism degree from the University of Missouri, coupled with four years of active U.S. Army duty, including a year in Vietnam, got me picked up by the Foreign Broadcast Information Service (FBIS; now the Open Source Center) to work on Vietnamese and other Southeast and South Asian press reporting. After that assignment, I did a stint on the FBIS Daily Report for the Soviet Union. Then I went in to ask my boss, the chief of ops for FBIS, for an overseas assignment in the following year.

I don't know if he was waiting for me to come in, but in response to my request, he said, "How would you like a two-year tour in Bangkok starting in six weeks? And (wait for it), if your answer is yes, you can take the whole six weeks to tell us yes, but if your answer is no, we have to hear that tomorrow. No one else in your grade has your experience in Southeast Asia and on our wire service. We'd have to use the six weeks to train someone in at least one of those areas."

I said, "I'll have to consult my wife about that," and so I did. In the previous six weeks, Julie had changed jobs and found out she was pregnant, and we'd bought a house that we hadn't yet moved into. Oh, and I also had to do two weeks of Army Reserve active duty in Arizona. In August. Fortunately for us, another FBIS couple with a small child was just back from Thailand and, reassured by them about U.S. military medical care, we agreed to go. Even after they told us not to take anything with us that we couldn't leave behind or carry onto a helicopter. In the wake of the fall of Saigon, the jury was still out on whether the rest of Southeast Asia would fall like dominos.

The excellent U.S. military medical care vanished soon after our arrival. The Thais had told U.S. officials that they must not stage a rescue mission of the *Mayaguez* cargo ship (seized by the Cambodians) from bases in Thailand, or Thailand would have to demand closure of those bases. Well, we did and they did. So all English language signage, American medical services, and Armed Forces Radio and TV vanished within a month or two of our arrival. Fortunately, Thai medical care proved to be excellent and our son Matthew was born early on a Sunday morning at Bangkok General Hospital, a bicentennial baby.

By the time we returned to the States, I'd spent 10 percent of my life in Southeast Asia. And the FBIS chief of ops' wit had only improved in my absence. During my debriefing with him, he said FBIS was thinking of opening a bureau the following year in Botswana. I prided myself on obscure geography, but I stepped into the trap. "Botswana," I said, "where the hell is Botswana?" He calmly took out a notebook and wrote in it. "Ah," he said, "you've expressed an interest."

Fortunately, I returned to stateside foreign press reporting, and after another year I applied for agency help with tuition to get a master's degree in Asian studies at George Washington University. After my first three evening semesters, I asked if I could take a year off to complete the degree. FBIS managers came back with a counteroffer: How would I like a year's leave with pay?

Yes, I was gobsmacked over that expression of trust. For two semesters and the intervening summer sessions, I was a full-time student. When I returned, FBIS put my shiny new degree to work when they made me a propaganda analyst on North Korea for the next three years. Pyongyang didn't make as many headlines then as it has recently, but analyzing their propaganda proved to be, as described to me, like trying to nail Jell-O to the wall. One of my accomplishments, probably spoken in hushed tones still today, was to predict the North Korea succession after Kim

Il-sung. I said with confidence that there were only two possible outcomes: his son Kim Chong-il would take over and run things, or Kim Chong-il would appear to run things while the Army pulled his strings. Nobody laughed, but there were plenty of scowls. "When would we be able to know the difference?" I was asked. "Maybe in two or three years, depending on other sources besides press reporting." My prediction was viewed as a cop-out, but it was borne out a few years later. The younger Kim was really running the country, but with older-generation military guidance.

After those years in my first analytical assignment, I spent a year-long rotation in the CIA's Office of Communications/Security Branch, during which I was part of a three-man delegation that went to communications sites around the world. When I attended the mid-career course at about the ten-year mark of my career, I learned of a small shop (a single Directorate of Intelligence [DI] branch) that had been set up at headquarters to work on terrorism analysis in the wake of the Beirut Marine Corps barracks bombing. I applied, was accepted, and FBIS let me go.

I began working on terrorism in Asia and Africa as one of more than a dozen analysts who worked more glamorous and important accounts. But in short order, the branch expanded, split in half, and I was given the further duty of editing the biweekly *Terrorism Review* that circulated to many government agencies. During this stint, I was delegated to be on a multiagency briefing team to talk about Middle East terrorism spillover into Western Europe, a major issue at the time. I gave the same talk thirteen times in seven countries in twenty-one days. In my absence our branch was absorbed into the new Directorate of Intelligence–Directorate of Operations Counterterrorism Center (CTC), one of the first places where analysts like myself sat cheek by jowl with operators, the collectors of intelligence on terrorism. So by default I became a founding member of CTC.

Now part of the new center, I put together a team of four database inputters and three other analysts and we got a needed publication out six months ahead of its expected release. I had already received several monetary awards for my FBIS and DI work, but when my branch chief said CTC management wanted to give me a $2,000 award for this timely work, I reminded her that seven other people had helped make the accomplishment possible. We were honored at an assembly and each of us received a check for $250. I was always proudest of that certificate.

That year we put out the CIA definition of terrorism as the intelligence community's definition, and one by one, every agency adopted it: "Terrorism involves premeditated acts of politically motivated violence committed against noncombatant targets by non-state groups or clandestine state agents. International terrorism involves the citizens or territory of more than one country."

Another of my fondest memories involved the dreaded phone call in the middle of the night. I didn't have a secure phone at home at that time, but I got a call from a young officer at the ops center sometime after midnight.

"Mr. Kresge, sorry to disturb you, but you know the G-7 heads of state [United States, Britain, France, Italy, Germany, Canada, and Japan] are meeting in Venice tonight? Well, there's been an unidentified object spotted floating in Venice harbor."

"I take it we don't know what it is yet, but efforts are under way to find out."

"Yes, sir."

"Thank you for the call. Let me know what it turns out to be."

About ninety minutes later, the officer called me back.

"Mr. Kresge, that object in Venice harbor turns out to be an abandoned refrigerator."

"Well, thank you for calling me back on this. I'm glad you were able to resolve the matter. I'll sleep more soundly knowing that."

Two hours later came the third call.

"Mr. Kresge, a bomb has gone off aboard a bus near the back gate of the U.S. embassy in Rome. The British embassy gate has been the site of a bomb explosion and rockets have been fired into our embassy grounds from a hotel room across the street."

"Thank you. I'll be right in. Please call my branch chief and give her my assessment."

When I arrived at the office, after a quick shower and dressing but no shave, my branch chief told me to go up to the seventh floor (where the agency's senior leadership resides) immediately and brief the deputy director of operations who would be briefing on Capitol Hill that morning. I did; he asked few questions and accepted my analysis that the perpetrators were members of the Japanese Red Army (JRA) acting at the behest of, or paid by, Muammar al-Qaddafi of Libya. The JRA had conducted an identical series of attacks in Jakarta, Indonesia, during the previous meeting of the G-7 in Tokyo. JRA members could not get into Japan to stage an attack there, so they chose to attack in Jakarta. The JRA must have known they could not get near the Venice venue either, even with their homemade rockets.

Back at the branch, as the analysts arrived, my chief was telling all and sundry that we couldn't have solved this attack so quickly if we didn't have Rob Kresge on the account. I demurred, saying any analyst who'd been on the account for the last year would have connected the dots as easily as I did. The JRA tried to set off a bomb in a parked motorcycle near the gate of a U.S. airbase in Spain during the next G-7. That device failed to go off. And a year after that, JRA member Yu Kikumura was arrested by an alert New Jersey state trooper at a turnpike rest area. His car was loaded with explosive devices contained in fire extinguishers that were due to be placed in a federal office building in New York City. All of these attacks had come as retaliation for the U.S. bombing of Libya following its role in a terrorist bombing of U.S. service personnel at the La Belle discotheque in Germany.

DI analysts rotate into other job areas every few years. As I prepared to end my first five-year tour in CTC, North Korea stepped up attacks designed to scare away attendees at the 1988 Olympics in Seoul. Pyongyang was behind a bomb set in a trash can at the Seoul airport, and then escalated to the most daring attacks on a civilian airliner before 9/11. A North Korean couple got off KAL

Flight 858 in Dubai, leaving behind a couple of timebombs that used liquid explosives. The plane disappeared over the Andaman Sea and the wreckage has never been found. It might have been chalked up to a simple accident from an unknown cause except that local police in Dubai immediately questioned the pair who had left the plane. The elderly man bit into a cyanide capsule in a cigarette and died. His young female companion was prevented from doing the same thing and told her story to authorities. International condemnation of North Korea did not involve military action or additional sanctions, but the country was deterred from any further actions and the Seoul Olympics were held without incident.

I went back into my home office, now renamed Resources, Trade, and Technology (RTT) and worked on gray market arms dealers for a few years. We liked to say they were a lot like terrorists, only they wore expensive suits and had their own airplanes and yachts.

Closely associated with gray markets was the RTT Transportation Branch, which became responsible in the early 1990s for reporting on and coordinating with other U.S. agencies in support of sanctions against the former Yugoslavia aimed at ending the genocide of Bosnian Muslims. With my predilection for current intelligence, I was a natural fit for writing daily reports, and over the next few years I turned out hundreds of pages in the agency's five-days-a-week *Sanctions Situation Report* on border controls, smuggling, and economic woes in Belgrade. In this role, I got to take more foreign trips accompanying senior officials. A favorite stop was Vienna, where I took advantage of the wonderful cuisine and rode the iconic Ferris wheel that appeared in the movie *The Third Man*. Yes, I hummed the famous theme music during every revolution of the wheel. When my wife and I visited Vienna as tourists in 2013, I managed to show her the converted concert hall where we'd held our meetings.

Much of my Balkan travel involved countries bordering Serbia to assess the success of economic sanctions and how tight enforcement was. I have a five-hundred-billion Yugoslav dinar note near my desk as I write this, in a frame that asks the question, "What Did You Do in the War, Daddy?" I helped to wreck the Serbian economy and drive Slobodan Milošević to the bargaining table.

When he capitulated and we moved the sanctions effort inside the former Yugoslavia and applied the effort to the Bosnian Serbs, I was sent to assess the effectiveness of the new control points at seventeen locations along Bosnia's eastern border, entering the "belly of the beast," so to speak, of the regime we had been strangling. At one point, I walked into Bosnia itself at the village of Metaljka and was told by my interpreter that a German soldier named Adolf Schickelgruber (Hitler's birth name) had been stationed there during World War I. I said, "Well, I'm glad they haven't put up a commemorative marker."

With the success of the Dayton Peace Accords, sanctions were lifted and I cast about for where to spend the remaining five years of my career. The now much larger Counterterrorism Center beckoned and I joined the brand-new Terrorism Warning Group as the CIA representative. Other organizations that sent analysts were the FBI, the National Security Agency, the Defense Intelligence Agency, and the State Department's Bureau of Intelligence and Research. They even printed business cards for us—the only time I received such credentials. For the next five years, we monitored the reporting of all five agencies and issued periodic terrorism assessments and advisories and the rare but much more serious terrorism warnings, which merited Director of Central Intelligence George Tenet's signature and were hand-delivered to the heads of several select cabinet departments and intelligence agencies.

My fondest memory of writing and delivering those documents is of a warm afternoon when my immediate boss, the National Security Agency's Frank Hyland, and I delivered one copy of a warning to the Justice Department only to find that Attorney General Janet Reno had just left the office and was walking home. We returned to our chauffeured agency vehicle and found her and her FBI escort officer at an intersection. Rather than alarm her escort, I waited by the car while Frank took her the document, waited while she read it, and then returned to the car. We took her copy back to her office and her staff locked it up.

Where were you on 9/11?

Every American alive at the time will always remember their answer. All through the summer of 2001, reporting from the various agencies indicated there was a Bin Laden plot afoot against U.S. embassies that would come to fruition by the end of summer. The head of the Terrorism Warning Group and I attended video conferences every afternoon with the White House, the State Department, the FBI, and the Pentagon to be briefed on the most significant reporting of the day. Because these agencies cooperated so fully at the time, CTC was represented by its deputy director, a career FBI agent. The FBI counterterrorism chair was held by their deputy director, a career CIA officer. The irony of that was not lost on anyone who attended these daily briefings.

As the 9/11 Commission's report made clear, there was no intelligence reporting that indicated what would happen on that fateful day. When the first plane struck, I had CNN running behind my intelligence reports screen and switched to it immediately. Those of us who have studied U.S. military history know that on a fog-shrouded early morning in 1939, an Army Air Corps plane crashed into the Empire State Building and fell into the street. Only the two pilots were killed. On 9/11, TV showed a cloudless day. There was no known video of the first plane until a citizen who'd filmed Manhattan from a taxi on a bridge that morning sold it to the news media three weeks later.

When the second plane went in, we all instantly thought, "Bin Laden." He was the only terrorist leader who conducted simultaneous attacks, like he had in 1998 against U.S. embassies in Nairobi and Dar es Salaam, and the only one who returned to attack a target he previously failed to strike. He returned to attack those two cities after al-Qaida elements there were found out, deported, or jailed. The abortive van bombing of the World Trade Center in 1993 leapt to our minds. Likewise, after a Bin Laden attack on one U.S. warship failed near the Suez Canal in 1999, his followers successfully attacked the USS *Cole* in the Red Sea in 2000.

While we desperately mined intel reporting to see what we could have missed and whether further attacks might be imminent, my wife Julie called. I had telephoned her after the first strike and told her to get to a TV in her Department of Agriculture office along Interstate 395 south of Washington. She told me that her officemates had just seen a commercial airliner flying north up the interstate at an altitude below their fourteenth story office window. It went over the hill toward Washington, and a sudden plume of black smoke had erupted beyond the hill. I barely had time to say thanks and goodbye. I ran to the CTC chief Cofer Black's office to tell him it looked like another plane had attacked a target in Washington. He told me to stay put while he called Director George Tenet to report the likely attack. CNN reported the strike minutes later, and soon video was available.

By presidential order, the U.S. government shut down. If buildings in Washington were being targeted (and at that point no one knew where a missing fourth airplane was), it was safer to jam the streets with traffic than to leave buildings occupied. Even the CIA began to evacuate. Cofer called the director and pleaded for CTC to be allowed to remain open. "If this building is the target, we'll ride it down, but we need to be able to work here and look for signs of other attacks. We can't do that rapidly if we relocate." As the rest of the CIA evacuated, many departing officers came into CTC and said variations on "I don't want to leave. I want to stay and make a contribution. Can you put me to work?"

And so we did. At every available computer and phone line. By the following week, CTC had doubled in size.

As subsequent investigation by staffers of the 9/11 Commission found, two of our five sister agencies in the Terrorism Warning Group knew that there were Middle Eastern pilots without airline sponsorship training on four-engine jets in U.S. flight schools, but none of that knowledge was ever turned into intelligence reports that we could have seen. But learning that information was still weeks in the future. When what could easily be called "The Longest Day" wound down and we passed our computers to volunteers who would use them all night on twenty-four-hour shifts, I paused at the door of the warning group's small conference room and changed the sign next to the door to name it for the Heroes of United Airlines Flight 93, the missing fourth plane that the passengers had taken down in a field in Shanksville, Pennsylvania.

After almost a year of compiling and editing the brand-new *President's Daily Terrorist Threat Matrix*, a collection of down-in-the-weeds suspicious incidents around the United States and the world, it was time for me to retire. In thirty years, I did lots of critical work at key moments, was given huge responsibilities on targets of high-level interest, and was entrusted with mentoring dozens of new analysts in various offices. I'd like to say I didn't regret a single moment, but considering that one day in 2001, that wouldn't be a true statement.

After retiring, we moved to the Southwest, where I began to write historical mysteries set in 1870s Wyoming, the first place in the world where women could vote: *Murder for Greenhorns*, *Painted Women*, *Death's Icy Hand*, *Warrior Hearts*, *Unearthing the Bones*, *Over the Brink*, and the Tony Hillerman Prize–winning Civil War spy thriller *Saving Lincoln*.

We're Not in Kansas—er, Missouri—Anymore!

MARY O'SULLIVAN

S cene: 1982, The Bund, Shanghai, China. Postprandial stroll. Strains of "Take the A Train" played by a white-coated combo wafting from the lounge of the Heping Hotel.

In my head: Today is my thirty-fifth birthday and I am—literally—on the other side of the world! And I can actually understand what people are saying. Geez! That's pretty special! Guess I've done all right.

Several more of those moments happened during my twenty-eight-year stint as an analyst at the Central Intelligence Agency. I characterize them as the "pinch-me moments" and the "Yogi Berra moments"—"you can observe a lot just by watching." The pinch-me moments primarily happened abroad when I was stunned by a sight I never expected to see. The Yogi moments largely were observations of leadership in action.

A pinch-me in the United States came in 1986 during a rotational assignment to the Department of Defense. My Defense colleagues and I were preparing the agenda for Secretary of Defense Casper Weinberger's visit to China. Each agenda item had to have accompanying materials: remarks upon arrival, talking points for meetings, banquet toasts, and even a letter from President Reagan to Premier Zhao Ziyang. When I asked who would be preparing the various agenda materials, my colleagues said, "We will! Why don't you do the letter and a couple of banquet toasts? We need to focus on the substantive talking points on arms sales and resumption of military exchanges."

My demeanor belied what I really felt. My outside voice said, "Sure! Why not?!" My inside voice said, "What? Write a letter for the president? Sister Theophila's English class at St. Elizabeth Academy never covered presidential letters!"

That same Secretary of Defense visit to China resulted in one of my first Yogi moments. My Defense colleagues, for whom I still have the utmost respect, worked harder than anyone I had ever seen to prepare and coordinate all the required materials. The official party was going to be "wheels up" at Andrews Air Force Base early on a Saturday morning. I was in bed—exhausted—when the phone rang. I assumed it was a call from the flight line. It was! My stomach started churning! What had I forgotten? I was stunned when Assistant Secretary of Defense Rich Armitage said, "Thank you, Mary. I hope we do you proud!" Although I had already experienced good leaders at the CIA and many more were to come, this conversation was my first lesson in leadership. A word of gratitude means a lot!

Another senior Defense official provided my second Yogi moment. I was chief of a branch of the CIA that specialized in political psychology and produced profiles of world leaders. It was a very challenging assignment because my "subordinates" were higher in rank than I was and were board-certified physicians. Last I looked, I did not have an MD behind my name! Skeptics of our work abounded, yet Deputy Assistant Secretary of Defense Karl Jackson called me one day to say, "I don't always agree with what you write, Mary, but I'm now smart enough to always read it." I consider that message the highest praise an analyst or manager of analysts can receive! Impact, respect. Those words are golden for analysts who often work out of the limelight.

In the late 1980s, a pinch-me moment was followed by a "bite of the reality sandwich"—my term for coming down to earth or coming to grips with a situation. Upon my return from the Department of Defense, I became an editor for the President's Daily Brief. At that time editors filled in periodically for the appointed senior official briefers; I had the good fortune to be Vice Presi-

dent George H. W. Bush's briefer as well as to substitute periodically for other briefers. When the car that was taking me to the
White House drove through the White House gates on my first
day as a briefer, my heart fluttered. As we left the White House
grounds, a self-satisfied smile was on my face. "Not bad for a
gal from St. Louis," I said to myself. As I sat at my desk back at
the CIA drafting my post-briefing report, the outside line rang.
When I answered, I heard a small voice on the other end saying,
"Mommy, I just used the big potty." Well, now! That last piece
of news actually had a more direct effect on my life than a drive
through the White House gates! So there, big shot!

Yogi moments abounded during the mid-1990s when I worked
for extraordinary leaders and sharp colleagues who went on to
assume senior positions in the agency. One of the popular management approaches at the time was the use of process action
teams to address thorny issues or solve problems. Because he was
dissatisfied with the quality of analysis produced by the Directorate of Intelligence, Deputy Director for Intelligence Doug
MacEachin appointed me and five others to a team to redesign
the new analyst training course. In a meeting with MacEachin a
few weeks after our commissioning, the team rejected the assignment and instead recommended creation of Tradecraft 2000, a
two-week class that became mandatory for every Directorate of
Intelligence analyst and manager. Subordinates giving advice to
a senior? And the senior taking it? Yup!

Other Yogi moments centered on observing two extraordinary
managers with whom I worked directly. They were inclusive, yet
they set boundaries for decision making. They were courageous
even when their decisions made them unpopular. This team of
managers appointed an employee group to redesign the office
structure when the dissolution of the former Soviet Union made
some units obsolete. It worked! The team established the general parameters for the organization but honestly considered
and adopted the group's recommendations. There were messy
moments and difficult conversations, but those conversations

were honest. The result: most employees were actually happy even when they had to relocate their belongings from one side of the building to the other. I still see carts zinging around the halls on the first floor of the Original Headquarters Building.

When that organizational structure became untenable after a few years, I saw leadership in action when the office director abolished the office yet preserved the functional mission. It takes courage to reorganize oneself out of a job. The takeaway: sustain the mission, place the people, and you'll land on your feet. I had to apply that lesson myself a few years down the road.

My service as chancellor of CIA University had many pinch-me and Yogi moments. Did I really visit the seventh floor (where the agency's senior leaders have their offices) on a regular basis? Sitting at the executive director's conference table, though never routine, became part of a regular pattern. Becoming part of a regular pattern meant delivering each and every time. The fastest way to be dis-invited was to drop the ball. I thanked my lucky stars that I had a boss who was smart, generous, and patient, and who had a good sense of humor and a knack for the ceremonial but necessary aspects of leadership. Memories of Rudolph noses and hula skirts that the leadership team donned for holiday parties and other festivities still make me smile.

My final assignment was as deputy director of an office with wide-ranging responsibilities—from cartography and graphic design to senior review of The President's Daily Brief to oversight of special overseas analytic programs. Seeing the Egyptian pyramids at dawn from my hotel room on the Nile, having my breath taken away at the beauty of the Taj Mahal in India, and flinging the hotel room drapes open wide to see Hong Kong Harbor at night! Wow! Pinch me! Having senior leaders who give you general direction and let you figure out the details—ideal! My boss and I often joked that we were the "Office of Hard Problems," but we figured things out, in large part due to her persistence, patience, and willingness to tolerate some messiness. And we had smart colleagues who worked hard to accomplish the mission, even when the first time we learned of a new agency-wide mission directed our way was during a Bubble (headquarters auditorium) speech given by the director of CIA. What!? Guess someone forgot to tell us that was coming!

What more could one ask of one's work? Great colleagues, dedicated leaders, fascinating puzzles to solve, sights and sounds I never dreamed I would see, and all done for a great purpose— securing the safety and security of our nation! Yep, sounds sappy, but those feelings were real and came relatively often. To be happy in one's work is a blessing from above. I was always happy!

7

My Thirty Years in Scientific and Weapons Intelligence at the CIA

JULIAN NALL

The Beginning

Plans Are Made to Be Broken

In the spring of 1957, I was a graduate student in the physics department of Vanderbilt University. One day it was announced that a recruiter from "The United States Government" was in the department and would like to speak with PhD candidates. The chair of the department came to me to say that no one had any interest in talking with the recruiter, but to be polite he would like for someone to do so. He asked if I would be willing. Recognizing that the chair would have a say in whether or not I received my degree, I immediately said, "Of course."

I was ushered into a small conference room and introduced to a very cordial gentleman. After he closed the door, the man said in a low voice that he was from the CIA. My immediate and naïve response was "What is that?" After he recovered from the shock of my not knowing about the real world, he went on to tell me a bit about "the agency." He did a good job of giving me a bird's-eye view of the CIA's mission. I explained that I planned on becoming an academic and that was why I was pursuing a PhD in physics. Therefore, I had no interest. We parted on a friendly note and I thought that would be the end of my contact with "the agency." A week or so later I received a letter from the CIA's personnel department inviting me to come to Washington for an interview. I responded as I had to the recruiter: "I have no interest." Once more I thought that would be the end of the matter.

Subsequently, however, I received a phone call from Dr. Donald F. Chamberlain, the chief of the Fundamental Sciences Division of the Office of Scientific Intelligence (OSI) at the CIA. Before joining the CIA, Dr. Chamberlain had been a professor of chemistry at Washington University in St. Louis. He encouraged me to accept the invitation to visit the CIA and said that he would personally meet with me. Hard to turn down, but I did. Surely that was the end. But one never knows, and later Dr. Chamberlain called me again and made a suggestion that did appeal to me. He proposed that I come to Washington and not plan on a long career at CIA, but instead join the organization for two or three years on a trial basis. If I did not wish to stay, I could return to academia. Yes, that did appeal to me, and after receiving my PhD in 1958, my wife, our eighteen-month-old daughter, a nurse maid, and I moved into a rented home in Arlington.

Intelligence Analyses

Fundamental Sciences

My position at the CIA was chief of the Physics Mathematics Branch in the Fundamental Sciences Division headed by Dr. Chamberlain. This division was a component of OSI, which in turn was a component of the Directorate of Intelligence, which was responsible for the analysis and production of foreign intelligence. Collection of various types of intelligence and covert action were the responsibilities of other directorates.

I found myself in charge of preparing analyses primarily of research in physics and mathematics in the Soviet Union and the People's Republic of China. Our interest included research in various branches of physics, such as solid state, infrared, and high energy, as well as computers and mathematics. OSI was housed in Barton Hall, one of three former World War II WAVE barracks located south of the National Mall near the Tidal Basin in Washington DC. The two-story wooden barracks were named for three famous women: Louisa May Alcott, Clara Barton, and

Marie Curie. My office was on the second floor of Barton Hall, overlooking the Tidal Basin with its world-famous cherry trees. During the height of their blooming I could have made a fortune if the Office of Security would have let me sell tickets to tourists to visit my office. But Security would not cooperate!

High-energy physics was a priority subject in part because of the competition between the Soviets and the United States. The Soviets had a major facility at Dubna, near Moscow, and the United States had the Bevatron at the University of California at Berkeley. (Bev—for billion electron volts—was in use before it became common to use Gev—for giga electron volts.) In 1958 the Soviets hosted a major high-energy physics conference in Kiev in the Ukraine. It was important to find out the latest Soviet progress in the field. Rather than receive reports indirectly from non-scientists who might be able to attend the conference, it would be much better to get the reporting from the prominent scientists who would normally attend. In addition, it would help if the scientists were to meet afterward to discuss the findings with a representative of my branch. Dr. Chamberlain asked me to meet with them and then visit several CIA stations in Europe to brief them on the highlights of the conference and the need for certain additional information. The project proved to be quite successful. My wife traveled with me, which was encouraged, as long as I paid for it!

Computers were just beginning to blossom. The analyst responsible for keeping track of Soviet progress probably knew more about Soviet computers than anyone outside the Soviet Union. Despite his field of expertise, he used shoe boxes to keep his records. He continued to use them successfully many years after computers were well developed!

Because of our interest in Soviet aviation materials, I had the good fortune in 1960 to visit the Lockheed "Skunk Works," where Clarence "Kelly" Johnson, its director, showed me the SR-71, which he designed and which was under construction at the time. I remember standing on the wing of the plane with him while

47

he discussed features of the aircraft and the materials used in its construction. He had also designed the famous P-38 fighter with two fuselages used in World War II and later the U-2 reconnaissance plane, among others.

Antiballistic Missile Systems

The move to the new CIA headquarters building in Langley took place in 1961, after my three years in Barton Hall. Because of the increased interest in antiballistic missiles (ABMs), an antiballistic missile working group, led by Chuck Ahern, was active for a year or so before the move. At the time of the move, OSI changed from being organized by disciplines, such as fundamental science, applied science, and nuclear science, to being organized by weapon systems, such as offensive, defensive, space, and nuclear. In the area of science and technology analyses, the fields of offensive missiles, defensive missiles, space systems, and nuclear weapons were of highest priority. The ABM working group became the ABM Branch within the newly created Defensive Systems Division; and I was named chief. That move made my planned return to academia out of the question, so my family and I bought a home. That was the best decision I ever made, other than choosing my wife!

A group of scientists and engineers in the field of ABM research met periodically under the auspices of the Department of Defense to discuss progress in the field. They closely followed the Nike Zeus program, which was the U.S. approach to its own ABM system. During one of these meetings I met a professor of electronic engineering at Stanford University. I mentioned my new position and that I needed some expertise from the academic community to help me. I asked him to join several other persons who had agreed to help me, and he accepted. That was in the days before Vietnam, and most academics were generally supportive of government research.

This ABM advisory group, which included a future Nobel laureate, came to the attention of Bud Wheelon, who worked with a contractor doing weapons system analysis for OSI. When the advisory group met in the Los Angeles area, Bud met with them and invited them to his home for dinner. Bud was destined to join the CIA as assistant director of scientific intelligence less than a year later, to take the place of Herbert (Pete) Scoville, who became director of the newly created Directorate of Research.

After Bud Wheelon had been the director of OSI for about a year, he proposed to Director of Central Intelligence (DCI) John McCone that there be a new Directorate of Science and Technology (DS&T). It would include the mission of the Directorate of Research, whose director had moved to another senior government position. This proposal was not controversial. An additional proposal, however, to move the OSI from the Directorate of Intelligence, where all analysis was carried out, to the newly formed DS&T, was very controversial. The question was, should all analysts regardless of field be together in the Directorate of Intelligence, or should all scientists and engineers, whether research or analytic, be brought together in the DS&T? The proposal resulted in a bitter divide between Bud and Director of Intelligence Ray Cline. DCI McCone decided in favor of Bud. The OSI was moved to the new DS&T and Bud was appointed its first director. He was replaced as assistant director of scientific intelligence by Dr. Donald Chamberlain, the former chief of the Fundamental Sciences Division, later the chief of the Nuclear Division, and the person most responsible for my being at CIA.

In the early 1960s Nikita Khrushchev boasted that the Soviet ABM system could "hit a fly in the sky." Even though no one took the statement literally, the priority to know more about the Soviet research program increased considerably. Much Soviet research was carried out at the Kapustin Yar/Sary Shagan (KY/SS) medium-range missile test range in Kazakhstan. A U-2 plane was sent to take pictures of the terminal end of the range at Sary Shagan on the shores of Lake Balkhash. The results were startling. The pictures showed a huge electronically steerable radar (nicknamed Hen House), which was much larger than any in the

Western world, a very large mesh antenna (Hen Roost), and a few dishes with domes (Hen Eggs). The Hen House had the advantage of moving its beam electronically, whereas the beams of most radars at the time were only steerable by rotating the radar itself.

The importance of this discovery was such that the next U-2 mission was targeted to include Sary Shagan. Tragically, that was the ill-fated flight of Francis Gary Powers. It was fortunate that within a short period of time the first satellite photographic mission took place and included Sary Shagan. The quality of the photography was poor by U-2 standards, but the photographs were still helpful. Of special importance was to know more about the characteristics of the various radars, especially the Hen House. The radiation from the main radars passed over Europe, where there were intercept stations. Unfortunately, the radar beams were too high to be intercepted by these ground-level stations.

Then we had a piece of good luck. During the fall of 1962, the Soviets were conducting some unusual experiments on the KY/ SS range. On several occasions they would launch from KY to SS a missile with a nuclear device aboard. While the missile was on its trajectory, a second missile with no nuclear device aboard would be launched on the same trajectory. Before reentry the nuclear device on the first missile would be detonated. The purpose of the experiment was to find out how effective the radars were in detecting the presence of the second missile. They were testing the so-called blackout effect, which could be used in a real attack as a technique to blind the defensive radars.

At the time, the CIA operated an intercept site known as Taksman II, located on a mountain in northeast Iran during the days of the shah. On one occasion, and only one, some of the radiation from the Hen House was scattered south from the nuclear cloud toward Taksman II. This gave us the first look at the radiation from this radar and helped us determine some of its characteristics.

The need for a more reliable means of detecting the radiation from the radars at Sary Shagan was apparent. A very bright analyst noted that when the moon was in the right position the radiation from the radars at Sary Shagan would be reflected and could be detected by a 150-foot dish antenna at Chesapeake Bay Annex near Washington DC. Fortunately, we had just hired a young analyst who had recently earned his master's degree at Stanford University. His first assignment was to use the large dish to intercept the radiation from the radars at Sary Shagan after it had been reflected by the moon. This had to be done at night because the Soviets would be active during the daytime. The young analyst had recently been married and he could not tell his bride why he was away from home at night! Fortunately, she was understanding and made the best of it for the sake of national security.

Soon afterward a defense attaché photographed a huge A-frame antenna near Moscow, dubbed the Dog House. It was to be part of a deployed ABM system to protect Moscow and was the only part that was detected. It was a mystery to all of us that the Soviets would deploy a strategic ABM system without testing it on an intercontinental ballistic missile (ICBM) range such as the one they had at Tyuratam, where they launched long-range missiles across Siberia into the Pacific Ocean. All of their ABM testing had been medium-range tests between Kapustin Yar and Sary Shagan.

On Shemya island, at the end of the Aleutians, the Soviets used an FPS-17 radar to monitor the Soviet ICBMs they had launched from Tyuratam into the Pacific Ocean. On occasion the radar detected objects that appeared to be launched from the Kamchatka Peninsula in a trajectory that was in contrast to the usual trajectory of an ABM, which was directly opposite that of the incoming missile. Some analysts, including some very senior managers, believed this might be a novel way to launch ABMs and that it would solve our dilemma about the Soviets not testing their ABM system against ICBMs.

Observation planes were immediately dispatched along the Kamchatka Peninsula to take photographs of the area from which the ABMs seemed to have been launched, according to the backtracking of the data from the FPS-17 radar. They could not, however, observe any object until it was at a very high altitude. No evidence of ABM activity was detected. The mystery deepened.

Sometime later a consultant from Bell Laboratories was in my office to review some of our work. We showed him the data from the FPS-17 and asked for his opinion. His reply proved to be a great embarrassment to all of us. He said that such objects had been observed frequently at Kwajalein Atoll, the terminus of the U.S. ICBM test range. They were merely pieces of the ICBM tank that had broken up when it entered the atmosphere; those pieces skipped on the upper atmosphere somewhat like a rock skips on water. Mystery solved. But it was still surprising that the Soviets would begin deploying a system against ICBMs that had only been tested against medium-range ballistic missiles.

Physical Sciences and Technology

After serving for three years as chief of the ABM Branch of the Defense Systems Division in the Office of Scientific Intelligence, I was promoted to chief of the General Sciences Division, later known as the Physical Sciences and Engineering Division and still later as the Physical Sciences and Technology Division. This division did not usually write the intelligence "headlines" that were the responsibility of the weapon system divisions. Our mission was to appraise the advances in foreign science and technology that might lead to improved or new weapons systems. On occasion there would be something of sufficient importance that I believed the assistant director of scientific intelligence should be briefed (despite the title, he was actually the director). I met him in his office and started the briefing. I was pleased that he seemed to be very interested. While I was facing the blackboard (yes, we used them in the old days), I made a remark, and the boss responded, "Very, very interesting." I was elated. But when I turned around, I saw he was looking out the window through binoculars. I was deflated when he explained. "That is the first time I have ever seen one of those birds in this area!" Yes, I should have remembered that he was an internationally known birdwatcher.

Upon my return from a year at the National War College, a Future Threats Branch was created in my division. Emerging technologies that were of high interest included high-energy lasers, millimeter waves, and particle beams that could be used as weapons against personnel and equipment. Given the importance of these technologies, two senior analysts were assigned to the National Security Agency for an extended period, which proved to be highly effective.

Technology Transfer

During the 1970s the Soviets' efforts to acquire advanced Western technology were succeeding and becoming a major problem for the United States and its military allies. The loss of Western military technology to the Soviet Union via illegal and clandestine means was called the technology transfer (TT) problem. The National Security Council conducted a major review of the problem and concluded that TT losses were serious and growing.

The CIA would take the lead for the intelligence community on a new countermeasures program. Because the Physical Sciences and Technology Division had focused for years on advanced weapons technology, it would provide both technological intelligence expertise and leadership.

When President Reagan took office in 1981, one of his administration's top priorities was stopping the TT losses to the Soviet Union. President Reagan assigned Vice President George H. W. Bush, who was a former Director of Central Intelligence, to take the lead on the effort to stop the Soviet Bloc activities. The intelligence gathered provided astonishing insights into the Soviet program to acquire Western technology and how it had advanced Soviet weapons systems development. For the first time it was apparent how comprehensive the Soviet acquisition program was, beginning in the early stage of military technology development at universities, through early industrial development, and concluding at U.S. and allied defense company contractors.

One of the first pieces of finished intelligence on TT was an unclassified white paper, "Soviet Acquisition of Western Technology," intended to alert the U.S. and allied defense industries and academic communities that they were both prime targets for and current sources of Soviet bloc TT intelligence operations.

Subsequently, the DCI directed that an intelligence organization be created within the CIA to analyze TT intelligence to help stop the Soviet bloc acquisitions. Thus the Technology Transfer Assessment Center and the Technology Transfer Intelligence Committee were established. Over the next several years, these two entities provided the intelligence support necessary to organize the United States' and its NATO allies' countermeasure operations in effectively shutting down the Soviet bloc acquisition program.

Intelligence Community Committees

The intelligence community had a number of committees that discussed select topics on foreign intelligence. These committees also prepared reports for the DCI and others. Among them were the Guided Missiles Intelligence Committee (GMIC) and the Scientific Intelligence Committee (SIC). To clarify the missions of the two committees it was decided that GMIC would be renamed the Guided Missiles and Astronautics Intelligence Committee (GMAIC) and would only address current foreign weapon systems. SIC would be renamed the Science and Technology Intelligence Committee (STIC) and would address foreign sciences, technologies, and advanced future weapons systems such as directed energy weapons.

Because of my belief that our analysts could benefit from the expertise of scientists and engineers in academia and the private sector, I proposed to DCI Bill Colby that a scientific and technical advisory group be formed. It would report to the DCI, work closely with STIC, and be known as the Science and Technology Advisory Panel. He was in full agreement and instructed me to proceed to form the panel. The first chairman was a former director of the Advanced Research Projects Agency. Members were approved by the DCI and included a Nobel laureate.

In the summer of 1975 I met John Deutch at a conference in Newport, Rhode Island. He was a young professor of chemistry at the Massachusetts Institute of Technology. We became friends right away and had a lobster dinner together one evening. I asked him to become a member of the newly created Science and Technology Advisory Panel and said I would arrange a meeting with the DCI. Before the panel was formed, George Bush became the new DCI. Bush developed a special interest in the panel and typically met with its members. In early 1976 he met with John and welcomed him onto the panel. This was John's introduction to intelligence and he became a valuable panel member. Many years later he became the undersecretary of defense for acquisition and technology and later still the deputy secretary of defense, when Bill Perry was secretary of defense. John did not achieve his ambition to become the secretary of defense, but President Clinton did appoint him to become the DCI—a big step from his formative days with intelligence in 1976!

Space Systems Division

After many years as chief of divisions concerned with various foreign sciences and technologies, I became the chief of the Space Systems Division in the early 1980s. Soon after taking over, I became concerned that all of our projects were conceived within the agency, and that we did not always know the needs of policymakers and leaders of major defense programs. With this in mind, I asked a senior analyst in the division to meet frequently with policymakers and leaders and create a document to help plan our future intelligence projects.

When Admiral Stansfield Turner became the DCI, he also liked the idea of using outside expertise. While I was chairman of the Scientific and Technical Committee, he directed me to arrange a conference on advanced technology to be held in Annapolis. The conference included some of the country's top scientists and engineers, including Bob Noyce, the founder of Intel Corporation. Admiral Turner attended and was very pleased with the results.

The National Intelligence Council

The National Intelligence Council was composed of a dozen or so national intelligence officers (NIOs) who were specialists in their substantive field or geographic area, such as economics or Africa. NIOs served as senior advisors to the DCI and were responsible for supporting the chairing member agencies of the intelligence community in the preparation of National Intelligence Estimates, which were reviewed by the United States Intelligence Board and approved by the DCI. I suggested to senior management that there should be an NIO for science and technology. They agreed and an especially capable officer received the position. He resigned after about six months to go to the private sector. The DCI recommended that I serve as his replacement, and his recommendation was accepted. I held that position for five years before retiring from the agency. During that time we prepared several National Intelligence Estimates and I had many sessions with the DCI. I also became a close friend of the science advisor to the U.S. president, who helped me a great deal.

Shortly before retiring from the agency, I had become concerned that intelligence officers in the field did not have access to senior government officials to know of their intelligence needs. I suggested that senior officers from various stations in Europe meet in Frankfurt, Germany, to be briefed directly by leaders of major technological programs, such as the Strategic Defense Initiative and stealth research. The meeting proved to be quite successful.

Unexpected Events

In Honor of Nikita

In the late 1950s when the dome of the U.S. Capitol was refurbished, the first coat of new paint was a protective red color. Nikita

Khrushchev and his wife visited the United States in 1959, and one can imagine the jokes that went around when Washington welcomed the leader of the USSR to the Capitol with a red dome "in his honor." From my office by the Tidal Basin, I remember seeing the Khrushchevs drive by.

The Slot Machines

While we were still in Barton Hall, the Scientific Intelligence Committee, a group that produced and coordinated scientific analysis for the intelligence community, arranged a trip to Oak Ridge, Tennessee, and various facilities in the Southwest. I was invited to join. While in the air over New Mexico, one of the two engines on the Convair plane stopped. I was startled, but the pilot assured us that there was no problem because the plane could easily fly with just one engine. However, we would stop in Las Vegas to have the failed engine repaired. On the tarmac a mechanic asked me what I thought was a dumb question: "Is there something wrong with one of the engines?" Seeing my startled expression, he explained that pilots of private planes often cut one engine so they can stop in Las Vegas for a short time at the casinos!

Almost a Nobel Laureate

Soon after my arrival in Washington, I met Clyde Cowan, a professor of physics at Catholic University. He and his wife Betty became my good friends, and my wife and I spent a happy evening with them at the officers' club at the Washington Navy Yard. Clyde was well known in the physics community as the co-discoverer, with Frederick Reines, of the neutrino, a nuclear particle predicted theoretically by Enrico Fermi. Unfortunately, Clyde died prematurely, but Reines was awarded the Nobel Prize in physics for the discovery of the neutrino in 1995. We kept up with Betty for a few years but eventually lost touch. Years later I was talking with a friend from the National Research Council of the National Academy of Sciences, Sid Reid, and we both commented on how sad it was that Clyde had not lived to become a Nobel laureate. I asked him whatever happened to Betty and was shocked when he said, "I married her!"

One of My Real Heroes

Almost everyone knows of the heroic act of Jimmy Doolittle in leading the air raid on Tokyo in 1942—a most remarkable man. I was fortunate to be with him at a small meeting shortly after my arrival in Washington. We had a good conversation, and he could not have been more cordial. The encounter was even more meaningful for me because I served in the Pacific theater with the navy during World War II. I was happy that he later received a promotion to four-star rank and received the Congressional Medal of Honor.

A Fortunate Error

In early 1962, shortly after John Glenn orbited the earth, I was on a flight with him from Washington to Los Angeles. Not surprisingly, he was seated in first class. When I got off the plane and entered the airport, there was a large crowd, including reporters, surrounding him. A few days later when I returned to the Los Angeles airport, there were very few people there. Much to my surprise, I found myself walking side by side with John Glenn! After quickly congratulating him, I got up my nerve to ask him if, once we'd boarded, he would sign a postcard for my young daughter. He graciously agreed. During the flight I told the flight attendant about my conversation with Glenn and asked if she would take a postcard to him. I wrote down my daughter's name, the southern double name of Sallie Chris. Shortly afterward, she returned with *two* postcards, one to Sallie and one to Chris! I was disappointed but did not have the nerve to ask him to autograph another one. When I arrived home, I gave my five-year-old the card addressed to Sallie. Her interest was marginal. Then I gave the other card to my wife Chris and she was overjoyed! Sometimes mistakes can be helpful.

A Smart Man

Soon after becoming division chief, I had the good fortune to be one of four CIA officers selected to attend the National War College at Fort McNair in Washington for the 1966–67 academic year. There were typically 140 students, 35 each from the army, the navy, and the marine corps, with the others coming from the air force, the coast guard, and civilian life. The speakers included President Eisenhower, senior government officials, ambassadors, and others. A highlight of the year was a trip to our choice of one of five areas in the world. I chose Africa because I knew that if I didn't go then, I never would. Our group had its own C-141 and traveled to Congo-Kinshasa, Ethiopia, Ivory Coast, Kenya, Morocco, Mozambique, and Nigeria. We met with senior U.S. officials as well as officials from each country, including the presidents of Nigeria and Congo-Kinshasa. A member of our group asked the president of Nigeria, Yakubu Gowon, why he was known as "Colonel" rather than "General" as head of state. He immediately replied: "They shoot more generals than colonels! Long live the colonel!"

Two of my fellow students at the War College became chiefs of staff of the U.S. Army, one became chief of naval operations, one became commandant of the Coast Guard, and one became commander-in-chief of the Strategic Air Command.

China

In August 1979 a traveling companion and I were chosen for a fascinating tour of China. We had an interpreter at each stop, which included Beijing, Xi'an, Shanghai, Hangchow, and Guangzhou. A special highlight was our visit in Xi'an, where we were allowed to see the famed army of life-sized terracotta warrior sculptures that had been discovered only a few years earlier. The official opening of the warriors exhibit was to take place in October to coincide with the thirtieth anniversary of the Communist Revolution. We were allowed to enter the huge Quonset hut with our interpreter to see where the figures were being restored. We walked just a few feet from archeologists who were carefully removing dirt from the figures with spoons and other small implements. Initially we were not allowed to take pictures, but after we made several requests, we were told that if we paid fifty dollars, we could take one. As one might guess, no photos were taken! We were permitted to visit the facility because Vice President Mondale and his wife were scheduled to visit the site a few weeks later; our visit was probably a test run.

The Dream Rocks

While I was serving as chief of the Space Systems Division, a senior analyst and I journeyed to Australia. I stayed with Australian friends I had known when they were stationed in Washington. One day my host asked if I would be willing to help him and a friend remove the fences around the "dream rocks." I had no idea what he meant, but because he was my host I agreed. It so happened that there had been a race there the previous weekend, and there were many large rocks along the route that were sacred symbols to the Aborigines. These rocks had to be fenced off to prevent the crowds from desecrating them. Thus, my job was to help take down the fences—a most unusual task for an intelligence officer!

The Supreme Court

One never knows whom one might meet in Washington. My wife and I were invited to a party at the home of close friends, where we were introduced to John Paul Stevens, associate justice of the Supreme Court. He and our host played tennis together. During my brief conversation with him, I mentioned where I worked and he replied that he and his wife were going to visit the Soviet Union soon. They had not been before and did not know what to expect. I asked him if he would like to come to the agency and have our director of security brief him. He was enthusiastic and immediately accepted. I informed the director of security and he was glad to have the opportunity. A meeting was arranged and Justice Stevens was highly pleased with the results.

A Fifty-Cent Postage Stamp

Another unusual encounter occurred when the CIA hosted a meeting with representatives from the RAND Corporation in Santa Monica, California. Included was Nancy Nimitz, the daughter of Admiral Chester Nimitz, commander in chief of the Pacific Fleet during World War II. About a week earlier I had bought a sheet of fifty-cent postage stamps with Admiral Nimitz's image on them. When I asked Nancy if she had seen them, she replied that she had not but that she had furnished various photographs of her father to the artist who designed the stamp. I called my wife and asked her to bring my sheet of stamps to the agency. Nancy was thrilled to have them.

A Doctor Known to Everyone

In the early 1980s I attended a conference at the CIA that included many well-known persons from outside the intelligence community. Dr. Jonas Salk, who developed the polio vaccine, sat on my right during lunch. I was absorbed in talking with him and more or less ignored the person on my left. After a while I turned to my left to ask what the person did. He turned out to be the chairman of McDonnell Aircraft Corporation! I was certainly taken aback. That evening at a reception at the Kenwood Country Club, I introduced my wife to Dr. Salk, who was unhappy with the various reporters around him. He began talking with my wife as a means of eluding the press, then escorted her to her table before going to the head table. My wife was thrilled.

A Hero from World War II

In the 1980s I met R. V. Jones, who had been the junior science advisor to Winston Churchill during World War II. He referred to Churchill as "Winnie." Jones developed a method to distort the crossed radio beams the Germans were using to designate places where bombers were to drop their bombs. His method caused the bombers to drop their bombs on unpopulated areas.

Jones and his wife visited Washington often. We became good friends, and my wife and I entertained them at the Washington Golf and Country Club on several occasions. When we were there with a small group in the Virginia Room, someone suggested that Jones play his harmonica. That was all that was needed. He pulled a harmonica from his coat pocket and entertained the group for quite a while!

Postscript

Many years after I retired from the CIA, while I was working at the Institute for Defense Analyses in Alexandria, Virginia, the spy Aldrich Ames was exposed. Many of my associates asked me if I knew him, and my answer was always a resounding "No, and I am glad I didn't." A year or two later I was with a briefer at a Frankfurt meeting, and the briefer told me that Ames was at that meeting and I was to be his host. What a shock!

My career at the CIA lasted for thirty years and was as rewarding a career as anyone could ask for. The experience of having a CIA career also makes one attractive to nongovernment organizations. After my retirement, I served as an official at the Institute for Defense Analyses for eighteen years. I retired for good at age eighty-five with no regrets.

8

The Pathway of a Life Unnoticed

MICHAEL DOUGLAS SMITH

In May 1973 I put my DD 214 (army discharge) on the seat of my MG, filled the tank with thirty-two-cents-per-gallon gas and headed to Yale University to attend its summer language institute. I had just finished two years as a Korean language voice intercept operator for the Army Security Agency (now the Intelligence and Security Command) and wanted a grounding in Russian before starting my PhD program in Russian history at Florida State University. As I left the gate at Fort Hood, Texas, I told myself that I would never take a job that required a security badge as jewelry. Fate had other ideas.

Seven years later, PhD in hand, and with a few years of teaching at a very small Georgia college under my belt, I joined the analytic ranks of the CIA, at that time collectively called the National Foreign Assessment Center. My first job was in the Soviet Division in the Office of Central Reference and focused on the Soviet foreign ministry and biographies of its personnel. For the next eighteen months the office introduced me to the inner workings of the CIA and realities of surviving and thriving in a bureaucracy. I quickly learned that a PhD made no difference in a community that aspired to equality through the use of first names, not titles, until you were dealing with the senior leadership.

Four months after I began, the supervisor who had hired me moved to a different position. His replacement became my bête noire. The source of the disharmony arose one day while she was away from the office. I was tasked with contacting a number of U.S. embassy officials while researching a future study, and

I received bad information from another (non-Soviet) division, which led me to use incorrect wording in my tasking (request for information from our colleagues). My senior analyst had not caught the error when she reviewed my work and the tasking went out with the wrong language. The manager in the other division immediately raised his concern, which embarrassed my supervisor, who was his bureaucratic rival. I was called on the linoleum (there was no carpet in analytic offices at the time!), and my next performance appraisal placed me in the marginal category—down from the previous fully satisfactory employee group. There is a little irony in this in that the non-Soviet manager in this vignette would work for me twenty-plus years later when we were both contractors.

About sixteen months into my job, I received a call from the head of the CIA Operations Center, whom I had never met. He had my personnel file in front of him when we talked, and he said that my immediate supervisor was doing a skillful job of trying to get me fired with this appraisal. He had heard of my predicament from unnamed officers and had talked to others who knew my work and thought highly of it. He offered me a job as a watch officer. This was the first and most important watershed in my agency career, as promotions would come regularly thereafter and my performance appraisals would be uniformly favorable. My experience highlights an important feature of a CIA career—there are many opportunities in the agency, and if you find yourself in the wrong position or with a boss with whom you don't work well, you can move to another job that is a better match for your talents and personality.

Although short, my time as a biographic analyst produced several rewarding experiences. Two of my research studies for the new Reagan administration made indirect cameo appearances in the *Washington Post*. To produce them I was able to pillage the extraordinary collections of historical and current documents in CIA files—truly a historian's delight. Not so the grilling I received when Alexander Haig, the newly appointed secretary of state, misremembered part of my paper and was publicly corrected by the Soviet foreign minister, Andrei Gromyko. The next morning my supervisor and senior analyst were waiting for me to arrive at my desk. Happily, I could easily prove my study contained the correct information and it was Secretary Haig who had erred. The second paper caused no stir as it led to effective action by the administration. It was also during this time that I debriefed a Soviet defector in a "safe" location and under an assumed name. This experience challenged my Russian language skills but was fun.

The new job was in the Watch Office of the operations center, a dramatic change from my biographic work. It was shift work—twelve hours on and twelve hours off in a rotation of nights and days that changed each week. After two weeks we got one week off for training or filling in for officers who were sick or on assignment outside the Watch Office. The work was fast-paced with constant interaction with analysts and managers in the Directorate of Intelligence, the original name of the collective analytic corps. We also worked closely with the Directorate of Operations, the Watch Office of the clandestine service. The central function of the Watch Office was to screen incoming information from all sources and alert analysts and the leadership to breaking stories or information that added to stories of interest. This meant daily contact with the staff that produced the President's Daily Brief (PDB), which is delivered to the president six days a week, and sometimes meant alerting an analyst to a new piece of data. A good watch officer was one who stayed on top of events in his or her part of the world and who thrived on juggling knowledge of the content of ever-changing publications and the interests of scores of analysts. In this twenty-four-hours per day, seven days per week environment, a watch officer quickly accumulates a batch of experiences that make work memorable. I had a blast, and two years after joining the Watch Office, I was chosen to join the watch teams at the White House Situation Room—the pinnacle of the watch business.

The situation room is in the West Wing of the White House, which is where the president works (in the Oval Office). It is both less and more than that portrayed in television shows and movies. The work in many ways replicated the Watch Office routine I had experienced at the CIA, but the people we supported included the president and vice president and their staffs. We interacted with all the other watch offices in the U.S. government, the intelligence community, and nonintelligence offices alike. We were the president's frontline alerting center, which added an adrenaline kick beyond any we experienced in our home organizations. The watch staff was largely made up of CIA staff, along with a few from the National Security Agency and State Department as well as some military officers. This has changed, and the CIA doesn't dominate these teams today. We had daily contact with the president's national security advisor or his deputy, with the National Security Council staff, and occasionally with President Reagan or Vice President Bush. On rare occasions we had to visit the family quarters of the White House. My two and a half years in the White House Situation Room were gratifying, and I learned how foreign policy is made at the highest levels of our government. This knowledge was central to my understanding of how to provide effective support to policymakers and served as the basis for my actions in future jobs.

Every watch officer accumulates stories of major events in history, and the White House Situation Room provided those in abundance. There are no quiet periods in history and a watch officer develops a craving for chaos, turmoil, and disruptions of the normal, for these quicken the pace of work and make a current affairs "junkie" high! My memories of this time are filled with such stories as the release of Father Benjamin Weir from Hezbollah captivity in Lebanon, the hijacking of the *Achille Lauro* by Palestinian Liberation Front terrorists, which resulted in the death of American Leon Klinghoffer, and many others. It was stressful and I was sorry to have to leave (just before the Iran-Contra scandal in 1986), but I had topped out in rank there after elevation to the senior duty officer position. (Senior duty officers lead watch teams; there are five serving at any one time).

I arranged to do a rotation in the Office of Soviet Analysis (SOVA) on my return to the CIA, and there I learned another lesson in bureaucracy. My assignment was to produce a study of the Soviet foreign policy establishment. As I neared completion of the paper about my study, the SOVA leadership decided that the core of my work would be folded into another paper, which was being written by a member of the SOVA analytic ranks. I wasn't happy, but I was "only" a rotational staff member whose career wouldn't be affected by the change (if I didn't transfer to the SOVA career service). Again there were professional satisfactions: I wrote a PDB piece once a week on average for nearly a year (at that time a very unusual feat) and participated in the preliminary drafting of a speech for President Reagan.

Just before my rotational assignment was to end, the director of the operations center that included the Watch Office invited me to return. At that time, they were short on experienced senior duty officers. His inducement was an imminent promotion. I was torn between staying in a mainstream analytic position or reentering the somewhat chaotic world of the operations center. I chose the operations center.

The excitement of watch office work again provided plenty of memorable moments, but I also learned that after a year off, my body's tolerance of shift work was much reduced. I was part of a group of officers who asked management to authorize a change in the schedule, citing research studies showing our rotation was one of the most stressful. But the rank-and-file watch officers voted down a change because they liked the amount of time off the current schedule offered. As I approached the three-year mark, I began to look for other opportunities, the most interesting of which was joining the staff of the national intelligence officer (NIO) for warning, a legend in the intelligence community, Charlie Allen. After some negotiation, he agreed to bring me on board on rotation as his senior warning analyst. The first paper I asked to write was "The Coming Dissolution of the Soviet Union," a topic that had been on my mind for a while, but Charlie declined because he said that it would never survive review by the agency's leadership. I should have pushed more but didn't, and failing to write this paper two years before the USSR actually collapsed is one of the two regrets I have concerning my career in the agency. I'm sure there are other analysts who had the same idea but for one reason or another didn't publish it.

I had thought my time with the NIO would last at least a year, but sometimes you aren't truly in control of your career. This I learned just four months into my rotation. The head of the operations center, a friend and supporter of mine, called me down to his office and alerted me to a conversation the career service panel had had concerning me and the needs of the office. A career service, as the name implies, determines the professional progression of its members, and it is a brave person who defies it. Shortly after this conversation, my office director and head of the career service called me down to her office and basically said I should bury my personal preference to stay with the NIO and return to the office that housed the Watch Office to take a difficult assignment. An unhappy NIO let me out of the agreement and I started the most draining assignment of my career.

The CIA took charge of the publication of the president's daily intelligence summary when it was created in 1947. There was little change in the process or form of this paper until the Kennedy administration, when the CIA rolled out a new publication specifically designed for the new president entitled "The President's Intelligence Checklist." It was abbreviated PICL and pronounced "pickle." Soon the room in which the PICL was produced became known as the "Pickle Factory" and the officers who produced it as "picklers." The PICL was continued after Kennedy's assassination, but the new president, Lyndon Johnson, wasn't completely happy with it and the CIA developed a new publication, the President's Daily Brief, for him. During the next several administrations, differing formats and styles were tried, but the focus on the president's needs as leader of the nation remained paramount. Within the CIA, however, the evolution of the publishing side of the business had grown dysfunctional, and my new job was to fix it.

How to do that while ensuring the production of the PDB six days per week would entail long hours and careful handling of an ineffective management structure that oversaw a processing section rife with racial and age-related tensions. Just before I started the position, there was a night when the PDB almost was not published when a physical assault in the processing section had narrowly been avoided. My plan to fix the problems had two tracks: training to reduce the racial tension and ageism problems in the processing publication section and development of a new structure for accountability and personnel management. I was fortunate to have the creative support of my division chief in dealing with the management issues and finding two very talented officers to fill the position of night supervisor of the publication process. The latter became heads of a night team and were responsible for producing the PDB each night and supervision of their team members, which included the typical branch chief duties of personnel development and performance appraisal. Both tracks worked, though the lion's share of praise has to go to the team chiefs. I have bittersweet memories of many nights with Jim Lewek, a fantastic leader and accomplished economist, whom I hired back into the agency, after he left to work on a Virginia state commission, when I was looking for new leaders for the revised management structure. We were both part of the agency's Little Rock support efforts to President-elect Clinton and Vice President-elect Gore, and our duties included briefing the PDB to Gore, an assignment we both relished. Lewek returned to his analytic roots as an economist soon after I left the staff. He was killed in April 1996 in the airplane crash that killed Secretary of Commerce Ronald Brown in Croatia. His star on the CIA Memorial Wall is my personal connection to the hundred-plus other agency staff who have died on duty.

As my reward for fixing the daily publications processing staff, the office let me take a rotation as head of the Director of Central Intelligence (DCI) action staff, which was charged with handling the director's formal taskings to all of the CIA's offices, and managing his weekly meetings with a number of cabinet heads. The view of the workings of the DCI's office was fascinating, from the speechwriters who had an irreverent streak to the bureaucratic machinations worthy of medieval Italian court politics (think the Borgias!).

A favorite memory is of a spoof of a fictional DCI appearance on the *Late Show with David Letterman*. Letterman had many topical, mostly mildly humorous comments about the DCI, such as the "Ten Reasons Why the CIA Continues to be Vital to our National Security." Numbers 3 to 1: We can verify that Franco (former dictator of Spain) is still dead, but we cannot reveal sources and methods. We know where Elvis is. We can make your VCR stop blinking 12:00. Twenty-two years later, how many people have any idea what a VCR is, much less why it blinked 12:00?!

After a year of fun with the DCI staff, I moved to the Weapons Intelligence, Nonproliferation, and Arms Control Center. This turned out to be another enjoyable and satisfying assignment. I created an intelligence community interagency support committee to ensure questions were properly staffed to the relevant agencies. My committee received a presidential letter of commendation for our support. This was a gratifying end to an engrossing assignment.

Normally, two rotational assignments in a row would be frowned upon by a career service, even ones that were clearly beneficial to the agency. So, of course, when the agency offered a third rotation, I accepted. This time the assignment was to serve as a senior staff member of the Commission on Reducing and Protecting Government Secrecy, usually known as the Moynihan Commission after Senator Daniel Patrick Moynihan, who was the driving force behind the authorizing of the commission and served as one of its co-chairs. The head of the House Permanent Select Committee on Intelligence, Representative Larry Combest, was the other co-chair. Senator Moynihan was a legend in politics, a prolific author, and a former vice-chair of the Senate Select Committee on Intelligence. I jumped at the chance to work with him.

The staff was housed in decaying offices on Navy Hill, across from the Department of State, which was providing administrative support to the commission and its staff. Our work included interviewing experts, academics with an interest in government openness, and government officials, both foreign and domestic. I became the liaison with the Canadian government and with academia. An unexpected crossroads occurred just four months in, when the head of the Center for the Study of Intelligence approached me with the offer of a plum assignment, chief historian of the agency. I was torn between my roots as a historian and the opportunity to delve into the history of the CIA as no other person can, on the one hand, and the fulfilling work I was then undertaking on the commission staff, on the other hand. This is the second and last of my regrets of my choices in the agency: I decided to stay with the commission. The two years had some bumps, most notably the continuing suspicions of the very capable staff lawyer whose default was suspicion of anyone from the CIA, no matter how much I was promoting more openness of the agency's historical files. Still, watching Senator Moynihan work and having the occasional interaction with him was gratifying and informative. My favorite time was the Saturday that the senator, his chief of staff on the commission, and I spent working through three three-inch binders of CIA reports containing CIA assessments of the viability of the Soviet system. Seeing our thirteen-year record all in one place prompted the senator to comment that the agency had done a better job than he had previously believed.

After two years the commission concluded its work and I returned to the CIA to confront the consequences of my decision to stay on the commission. I discovered that my previous leadership and mentors had all moved on or retired, and I was on my own in finding a new job. The historian's job was no longer open, and my office had no openings either. Happily, a colleague asked if I could temporarily join the PDB staff, which was undergoing reorganization. This brought me back to the publication that had dominated my life for three years at a time when the agency was trying to reenergize its relations with the president. Most of my days were filled with administrative tasks—I became the unofficial chief of staff—and support for the PDB briefers. Because of my background as a historian, former chief of the PDB publications staff, and former PDB briefer, I was asked by the DI front office to produce a fiftieth anniversary issue of the PDB and its companion, the National Intelligence Daily. This was fantastic: it meant I had to read every PDB produced to date to select representative stories for the commemorative volume. Imagine the joy of a professionally trained historian and current affairs maven being "forced" to read this material—and get paid for it! Once completed, the volume was shown to recipients of the PDB, who were enthusiastic about its appearance. One reader suggested it be declassified and offered to the public, but that didn't happen and it remains in the vaults of the agency. During this time, I also filled in as a PDB briefer. This time my readership would be the deputy secretary of defense, John Hamre, the deputy director of CIA, General John Gordon, and the undersecretary of state for political affairs, Thomas Pickering. Again I felt the adrenaline rush and joy of juggling multiple stories for multiple customers over time. In hindsight, there was no job that I liked better than that of briefer (but senior duty officer in the White House Situation Room was a close second).

After over a year of looking for a permanent job, I was frustrated and beginning to tire physically. In June 1998 I realized that with my military service, I qualified for the early retirement provisions of the peace dividend after the demise of the Soviet Union, and I decided to put in my paperwork. At the time, you could choose a cash buyout or three months in a transition program, which included help in finding a new job outside government. I chose the transition program, and during my first weekend in the program the Army asked me to be in charge of its European analyst division in England. An agonizing Columbus Day weekend followed—I had lived as a child just a few miles from this post and would enjoy living there again—but in the end I realized my mind was already engaged with a new future. On December 31, 1998, I stopped being a CIA officer and entered the private business sector and returned to part-time teaching.

9

The DI Toolkit—Don't Leave Home without It

JANET M. STIEGLER

My thirty-two-year career at the CIA had an inauspicious start.[1] A foreign language major with degrees in German and Russian, I had been invited to interview with several different CIA offices on January 14, 1982. When my fiancé and I arrived in Rosslyn, Virginia, the evening before the interview, we learned that the city had just experienced two tragic accidents within thirty minutes of one another: Air Florida Flight 90 had crashed into the Fourteenth Street Bridge over the Potomac River killing seventy-eight people, including four on the ground, and the Orange Line of the Washington Metro had derailed, resulting in three fatalities and numerous trapped and injured passengers.

These incidents, combined with icy snow, paralyzed the region for the next several days. Buses, including the CIA's Blue Bird, which I was to take to headquarters for my interviews, ran sporadically, and some of my interviews were canceled, either because the transportation delays did not get me there in time or because the hiring managers had opted to stay home for the day.

I had hoped to land a job that would allow me to use my Russian language skills, but it appeared the only opening in the Soviet Division, where I interviewed, involved entering the names of Soviet leaders and facilities into a database for future research and retrieval. Believing a master's degree should lead to more intellectual work, and naïve to how the hiring system worked, I graciously declined, not realizing that my folder would likely be sent back to the Office of Personnel with a "no appropriate position" sticker on it.

Luckily, before sending it back, the manager showed my folder to a colleague in the division that followed European leaders. Many years and several promotions later, I learned from this manager that she was halfway out the door when the manager came by, took a quick glance at my résumé, and said she would give me a shot. What was probably an incidental decision on her part turned out to have a huge impact on the course of my life.

The first thirteen years of my career were thus spent in the Directorate of Intelligence (DI) as a leadership analyst and manager. Researching, analyzing, and writing thousands of profiles and several longer papers on European (and later Soviet) leaders for the executive and legislative branches of government was like being in college, only a lot more fulfilling. A briefing book is always prepared when a U.S. policymaker is going to meet with a foreign counterpart, and the leadership profiles are a key component of that book. I had the satisfaction of knowing that what I wrote was being read and used daily by our customers. (I still remember the sense of awe I felt when I learned that one of my first leadership profiles would be read by then secretary of state George Shultz.) On several occasions I was invited to State Department roundtables to listen to the very subjects of my analysis. I also had the opportunity to travel to a number of European embassies and consulates to debrief U.S. diplomats for a longer research paper I was writing on the next generation of foreign leaders. Over the ensuing years, it was fun to watch when many of these leaders rose to leadership positions in their respective countries.

One of my more satisfying projects was a piece I wrote for a U.S. ambassador and arms control negotiator on his Soviet counterpart. The U.S. requester was looking for ways to build rapport with his Soviet counterpart, who had a distant and often dour demeanor. I had recently transferred to a unit where we were teamed up with clinicians doing psychological studies of foreign leaders and was concerned that, as the newbie, I had been saddled with a dull and impossible task: outside of some basic curriculum vitae from his time in the Soviet foreign ministry, there was hardly any information on the subject in our files. It turned out, however, that the subject was well known to a Soviet defector who was living in the Washington DC area and was willing to be debriefed. My Directorate of Operations contacts kindly arranged the meeting at an undisclosed facility. It was a fascinating experience, and I gained much more knowledge about my subject from a man who knew him well. Two personal points helped humanize my subject for the U.S. ambassador. One was that his Soviet counterpart suffered from ulcers, which may have explained his pained facial expressions and curt behavior. The other was that he was a fan of Soviet literature, especially the nineteenth-century Russian poet and novelist Alexander Pushkin, and that he became very animated when discussing it. How exactly the U.S. ambassador used this information was never shared with me, but I received a very laudatory cable in response, suggesting that he had succeeded in making a breakthrough.

By and large, our leadership profiles and longer analyses were on the mark, and we often heard how they were the most popular products in the U.S. policymakers' briefing books. Every once in a while, however, we got something wrong, and we would hear about it. For instance, we had egg on our faces when one European leader with a known weight problem showed up looking a lot thinner than the portrait we had drawn. Apparently, he had been on a crash diet, something not evident from the information available to us at the time. A psychological profile of one Soviet leader I worked on described his behavior and motivations to a tee, but it assessed in a short paragraph at the end that he was unlikely to advance much higher in the Soviet hierarchy. At the time of publication, we received kudos for our "insightful analysis." Years later, however, and to my chagrin, this leader rose to some prominence.

Working in the DI, particularly on analyses of Western leaders, gave me a lot of writing experience, since leaders in these countries met regularly with our policymakers. The DI schools

all its analysts on BLUF (bottom line up front) and the importance of strong topic sentences with relevant supporting evidence
and examples. It also teaches its analysts how to evaluate various
sources of information for reliability and provides tools to help
them avoid common cognitive biases. The analytic and writing
skills I learned in the DI proved valuable throughout my career,
and I applied them to every other job I held in the agency.

From 1986 to 1988 I had the opportunity to serve two years as
a DI representative overseas in a European post. My role was to
serve as the analytic liaison to our foreign intelligence partners.
My husband, who also worked in the DI at the time, had a job
at the post as well, although he worked in a different unit and
building. We were very fortunate to have had that opportunity
as there were not many DI positions overseas at the time, and
it greatly enhanced our understanding of and appreciation for
what we do as an agency overseas. I believe it also gave us more
credibility with our Directorate of Operations counterparts when
we returned to the United States.

There were some rough patches during the tour, particularly in
the beginning. Being a young woman and a new mother, I faced
some initial skepticism as to whether I was up to the job. On top
of that, our infant son had to have surgery within the first month;
although not serious, working with the local bureaucracy added
to my stress. Finally, our two Siamese cats had been separated
from our flight and sent to another country for a few days. When
they finally arrived, they had terrible wheezing coughs for several weeks, leaving us to wonder where they had been stored in
transit and whether they would survive.

Over time, however, things improved, and I soon had a regular stream of DI visitors and analytic exchanges with our partner
service. Practically every DI office director came over, often leading an entourage of several analysts, and I would arrange multi-
day conferences with our foreign partners. During the rare lull
in my activities, I assisted the reports officer in drafting intelli-

gence reports based on documents provided by the foreign intelligence service. This permanent change of station turned out to be a highlight of my career, and my success earned me the respect of the partner service and my overseas colleagues, a promotion, and several job offers upon my return. My husband and I spoke about trying to go overseas again, but as our respective careers took off in different directions and our children became involved in school-related activities and friendships, the prospect of another tandem assignment faded.

There was one incident during the tour that in hindsight seems funny but at the time was quite embarrassing. I share it because it shows how even with the best-laid plans, there is always the unexpected, and how you react to the unexpected can be as important as the event itself.

Whenever a senior DI officer came through with a group of analysts, I would hold a party at my house for them and our foreign counterparts as a relaxing end to the substantive talks. It was not uncommon for the heads of the various analytic departments in the liaison service and their spouses to attend, along with the management of our organization. I was given funds to have these events catered, and they generally went off splendidly.

Before one event, I asked our administrative officer if I could have my apartment rugs cleaned. Our infant son had dropped food in some areas, and we wanted the stains out before the party. Our officer agreed to have one of the foreign nationals who worked for him rent a rug cleaner and take care of it. When we arrived home the night before the party, we noticed the rug was still a bit damp, but we did not worry too much about it, figuring it would be dry by the next night. We tiptoed around the apartment in order to keep the rug pristine.

By the night of the party, the rug was dry, so I happily got dressed and worked with the caterers to set out the food. The guests began arriving and everything seemed to be going smoothly. The first hint that something might be amiss was when one of the guests from the partner service asked if we had a chlorine pool in the basement. Then one of the DI analysts said he had to go back to his hotel because there was something in the air that was affecting his asthma. We quickly called him a taxi. As several more people commented on the smell, it soon dawned on me that whatever was used to clean the rugs was being dusted up into the air by the fifty-plus guests now trampling around the rug. It was making people uncomfortable and, in some cases, affecting their health.

I wanted to dig a hole and hide in it. My face must have registered my dismay, for the DI office director who was visiting at the time, Bob Layton, came to my rescue. He laughed and joked that it was no big deal, that everyone would just have another drink and not even notice. His lighthearted attitude put me and everyone else at the party at ease. If it were not unprofessional, I would have kissed him. The party continued for several more hours, albeit with fewer guests. Several weeks later I received a handwritten note from Mr. Layton, thanking me for a fabulous conference. I had received thanks before from visitors but never a handwritten one, and his gracious leadership left a strong impression on me.

Although the Office of Leadership Analysis (LDA) was disbanded as a bureaucratic entity in 1995, the function continued (and continues to this day) in the regional DI offices. I was now a part of the Office of European Analysis but sat in the same office and carried out the same function as I had as an LDA branch chief. Our new management did their best to make us feel at home, but for those of us who grew up in LDA and its predecessor organization (the Office of Central Reference), its dissolution was nevertheless heartbreaking. On top if this, I had recently undergone what would turn out to be the first of several surgeries for breast cancer. It was a challenging time, personally and professionally.

As a GS-15 I had been looking at other opportunities, and in less than a year I took a broadening assignment as one of two DI representatives to our comptroller's office. (Before the CIA had a chief financial officer, the comptroller was essentially the head of the CIA budget.) This was not my first choice; I was close to landing an assignment as a staff assistant to one of the executives on the seventh floor, but this fell through when a new CIA director (John Deutch) and executive director (Nora Slatkin) were brought in from the Department of Defense, and they wanted more senior staff assistants. I was steered instead to the comptroller's office, where I imagined being surrounded by people with green eyeshades whose passion was crunching numbers all day.

As it turned out, the number crunching was left to the real budget experts, and my DI skills were put to good use analyzing the CIA program plan for gaps and inconsistencies; drafting or editing the all-source analysis portion of the Congressional Budget Justification Book; and organizing DI briefings for examiners from the Office of Management and Budget. I also had the opportunity to participate in an interagency exercise that ultimately brought more positions to analysis. In fact, participating in the process of developing a CIA program and corresponding budget, submitting it to Congress, and then seeing how we defended it over the course of the next few months was such an eye opener that I wrote an article for *What's News at CIA* (the CIA internal newspaper) to explain it in layman's terms. Understanding this process and how agency programs are funded and executed was extremely useful to me in subsequent management and senior staff positions, and I have encouraged other new managers to take a tour there or in their respective directorate plans shops to gain similar understanding.

When my rotation on the comptroller's staff concluded, I took a risk and applied for a position at the newly formed National Imagery and Mapping Agency (NIMA, now the National Geospatial-Intelligence Agency). Having been formed from the Defense Mapping Agency, the CIA's National Photographic Interpretation Center, and several other smaller organizations that performed or supported imagery analysis, NIMA was undergoing a fair amount of internal turmoil, and I was discouraged from taking a position there. However, the DI was also undergoing change, and the position at NIMA would allow me to work for a leader I admired—Leo Hazlewood, the CIA's former executive director and then head of NIMA's Operations Directorate.

My job at NIMA evolved over the two years I was there: I first advised the director and deputy director of operations on workforce-related matters, performed research and skills analysis, and implemented several process improvements. In the second year, I served as deputy program manager of a small team developing a new human resource management system for NIMA. The rotation allowed me to use my DI research and communications skills while also learning more about human resources issues. I also wrote an article for NIMA's internal newspaper about the CIA's "rank in person" assignments process, since NIMA was exploring the implications of transitioning from a "grade in position" to "grade in person" system.

As I began making plans to return to the CIA, a mentor advised me that, after serving two back-to-back staff jobs, I needed to get back to management or the organization would forget I had ever been a manager. I wanted a position that would allow me to capitalize on the budgetary and human resources expertise I had built up in my last two rotations. My next stop turned out to be the Foreign Broadcast Information Service (FBIS, later the Open Source Center and now the Open Source Enterprise).

FBIS was formed during World War II to monitor radio broadcasts from the Axis powers, and it is unique in that it serves as both a collection entity and a reporting entity on openly available information. At the time I joined, it was at the tail end of a painful cut to its overseas bureaus, as some seniors felt that the growth of the internet was making it less relevant. This turned out to be shortsighted, since the explosion of open-source information still required experts to identify, translate, and put into context most intelligence-relevant information.

I stayed at FBIS for six years, first as deputy group chief for Europe, Latin America, and Africa and later as chief of production and analysis. As such, I

- Oversaw an effort to increase the volume and sophistication of FBIS analytic production;
- Developed corporate standards of quality for FBIS analytic products;
- Piloted the office's first efforts to publish open-source analysis based on internet exploitation; and
- Increased the production of media aids through in-house research, commercial acquisitions, and foreign partnerships.

I also worked with the senior analysts in FBIS to develop and implement two media analysis courses, my first foray into the training world. One year I planned and executed FBIS's annual management conference with a focus on how the organization would address the challenges posed by the explosion of open-source information over the next decade.

While at FBIS I was promoted into the Senior Intelligence Service, but the exposure to this often underestimated service with its linguistic and media expertise was far more rewarding. I was also in awe of FBIS managers, who at fairly junior grades were managing facilities abroad with a level of program management, budgetary, and technical savvy not generally expected of DI managers, who focused more on substance. One of my few regrets was not having the opportunity to work in or manage an FBIS bureau abroad. The timing simply did not work out, so instead I took advantage of other opportunities.

After a second bout with breast cancer (it returned after my initial surgery ten years earlier), I sought a lateral assignment that would afford more flexibility and time with family. The inspections staff in the Office of Inspector General hires officers from across the agency to conduct inspections on select CIA offices and specific agency activities. We worked in teams for six months on one topic, then began with a new team and topic for the next six months. Everyone had some common responsibilities like researching a specific topic and conducting interviews, but we also had some unique ones. For instance, you could be the team leader, the main drafter, or the survey lead; you could also be put in charge of developing and analyzing the interview questions or collecting and analyzing documentary data. There were standard team meetings twice a week, but apart from that, you were in charge of your own schedule.

The job, which included a lot of research, analysis, and writing, played heavily to the strengths of someone with a DI background. Often the DI analyst on the team served as primary drafter, but perhaps because of my varied career, I played different roles with each inspection: twice I served as team lead, twice as drafter. Another time I developed and analyzed a survey from scratch. Because they were congressionally mandated, the inspections opened doors for us across the agency, and I learned about agency activities and special programs that I would not have been privy to back in the DI or FBIS. I also traveled twice to the Far East and once domestically to conduct interviews with folks in our stations.

My last six years at the agency were spent in the Director's Area in a variety of staff or staff management positions, including three years as the CIA's executive secretary. I was again able to parlay the skills I had acquired in the DI into these assignments. For instance, I

- Oversaw production of the director and deputy director's daily meeting materials and trip books;
- Reviewed all executive correspondence and responses to external taskings that came to the agency; and
- Conceptualized and published the agency's monthly corporate report, a vehicle designed to provide the CIA's director and deputy director with insights and trend analysis on agency programs and corporate governance.

Supporting the senior leadership team gave me insight into the variety of issues they deal with each day and the importance of providing them with clear, succinct briefing materials that they could digest quickly before a National Security Council, foreign liaison, or internal decision-making meeting. My staff would edit and integrate the talking points that experts in the different directorates had drafted into a coherent whole on templates specific for each meeting. Often a National Security Council meeting agenda would be decided the day before the meeting, resulting in late nights for everyone involved in the production chain. With the directorates juggling other mission priorities and some offices not understanding how the information they provided would be used at these meetings, the input we received from across the agency could be quite uneven.

At the direction of the CIA's executive director, Scott White, I led a cross-agency effort to raise the quality of staff work in the agency. This six-month effort involved interviewing seventy executive managers and senior staff officers; benchmarking best practices at eight intelligence, defense, and policy agencies; developing online references and training guides, and creating an agency-wide brown bag speaker's series specifically for staff officers. Using a format similar to one we used in the Office of Inspector General, I drafted a white paper outlining our findings and recommendations for the executives on the seventh floor.

While not all of our recommendations were implemented at the time, they saw some light when a new executive staff officer (ESO) career service was created a few years later combining six of the Director's Area offices. Given the work I had done previously in this area, I was asked to lead a team to develop training for the new career service. With the help of a CIA University course designer, we conducted a fairly in-depth needs assessment and then designed, developed, and implemented an ESO tradecraft course. A three-week course including both online and classroom exercises, it targets senior staff who support the executive decision-maker and want to learn more about the functions of the seventh floor. The course continues to serve the ESO career service and business areas as well as those doing similar work in other parts of the agency.

Looking back, I had a fabulous career that took me places I would never have imagined I would go when I started out as a junior leadership analyst. The DI provided a solid foundation from which I could apply my critical thinking, problem solving, and writing skills to other areas in the agency. Moving across directorates exposed me to new knowledge and the phenomenal people who work for the CIA, whose expertise and dedication to its mission make the organization a gold standard in government.

Notes

1. The analytical arm of the CIA was called the Directorate of Intelligence throughout the author's career at CIA. The name was changed to the Directorate of Analysis in 2015, after the author's retirement, as part of a larger CIA modernization initiative.

TWO

Directorate of Operations Tales

10

A Nightmare Come True

ELINOR HOUGHTON KELLY

I was living a nightmare. I was being held by the Sluzhba Vnesh-ney Razvedki (SVR), the Russian external intelligence ser-vice, inside Sheremetyevo International Airport in Moscow. As I started to make a critical phone call for assistance, the left lens of my eyeglasses fell out and slid under the telephone kiosk. Now I could only see out of my right eye—the weak one. I felt myself in a fog. I strained to hear, but my normally acute sense of hearing was muffled and I was only dimly aware of several men standing close to me. My heart was thudding so hard that I was afraid the men would hear it.

I tried desperately to regain control of my body and my thoughts. Cold sweat trickled down my nose, ran down the inside of my silk blouse. My glasses were sliding off my nose, and the telephone receiver I was holding in my hand was slippery. I dialed the phone with one hand, while holding on to my glasses with the other. My legs trembled with fear, and I had to lean against the wall of the kiosk for support.

An embassy operator answered the phone. Exhaustedly, I asked for the officer on duty. When he responded, I said that I was in Moscow for U.S. embassy meetings. I explained that after the meetings ended, the Russians had physically prevented me from boarding a plane to return to the United States. Further, they had informed me that there was a "serious problem" with my Rus-sian visa and they were detaining me in the airport.

A few moments later the duty officer brusquely advised me that I wasn't listed in embassy records and that he could find no record of my meetings. Before he could hang up, I demanded that he review his records. He reiterated that he didn't know who I was—implying that he didn't care either—and then added with apparent satisfaction that since it was Sunday, neither the embassy nor the Department of State in Washington would take any action until the following day. I pleaded with the officer to recheck his records and told him that I would call him back. He had been speaking loudly, so I knew that the Russians standing next to me had heard his every word.

When I hung up the phone, the officials standing close beside me gripped my arms so hard they hurt and led me back to the stifling, windowless baggage room where they were holding me. The fact that an American official had been prevented from boarding a flight meant that the Russians were paying serious attention to me. And now they had heard the embassy officer's unusually negative and disrespectful responses to my plea for help. It was clear to me that if I weren't already in the hands of the SVR, I soon would be.

How had I ended up in this terrifying situation? Perhaps I should have expected it, given my long quest to fully "experience life."

I remember the day I was stopped for speeding in North Carolina in my spiffy little convertible. I had begged the kindly old southern judge to allow my friend Donna and me to spend the night in the local jail instead of paying a fine. We really wanted to experience jail! We were greatly disappointed when the judge refused, explaining that since it was "Sattidy" night, our delicate young ladies' ears would be exposed to the loud "cussin' going on." Fortunately, there were other opportunities for "learning by living."

I remember the exhilaration when I hitched a ride on a freight train. Actually, that had happened only because a friend and I were whiling away a boring summer afternoon waiting to return to college, and we climbed over a stopped train to get to Baskin Robbins. Once we climbed up onto the flat car, we were reluctant to climb down. We were up high, and although there was a huge threshing machine chained to the flat car, it really didn't block much of our view. We sat down and laughingly debated whether we should take a ride. We hadn't quite reached a decision when the train began to roll forward. We hung onto the chains as the train flew around curves at terrifying speeds, while the thresher creaked and slid and dripped oil on our heads. What a ride!

I was born into a wonderfully creative family in Bethesda, Maryland, in which my two brothers and I were each encouraged in our own very different fields of endeavor. We were also expected to remember our illustrious colonial forebears and to behave with dignity as they presumably always had.

To our delight, we discovered we had a "black sheep" in our ancestry known as "Hair Buyer Harrison." During the Revolutionary War, Hair Buyer paid bounties to the Indians for white men's scalps and proudly wore them hanging from his belt. When my older brother taunted our grandmother, a grand dame who lived and breathed our proud family heritage, by loudly discussing Hair Buyer in front of her aristocratic friends, she threatened to disinherit him. It was not an idle threat.

I discovered only recently in the Harvard University archives that Hair Buyer was actually Henry Hamilton, and he was a British general rather than an American renegade. He recruited Indian tribes to fight with the British against the American rebels, and apparently he did in fact collect white men's scalps. Although of questionable character, he was also an adventurer whose DNA I have inherited.

After leaving home, I did a stint as an au pair in France, graduated from American University's School of International Service, and took a couple of private sector jobs. I always had a penchant for foreign languages. Was it life taking a hand when an agency friend heard me speaking French and Portuguese and then recommended me to the CIA Directorate of Operations (DO)?

After months of interviews, testing, and background checks followed by intensive training, I was pleased to finally become a DO case officer—a spy. My first twenty years in the DO were fascinating, boring, and thrilling. But what happened in Moscow was downright terrifying.

My job at the time was to manage the National Resources Division's (NR's) operations against Russians in the United States, in close partnership with Central Eurasia Division. The National Resources Division was the DO division responsible for operational activities in the United States, and the Central Eurasia Division was responsible for operations against targets (foreigners with access to important national security information needed by the United States) from former Soviet Union countries.

I had just returned from seven years in the field, where my job, much like that of a journalist seeking well-informed sources, was to identify foreigners with access to information needed to address the U.S. government's intelligence gaps. The ultimate goal was to persuade those individuals to provide critical information to us. Now back at headquarters, my job was to energize new operations, to support field officers who were running operations, and to disseminate intelligence produced in those operations to U.S. policymakers.

My first days as a young headquarters manager were eye-opening. Case officers often could select their individual targets. But in spite of its importance, most officers in the domestic field were choosing not to pursue the Russian target. Headquarters had been sending out a litany of negative messages to field officers, denigrating their efforts. Who wants to be told repeatedly that they don't know what they are doing? And on those rare occasions when cases did begin to move forward, the headquarters pros from Dover leapt onto planes to take over the cases from the field officers. Obviously, field officers couldn't be trusted to handle things as well as the headquarters experts. The end result was a few field officers handling a few lackluster Russian cases.

My boss said he picked me for the job to ratchet up the quality and quantity of U.S. operations against the Russian target. I was also expected to improve morale among domestic field officers working that target. It was a tall order. I needed to persuade the talented but often arrogant Central Eurasia Division officers who "owned" the Russian target worldwide that we were just as competent at recruiting targets—that is, convincing foreigners with access to important national security information to provide it to CIA case officers—as they were. To make that happen, we also had to find valuable new targets.

My first day on the job I stopped all negative cables on Russian-related issues, regardless of which office drafted them. Instead, I edited the cables so that, while the bottom line remained the same, the tone and verbiage were positive and encouraging. Changing those pessimistic and dogmatic cables required stomping on a lot of toes. Later, as operations improved, more positive and supportive cables flowed from my office as well as from the Central Eurasia Division.

At the same time, I developed new ways to identify targets. During my field years I had been frustrated by the abysmally poor leads sent out by headquarters. I was convinced that case officers could recruit more targets and collect more intelligence if headquarters sent out better leads. So we implemented methodologies to systematically collect, analyze, and map data on certain foreigners visiting, studying, or working in the United States. We then sent our results to the field for action. This was a new way of doing business, and most officers in the domestic field fought it fiercely. They didn't want headquarters' help; they were sure they could find better leads themselves. Even more importantly, though, they saw it as a deliberate attempt to curtail their authority and autonomy.

Shortly thereafter, I was invited to visit Moscow. And on my way home, I ended up in a Russian baggage room.

The Russians did not physically torture me. However, being forcibly detained and interrogated by large, angry men in a small, crowded space for hours on end is probably not anyone's idea of a good time. And the fact that they knew I worked for the CIA, their sworn enemy, made it much worse.

After my meetings in Moscow had ended, I rose well before dawn to go to the airport to catch a flight home. I believed myself well on my way as I walked confidently down the ramp to board my plane, wheeling my small carry-on bag. Suddenly, I was grabbed from behind. My bag was yanked from my hand. Uniformed Russian officers surrounded me. One grim, heavyset man tersely informed me that my visa was no good. Therefore, he announced in a threatening voice, I was prohibited from leaving Russia. The men ignored me as I whipped out my passport and frantically pointed to my Russian visa.

Two Russian officers gripped my arms and pulled me back down the ramp. I was pushed through the airport to an out-of-the way room jammed with luggage and thrust into a metal folding chair. Then they slammed and locked the door. The next time the door opened, a man was wheeling in my suitcase, which I had checked that morning. Obviously it had been removed from the plane. I knew then that I was in deep, deep trouble.

The hard chair bit into my back as the Russian men leaned close to me and peppered me with questions. They wanted to know everything about me, and they grew enraged at my brief, uninformative replies. Finally, I had had enough. Girding myself, I stood up. I furiously reminded them that I was an American official and demanded to be allowed to call the U.S. embassy. The men muttered angrily in Russian among themselves. Eventually, crowding close to me on either side, they allowed me to exit the baggage room and walk to a telephone located in a kiosk. After I made the call, they grimly escorted me back to my chair in the baggage room.

As I tried to keep my wits about me, I remembered hearing that it was a tough time for Americans living in Russia. American officers returning from work might find that the orange juice in their refrigerators had disappeared. Tomato juice stood there instead. Or some might find that streets on their route home from the embassy were unexpectedly blocked by construction or mysterious police blockades. I knew I wasn't the only American being harassed.

Time passed. I looked at my watch and realized that it had been more than three hours since I had called the embassy. My Russian minders unlocked the door but deliberately jostled against me as they walked me back to the kiosk to make another call. They smelled hot and sweaty, and their arms were rock hard.

The duty officer answered and reluctantly admitted that he had located me in embassy records. However, he emphatically refused to ask the State Department in Washington to take action on my case. He was obstinate, insisting that he would not call people into work on a Sunday. He said the State Department would have to send an official diplomatic note, a démarche, to the Russian Ministry of Foreign Affairs to request my release. He flippantly suggested I rent a room in a hotel downtown while awaiting a reply. Through gritted teeth, I reminded him that the Russians were holding me in an airport baggage room. The Russians, listening intently, glowered at me as I pleaded with the duty officer.

Eventually, reluctantly acceding to my insistent demands, the duty officer angrily agreed to cable Washington to request the démarche. He warned me not to expect a response that day; he added that even if the State Department made the démarche, it was highly unlikely that the Ministry of Foreign Affairs would respond promptly. Then he hung up on me. I was incredulous. What a way to treat a fellow American officer in need of help!

The SVR officials returned me to my straight chair in the baggage room. My head flopped forward. I slid down in the chair. I deliberately slowed my breathing, trying to regain my composure. I knew I had to appear strong and unafraid, no matter how I really felt. The officers who had been guarding me for hours also appeared weary. All was quiet for a long, long time.

Suddenly, the door swung back hard on its hinges and a Russian wearing a suit and tie strode in. He ordered me to stand up and began hurling more intrusive questions at me than my previous interrogators. I realized immediately that the Russians had traced me in their records. They now knew a lot more about me.

Then the SVR officer demanded to know why I was perspiring so heavily. I wasn't about to admit that I was not at all sure that the duty officer would do what needed to be done to gain my release. My American passport was cold comfort to me. But I would never admit to this American enemy how afraid and vulnerable I really felt.

I stiffened my spine, lifted my head high, and defiantly responded that I had promised my teenage son that I would return that day. I needed to accompany him to an important medical examination the next day, and I was infuriated and upset that I wouldn't be able to honor my promise. I added that I was sure he could understand the importance of keeping commitments made to one's children. He jeered angrily at my response and continued to fire questions at me. The interrogation seemed to go on forever. My head throbbed as I tried to keep my wits about me.

Finally, he slammed his way out of the room. I fell back into my chair. Surprisingly, sometime later, one of my Russian guards offered me a soft drink, commenting that he, too, had children. As I began to thank him, a hardliner in the room exploded, telling me to shut up. He berated me for being American and, further, for innumerable U.S. transgressions against Russia. Steeling myself, I interrupted his tirade and demanded that he take me back to the kiosk to make another call to the embassy. This would be my third call. He smoldered with hate and hostility, but he led me out to make the call.

This time the duty officer grudgingly informed me that Washington had decided to make the démarche. He again commented that he seriously doubted that the Russians would respond that day. I asked him whether I should call to check on my status, but he told me flatly that it would be pointless. In acid tones, he said that the Russians would no doubt tell me if they decided to release me. The duty officer made it clear that he wanted no more calls from me.

My captor led me back to my lockup and my metal chair. I checked my watch. Unbelievably, the Russians had held me captive for more than fourteen hours. I asked the Russian who had given me the drink when his government might respond to the American request. He shrugged his shoulders. Three more hours dragged by. Nobody said anything.

Suddenly, the door flew open with a crash. A burly Russian bellowed that the flight for Frankfurt was departing momentarily. He pointed to the opposite end of the airport, motioning for me to run. Dragging my suitcase and my carry-on bag, I began running faster than I had ever run before. Perspiration ran into my eyes and I got a stitch in my side, and I dimly realized that people were staring at me. No matter. I would make that flight!

My heart pounding, I arrived at the gate. Unable to speak, I waved my ticket at the attendant. She grabbed my suitcase and gestured me forward. As I stumbled onto the plane, I noticed that all the other passengers were already seated, waiting. I sank into my seat and tried to catch my breath. I fumbled weakly with my seatbelt. A moment later the plane's engines roared, and we took off.

A stewardess walked past me. I grabbed her arm and asked her to tell me when we had left Russian airspace. Then I waited tensely. It seemed forever. Eventually she walked back toward me, leaned over, and in a quiet voice said that we had departed Russian airspace. I asked her to bring me a very large and very cold gin and tonic, and wearily closed my eyes.

11

How Hoosier Basketball and Spying Came Together in Moscow during the Cold War

GENE ARTHUR COYLE

t's hard to believe that more than twenty years have passed since my days in Moscow at the height of the Cold War. I spent two years in the mid-1980s working in Russia as an operations officer for the Central Intelligence Agency. As a native Hoosier, naturally I had grown up playing basketball, and I found it an enjoyable pastime while in the USSR. The Cold War is over, thankfully; the Soviet Union no longer exists; and as of 2006, I'm no longer a spy. Even the fact that I used to be with the CIA is no longer a secret. My basketball-playing days are also behind me, but with that passage of time has come the liberty to talk of events and operations that were once considered state secrets. I had the opportunity to be involved in one of the most spectacular CIA operations ever conducted in Moscow, which earned me the agency's Intelligence Medal of Merit. Some aspects of the operation are still considered classified, but enough can now be told to make a good story.

My story begins in 1983 while I was preparing for my assignment in Moscow. My preparation included intensive Russian language study for almost a year, followed by training for an assignment in a hostile environment. The KGB was a first-class security service, and the component responsible for keeping a watch on foreign diplomats had almost unlimited resources. Many Western diplomats experienced surveillance by the vigilant Seventh Directorate as they traveled about the city and had their phone calls monitored both at work and at home. The KGB was also known to place microphones and possibly even video cameras in the apartments of foreigners suspected of being intelligence officers. (Upon hearing that, my wife, Jan, commented that she was going to start a diet before we went to Moscow. "I'll put up with them seeing me naked, but they're not going to see me overweight and naked!")

Along with all the other training, the CIA prepared me to play a role in a "compartmented" technical operation, code-named GTTAW. A compartmented operation was a top secret one for which a person had to be on a BIGOT list to even know that it existed. (The concept of the BIGOT list came from WWII. The British were sending a group of men to Gibraltar, but to cleverly hide the destination from people who might see the subject line of the list, the abbreviated term TO GIB, was reversed, making BIGOT. The term soon came to cover any situation wherein only specifically named people on a list were allowed to know about something.)

The target of the GTTAW operation was the buried telephone trunk line that ran to Moscow from a military research facility in a "closed" city near Moscow. "Closed" meant that foreign diplomats were not permitted to travel to that city. The memoirs of Rem Krassilnikov, a KGB official who was in charge of keeping an eye on the Americans in Moscow in the 1980s, had indicated that the targeted facility located in Troitsk did defense research associated with laser development. Satellite photography had revealed the digging of this new telephone trunk line in the early 1980s, and thus was born the idea of tapping the phone calls that scientists and officials at this secret facility made to colleagues in Moscow, during which they might talk about their secret research work. Access to the phone cable would be through one of the manhole covers placed along the line that ran parallel to the Kaluzhskoye Highway. According to Krassilnikov, the tap was installed within the conduit pipes below ground and connected to a metal box buried nearby, just under the surface of the dirt. It was that box, full of recordings over a period of several months, that needed to be exchanged periodically by a CIA officer.

The CIA had built a small-scale version in America of the telephone lines and junction box, and it was on that working model that I and a few others trained to work with all aspects of the GTTAW operation. During this training we were cautioned that conduit holes were a popular spot for snakes to lounge and to look carefully before reaching into one. As for the real site in Moscow, we were told that there was some good news and some bad news. The good news was that there were very few snakes that far north in Russia; the bad part was that those that did exist were poisonous. One afternoon another colleague who was scheduled to serve in Moscow and I were down in the large manhole area, practicing. Let's call my colleague Bill. Bill was quite tall; and he and I frequently played basketball during our downtime at the training site. He looked into one of the conduits and told me there was a snake. I assumed he was joking, so I leaned over to look, and sure enough there was a snake head looking back at me. I turned around to say something to Bill, but all I saw was the last of his feet going out the manhole opening some seven feet above the floor. We were informed a few minutes later that it was a harmless garden snake. This became a running joke with us over the years—how Bill hadn't even used the ladder to get out, and how if he had regularly had such a vertical leap, he could have been playing in the NBA!

Once Jan and I arrived in Moscow in the summer of 1984, I settled into my cover duties. This included purchasing books published in the USSR that any U.S. government agency would want a copy of, which required that I travel around the city and the entire country. Contrary to what the movies suggest, a real spy in such a situation doesn't go about trying to outrun or lose surveillance. Rather, the spy tries to bore the surveillance personnel to death. I was just doing my cover job, traveling back and forth to my apartment, and often driving to the compound of my workplace to play basketball on the outdoor court in decent weather, especially on weekends. Some days I was followed around. Some days I was not. My basketball playing got me invited to play in a longstanding, friendly pick-up game between Americans and Russians at the Moscow State University on Sunday mornings. One of those games turned less friendly when then senator Bill Bradley, formerly of the New York Knicks, came to play with us. Even such a trivial game had political significance from the Soviet perspective, and on that Sunday a center from the Red Army basketball team "just happened" to show up to play—to ensure that the Soviet side won. Senator Bradley announced to us that as he hadn't played in years, he'd have to play easy and we should play zone defense. The Russians trounced us in the first game. You can take a player out of the game, but you can't take the desire to win out of a former NBA champion. After the first embarrassing game, Bradley was a changed man, diving to the floor for balls and quickly giving his young Russian opponent a lesson in how real basketball is played. In the fifth and tie-breaking game, I tied the game up with three jump shots in a row and we won on a Coyle-to-Bradley pass for a layup. I was insufferable with my fellow basketball buddies around the American community for weeks thereafter! Bradley's signature and inscription on my water bottle from that game—"Thanks for pulling us through in Moscow. You didn't miss."—is one of my favorite souvenirs from those days.

When it came time for one of the periodic exchanges of the GTTAW black boxes, I was selected to carry out the operation because I was only rarely getting surveilled at that time and I had a successful track record with other operations. I had established the pattern on weekends of driving to my workplace to shoot some baskets and wash my car. There was a militia man on guard 24/7 at all the apartment buildings where foreigners lived. Ostensibly he was there to protect us, but he was really there to keep track of our comings and goings. On the days that I went to play basketball, I would carry a very large gym bag containing my sports clothes and ball out to my car and drive off.

A few days before the actual operation, our CIA chief had the good idea of making me go through all the technical steps that would be required at the GTTAW site, while he and a few others watched to add some pressure to the exercise. This occurred just after lunchtime. About ten minutes into my "practice" I heard snoring. I looked up and saw our chief, who was close to retirement age and who had just eaten a heavy lunch, sound asleep in his chair. So much for the pressure of being watched! My snake and basketball buddy Bill had a hard time holding back his laugh.

On the day of the operation, Jan and I left our apartment building, waving and smiling at the militia guard as always. I carried my gym bag as usual, but this day it also contained a fairly large and heavy metallic box in addition to the basketball. We headed first toward the basketball court, but then we veered off in other directions. As time passed, we became convinced that no one was following us that day. However, the extreme tension of the day had gotten to my wife's bladder and she informed me that she could wait no longer. The paranoia about microphones in our apartment extended to our automobile as well, and she actually had to convey her need to me through body language and voiceless mouthing of words. God knows what nearby drivers thought was going on in our vehicle. There were no fast food restaurants or even gas stations where one could easily find a restroom in those days. We pulled down a side street with some bushes, and she made use of a bit of privacy, as was common practice among Moscow citizens in similar circumstances. We joked later that if anyone had been following us, they would have been "flushed out" as they came forward to see what espionage ploy Jan was up to in the bushes!

Posing as a couple out for a walk in the woods in the suburbs of Moscow, we finally reached the desired manhole cover. Thin bushes hid us from the view of speeding cars on the highway about ten yards away, but there was a footpath close by, and no sooner had we arrived than another young couple, holding hands, came along that path.

To "explain" why we were sitting in the bushes, we immediately started necking. Ah, the things I've done for my country! Housing space was at a premium in Moscow, and many young couples had to live with one or the other set of parents. This afforded young people little privacy in one-bedroom apartments, so seeing couples necking out in the woods in good weather was fairly common.

I began exchanging the recording boxes. The box was buried much deeper in the ground than I had expected and it required a good bit of digging. Jan kept a look out, passed me tools, and took pictures of the area. To say there was stress is an understatement. I had her take one of me making the "we're number one" gesture and grinning. When I later saw the picture, I could tell just from my taut face how much strain I had been feeling at the time. That, of course, is where one's training—to learn to function under pressure—comes into play. The CIA's search process—for people to become field operations officers and the even smaller circle of those who can serve in the USSR—looked for the trait of grace under fire. There were and are many fine CIA officers around the world, but those of us who served in Moscow during the "evil empire" days felt we were pretty special. I had always been a self-confident, cocky kid growing up in Indianapolis, and my attitude didn't change much during my years at the agency. While I respected the capabilities of the KGB, in my heart of hearts I knew I was better than they were and that they'd never catch me—and they never did.

Several hours later, we were finally back in our car and almost at my workplace with our buried treasure box. I pulled out my victory Snickers bar. I had happened to take one with me on my very first Moscow operational outing, which had ended successfully, so it became my superstitious habit to carry one on every operation and eat it once I knew I had succeeded on my mission. I was enjoying my Snickers, listening to a Bruce Springsteen tape, and "Born in the USA" began to play. We smiled at one another. That tune captured perfectly our feelings of exhilaration and triumph. I never felt antipathy for the average Russian citizen, but it was hard to spend time in the USSR, seeing how badly the government treated its people, and not come to detest the ruling circles and the KGB. Call it by any term you want, but I saw it as a brutal dictatorship and it felt good to beat them on their own turf.

To keep up the story of having come to play basketball that day and wash the car, I pulled the car into the car wash area and gave it a quick rinse. I then quickly changed clothes and spent the next twenty minutes shooting baskets. As a former varsity gymnast at Indiana University, even at only five feet and seven inches tall I could touch the rim on my good days. On that afternoon, with the adrenalin still flowing, I was doing it easily. Jan had gone on in to the main building to give the good news to the chief and Bill, who had been sweating it out for hours, waiting for our return or the dreaded phone call reporting our arrest. When I finally got to the office, they had already started drinking champagne in celebration. Even Mother Nature was on our side that day. It rained heavily that night, erasing any trace of our presence near the manhole. According to various sources, the KGB used special chemicals to allow them to track suspected CIA officers about the city. The rain would have washed away any such chemicals as well. All in all, it was a great day of espionage and basketball.

After my return to CIA headquarters in 1986, I was presented with the CIA's Intelligence Medal of Merit. Did that operation change the course of the Cold War? No, but it allowed the U.S. side to know what the Soviets were working on in relation to future, highly advanced weapons systems and to prepare defenses. The value of a country's intelligence service is the cumulative contribution of many such operations. Rarely is it a single officer or a single operation.

POSTSCRIPT: No operation lasts forever, and according to many newspaper accounts, GTTAW ended as the result of a CIA traitor. I was the last officer to visit and make an exchange at the GTTAW site because a fired CIA officer, Ed Howard, became disgruntled and, according to the press accounts, began passing secrets to the KGB. He had been trained for the GTTAW operation and knew the general location of the site. While under FBI surveillance in September 1985, he fled from New Mexico, eventually reaching the Soviet Union, where he was granted political asylum and later even Soviet citizenship. He died in July 2002 from a fall down the stairs while drunk at his home near Moscow. In a newspaper interview with the former head of the KGB of that era, Vladimir Kruchkov, speaking of the CIA black box eventually found by the KGB in one of the southern regions of the city, stated that the project had cost $220 million. He declined to say how they had learned of the operation, but he said of the black box, "For us at that time, we couldn't even dream of such electronics!" The actual cost of the GTTAW project is still classified. I don't believe it was really that much, but for whatever it did cost, I'd say that American taxpayers got more than their money's worth over the several years that it was functioning. And to this day, when I watch the Hoosiers execute a great fast break or a sweet jump shot that rips nothing but net, my mind drifts back to that fine spring day in Moscow when I was young and fleet and the games of basketball and espionage intertwined.

12

How Intelligence Saved the Pope

TERRENCE L. WILLIAMS

In the spring of 1997 I was assigned by the CIA's Office of Military Affairs to be the chief of the National Intelligence Support Team (NIST), assisting the commander of the Stabilization Force (SFOR) in Sarajevo, Bosnia-Herzegovina. At the time I was a GS-14 operations officer, home-based in the Directorate of Operations, East Asia Division, with five foreign field assignments under my belt.

Our three-person NIST was one of three from national-level intelligence agencies deploying intelligence support cells to the conflict zone, where we would be housed with the National Intelligence Cell at SFOR headquarters in Sarajevo under the direction of the G-2. The other two participating agencies were the Defense Intelligence Agency (DIA) and the National Security Agency. The combined NIST was headed by an Army major seconded from Defense Intelligence. A senior analyst from the Joint Analysis Center, Molesworth in Cambridgeshire, England, rounded out the intelligence contingent.

The Republic of Croatia, the Republic of Bosnia and Herzegovina, and the Federal Republic of Yugoslavia had signed the General Framework Agreement for Peace in Bosnia and Herzegovina in November 1995, in Dayton, Ohio. Known as the Dayton Accords, the agreement set forth the terms by which the signatories would conduct relations with one another going forward.

By the time I arrived in Sarajevo that spring, the bloody three and a half years of ethnic conflict were largely over. Still, a year after the agreement was signed, there continued to be sporadic sniping in and around Sarajevo. In addition, the prevalence of land mines scattered haphazardly across the countryside made travel outside the capital a perilous undertaking. Tension along the line of demarcation between Serb-dominated Republika Srpska and Bosnia and Herzegovina was palpable.

Sarajevo was awash with troops, representatives of more than two hundred nongovernment organizations, and members of eighteen United Nations (UN) agencies. Some fourteen billion dollars in international relief aid was pouring into Bosnia, and there was a sense of optimism that the reconstruction of this devastated region was at last under way.

The ominous presence of hundreds of battle-scarred foreign mujahideen patrolling the streets stood in stark contrast to the humanitarian mission described above. These foreign fighters had come to battle the Serbs, who during the war had embarked on a devastating campaign of ethnic cleansing, shocking the civilized world. Under the terms of the Dayton Accords, these foreign fighters were to leave Bosnia in 1995. Their presence there in 1997 was a reminder of how difficult it was to implement the framework agreement.

In my previous foreign tours, I had had very little operational contact with the U.S. military. As a career trainee in 1980, I had been exposed to paramilitary operations, including air operations, where we were certified to jump; small boat operations; small arms and light weapons familiarization; orienteering; survival skills training; and explosives training. Up until the time I volunteered for duty in Bosnia, I had never been called on to employ any of this training.

On the day of my departure for Sarajevo, I boarded a commercial flight from Dulles International to Frankfurt, where those assigned to the NATO-led SFOR contingent were required to receive area familiarization and safety training. Days later I boarded a C-130 for the 850-mile trip to Sarajevo. I'll never forget flying into Sarajevo that afternoon. Many of the structures around the airport were riddled with bullets or reduced to rubble from intense Serb shelling. It was a somber reminder of the troubles in the region.

My NIST colleagues, an officer from the Office of Communications and an analyst from the Directorate of Intelligence, and I soon settled into a routine of sixteen-hour days. Most of our support to the commander of SFOR involved intelligence sharing, although from time to time we were called upon to assist the chief in his efforts to "de-conflict" operations with the military.

I was assigned a quasi-personal vehicle while I was in Bosnia and took road trips to Mostar, Zenica, and Tuzla during the three months I was there. I often invited two or three of my military counterparts to accompany me. They rarely had the opportunity to get off base and looked forward to these daytrips.

Shortly after I arrived in Sarajevo, we received word that Pope John Paul II was planning to visit Bosnia and Herzegovina on April 12 and 13. The pontiff had originally proposed visiting the war-torn country in 1994, but his visit had been canceled due to security concerns. At that time the Serbs had the capital city, Sarajevo, under siege. In 1993 NATO responded to the Serb aggression with Operation Deny Flight, originally intended to enforce the UN no-fly zone over Bosnia and Herzegovina. NATO subsequently expanded this operation to provide close support for UN troops stationed in Bosnia as well as to conduct sorties against Serb targets there.

John Paul's visit would mark his seventy-fifth apostolic voyage. He planned to meet with clergy, religious, seminarians, and senior church officials as well as civic leaders. The centerpiece of the pope's visit was to be an open-air mass at the Kosovo Olympic Stadium in downtown Sarajevo.

There were immediate concerns about whether the tripartite government of Bosnia and Herzegovina would be able to guarantee the pontiff's safety. Shortly after the visit was announced, there were explosions in the Croat (Catholic) section of Mostar and a spate of bombings aimed at churches and monasteries in Sarajevo. As late as one week before the pope was due to arrive in Sarajevo, a monastery forty miles south of the city was shelled, although the attack did not result in substantial loss of life or damage to the facility.

SFOR's position vis-à-vis security arrangements for the pope was that it was the responsibility of local officials—the tripartite federation made up of Bosnians, Croats, and Serbs—to guarantee the pope's security during his visit. SFOR offered to assist local security officials and the UN's International Police Task Force (IPTF) in their security efforts by organizing a joint security coordination center, providing airspace control in the skies above Sarajevo, making SFOR bomb detection units available during the visit, detailing a helicopter for the pope's use for travel to and from the airport, and in the event of a medical emergency, providing medical evacuation.

Several hours before the pope was scheduled to arrive, security officials discovered twenty-three land mines planted beneath a bridge along the six-mile route, aptly named "sniper alley," that the pope would take from the airport to his downtown meeting at the cathedral. This bridge had been inspected earlier in the day and had been declared clear. The anti-tank mines were set to be detonated remotely and would have demolished the glass-topped Mercedes popemobile.

Despite the concerns that this discovery raised about the pope's security on the ground, he remained adamant that he would travel into the city by land, turning down SFOR's offer of helicopter transport. This incident put everyone on edge, serving notice that there were forces conspiring to kill the pope. Not only would this be a tragedy for Christendom and the millions of Catholics around the world who revered the Polish pope, it would unravel the fragile peace in Bosnia.

Late on the evening before the pope's arrival, I was wrapping up our operation for the day. It was Friday evening, April 11. As I prepared to shut down our communications system, I received a message from headquarters. There was a threat report of an assassin traveling to Sarajevo, where he planned to assassinate the pope.

I spent the next several hours working with headquarters and relevant field stations to revise the original report so that we would be able to share it with our U.S. and foreign counterparts—in particular, the IPTF contingent. By the time we received these approvals it was near midnight. I needed to get the sanitized copy of the intelligence report into the hands of the IPTF, who were helping to coordinate security on the ground.

The problem was that Sarajevo had been shut down in a security lockdown. No personal vehicles were allowed on the roads. That meant that driving my vehicle was out of the question. The six-mile trek from the municipality of Ilidža, where SFOR headquarters was located, to the downtown offices of the IPTF was sealed up tight.

One possibility for making the trip remained open to me. If I could find an official vehicle and driver we'd be able to navigate the streets. I did not have a Humvee license, so finding a willing driver at that hour was the first order of business. I located an obliging lieutenant colonel, and within the hour we were wheeling northwest out of the base toward town.

It was eerily quiet. With the exception of roving vehicular patrols and manned checkpoints along the route into the city, there was no one on the roads. We made the six-mile trip in record time. Within minutes of my arrival I was ushered into the offices of the IPTF duty officer, where I explained my mission. He accepted the packet I gave him, asked some clarifying questions, and dispatched a subordinate to make copies of the material and ensure that it was in the hands of security officers on the street before daybreak.

I returned to the base, vaguely reassured that my efforts would prove useful in tightening security for the pontiff's trip. I remember sleeping fitfully in my barracks that night. Normally a light sleeper, I had adapted to barracks life, where troops were coming and going at all hours—packs, utility belts, weapons, and other gear making a din as they hit the ground and their weary owners clambered into their racks for much-needed rest. Along with them, I normally slept the sleep of the dead weary. But this night I could not fall asleep. A recent convert to Catholicism, I had followed Pope John Paul II's papacy since his elevation to pope in 1978, particularly his leading role in helping to end the Cold War. He couldn't die in Bosnia!

The pope's Alitalia aircraft landed in Sarajevo on Saturday, April 12, without incident. As promised, SFOR was providing air surveillance for the visit. We were able to monitor the live feeds from Predator aircraft flown by the Air Force Air Combat Command's Eleventh Reconnaissance Squadron, which operated out of Taszar, Hungary. The twenty-seven-foot-long aircraft has a wingspan of forty-nine feet and can fly up to five hundred miles at an altitude of twenty-five thousand feet. As it collected surveillance footage, the Predator could transmit live feeds via satellite to joint tactical controllers and command centers like ours. The day passed without incident, and we gathered again the next morning to renew our surveillance.

Throngs of people crowded the streets surrounding the Kosovo stadium. Some estimated that over fifty thousand crowded into the facility, which was only equipped to seat thirty-five thousand. It was bitter cold that day and there were brief snow showers. We were glued to our monitors. Despite the conditions, the resolution from the air surveillance was superb. We followed the three-hour mass from the introductory rites to the closing blessing. Later in the day, as we observed the papal aircraft take off from Sarajevo International Airport, there was a spontaneous round of clapping.

And what news of our purported assassin? Had our robust security posture persuaded him to look elsewhere for a softer target? We'll never know. He was not spotted on the streets of Sarajevo that weekend, the weekend Pope John Paul II brought his message of peace and reconciliation to this war-ravaged capital. Did the CIA have anything to do with that? I like to think that, in some small way, our intelligence made a difference that day.

13

Flirting with the Directorate of Intelligence

A Directorate of Operations Officer's Short Story

BOB PHILLIPSON

During a flap of some kind in the early 1960s, the Technical Services Division (TSD) in the Directorate of Operations left the Asian country in which it was based and moved to another location. My stepfather, a bookbinder and former World War II Marine Raider, was an employee of TSD, and when my family moved, I left home to return to the States. I was sixteen. Initially I thought I would live with my grandmother in Albuquerque, but realizing that I was more than a bit undisciplined, I asked my grandfather to help me get into New Mexico Military Institute (NMMI), a high school and junior college. He succeeded, but unfortunately he died two weeks after I entered NMMI.

During the summer following my senior year of high school at NMMI, I traveled to visit my folks overseas. That was when I got my first job with the CIA, as a summer employee working in a warehouse that handled communications and related gear for Army Special Forces assigned to Vietnam. I was a summer hire GS-1! The job was interesting for a young guy like me; I was the liaison between the local employees who moved the stock and the agency office employees who were accountable for that stock. The people in the office were all wonderful, and except for my encounters with one overzealous security guy, I enjoyed my three-month stint. One fine day the base security guy called me in and sat me down in a chair in the middle of an empty room. I wondered what kind of trouble I had gotten myself into. He asked me to name the organization for which I was working. After some hesitation I told him the CIA. He then launched into a scream-

ing fit to impress upon me that I should never say "the three letters." That lesson did have an effect, and I was quite sensitized
to the need for security from then on, but the lesson was a bit
brutal for a teenager.

After graduating from the University of New Mexico in 1966
with a degree in Latin American affairs and a minor in geography, I applied for a job at the CIA and was brought to Langley, Virginia, for an interview. I was escorted to a place that was
a library for photographs. I didn't realize it at the time, but it
was part of the Directorate of Intelligence (DI). I was told that
the function of the job was to handle all Latin American photographs and know where they came from. In that dismal library,
a room contained fourteen desks with fourteen people working
diligently and one supervisor with a small office. The thought of
being stuck at one of those fourteen desks every day for the rest
of my life was unsettling. I asked how one received a promotion
there and was told that when the supervisor moved up or died,
someone would take his place. The supervisor was, to my young
eyes, almost dead already, and I quickly and erroneously calculated that if I had to wait for fourteen people to die, I would never
receive a promotion, and therefore this job was a non-starter.

I thanked the recruiters and joined the U.S. Army, as I knew
I would be drafted to go to Vietnam and I really did not want to
be an infantry grunt. I enlisted, went to the Officer Candidate
School, and ended up as a first lieutenant tank company commander. Finally I was holding down a major's job as the S-3 (chief
of operations) for a tank battalion, with responsibility to train
soldiers to be tankers destined for Vietnam, primarily because
there was a lack of officers in stateside assignments. I put in my
10-49 (transfer papers) for Vietnam three times but was told to
withdraw them because I was a sole surviving son, and my father
had been a World War II glider pilot who perished in the last large
glider operation—code-named Varsity—in 1945. Perhaps more
importantly, we had a significant shortage of officers in the division at that time.

After my stint in the Army, I again spoke with the CIA and was offered the opportunity to go to Vietnam as a paramilitary officer. Later I learned much about this program, but as fate would have it at the time, I was also offered a job managing a small factory in California. By that time I was married, and with a child on the way, my wife and I moved to California and I began the daily grind of driving from Bellflower to Santa Monica and learning that folks in California did not know how to drive in the rain. After six months, I felt that the job offered little challenge; I was bored stiff. I contacted the CIA and asked them if they still had an opening in Vietnam. They said no, but they had a better one. They also told me that this would be the last time they would entertain my employment there. I offered to go anywhere, anytime, under any circumstances, and was signed up as a contract paramilitary officer.

Shortly after arriving in the Washington DC area, I found myself taken to an off-site location for two weeks with seven other men, all military veterans, for an orientation on the CIA acronyms and on what would be coming at us. After all, we were all contract employees, and knuckle draggers to boot, and should not be expected to think. Our group of eight joined another group of five knuckle draggers for a new program in June 1970, and the thirteen of us enrolled with that class of career trainees for more than a year of training in everything the career trainees received plus an extensive course in paramilitary activities. The training was long and intense but professional. We trained hard, but in between courses we went home, occasionally for a week. Four out of the thirteen of us placed in the top ten of a class of more than ninety.

After training, two of our original group were assigned to Thailand to work in the denied areas of Cambodia and the rest went to Laos or Cambodia. Two were killed in the first year in Laos. Only three of us made a career at the CIA. The others all left during the first tour or immediately afterward. The job was dangerous but probably one of the best I've ever had. Running intelligence nets into the denied area of Cambodia was very challenging. The area was rural in the extreme. Sixty reports in six months told the highest authorities in Washington DC what the Khmer Rouge were doing as they conquered new territory. Too bad no one in Washington would believe it. The word came back to me that "no government would do that to their own people." There was an unstated mission to protect the U.S. airbases in Thailand by providing early warning intelligence of potential attacks by North Vietnamese Army (NVA) sappers (combatants) living in northern Cambodia and Laos. In my area of operation in Thailand, a sapper group made several attacks on U.S. airbases. Fortunately, we were aware of all attacks before they occurred and not one aircraft was lost due to those enemy efforts. They did come close on several occasions, however.

Arriving at the office one morning, I found an airman trying out the cypher lock on our outer door. This type of lock has a round face and buttons that you press to put in the correct code. I told the airman he should be careful because if a certain sequence were put into the lock, a poison needle would shoot out and kill the person trying to break in. I do not believe we had any further attempts on our outer door cypher lock.

I hired an English-speaking maid named Pi Dee because neither my wife nor I spoke Thai at that point, and Pi Dee came with the highest recommendations. Pi Dee was quite sophisticated, and she was running away from her husband, a minor prince and bully in Bangkok. We found a small Thai house that looked like it might suffice for her, and I contacted the Chinese-Thai businessman-owner to negotiate to rent his house. The negotiation was conducted mostly through gestures. Later, we hired a guard/gardener, and when I asked the Pi Dee his name, she replied My Lou. For a month I called for My Lou, and he never responded. One day Pi Dee called him using the words *nai kheng*. I asked her what *nai kheng* meant, and she replied that *nai* meant "mister" and Kheng was the man's last name. Then I asked her what My Lou meant and she said "I don't know." I asked her why she didn't know. After all, she was a native Thai speaker and conversant in several languages. Then she told me that *my lou* meant "I don't know," and I realized that for a month I had been standing in my yard shouting "I don't know" with the expectation that my guard/gardener would respond. So much for the benefits of no language preparation before an overseas assignment. My wife and I began Thai language training with a private instructor.

During my time working border intelligence operations, liaison operations, and other projects in inner Thailand, we moved three times. I was the "old man" upcountry, and in 1975 I felt like I was the last to leave—"turn off the lights and close the door." I watched Laos and Vietnam fall to the Communists, but since my tour would be up a short time later, I was permitted to finish my time in Thailand.

Unbeknownst to me, our group of contract officers was being "riffed" (dismissed through job elimination). Representatives of all the operating divisions sat around a large table and reviewed our files to see if any of us would be useful. Apparently my obsolete degree in Latin American studies was still helpful, because the Latin America (LA) Division picked me up. The reductions in force (RIFs) continued within the employee ranks, but I was saved by a kindly LA personnel officer who sent me to Chicago to work in the Domestic Collection Division. I was there with several other folks who became very senior officers in the Directorate of Operations. I believe we were being tested to see if we had what it took to be case officers.

The murderous RIFs ended about the time my tour in Chicago ended. I had found a niche in recruiting assets and polished those skills. At the same time, I went to my boss and asked him to go to bat for me; I wanted to become a staff officer and needed a promotion. I told him that my ambition was to be a chief of station (COS) and that would never happen if I continued as a contract officer. He agreed and put my case forward. I received full staff status and the promotion before I arrived at headquarters, where I soon found myself transferred to a Latin American country that was having a revolution. Due to the unsettled situation, my kids (three of them by that time) were in five different schools that year. Our small office expanded and I became an acting (in name only) COS until a more senior LA officer was assigned. Since neither side in the conflict liked the United States, the tour was quite dangerous, and I felt that that year was more threatening to me than all my time in Southeast Asia.

Once the fighting ended, I was declared persona non grata and kicked out of the country. But the folks at headquarters were relieved when I requested another assignment in a Latin American hotspot. Apparently they were having trouble getting people to go to a country with multiple terrorist groups, drug issues, and general insecurity in the capital city. I viewed it as a target-rich environment. But I had worked briefly for the then COS, and I knew he would give me a good job. My three-year tour was very successful. Early in the tour a terrorist group captured our ambassador and many other ambassadors. A special military team was dispatched and they set up their operations in my office. Our successes in the hostage situation highlighted our need for a rapidly deployed intelligence team for similar events and helped spawn the formation of the CIA's Incident Response Team.

Another highlight of this tour was destroying the first of the major drug-trafficking organizations and linking the Cubans to that organization. As a result, the Cubans stopped their open facilitation of drug trafficking in the United States. Later I received an award for an important recruitment during that tour.

I next found myself on home leave in the United States, and then I was posted to another Latin American city as the deputy chief of station (DCOS). During that tour my children decided to learn to snow ski, and I took up the challenge as well. My kids said that with new skis and boots and in my old trousers and an old sweater, I looked like the farmer that won the lottery (*el campesino quien gano el pollo gol*). During this period of time, the Argentine government decided to attack the Falkland Islands and our liaison with the host country military intelligence increased in importance.

We returned to Langley and I became a branch chief within Cuban Operations. The highlight was the conduct of a unique operation in which I requested and received from the DI the assistance of a young officer. Because this operation ventured into previously unknown technical areas, the TSD refused to support the effort, but I found help in the DI television center. One of its members received a cash award for his work. Our operation was wildly successful and after assuring my division chief the method used in that unique operation could result in the removal of Fidel Castro, obviously I was deemed crazy because of the political risk involved.

As a result, I found myself transferred to another, larger Latin American country, again as a DCOS. We lived in a large metropolitan city and had an apartment overlooking the horseracing stadium. As one of my local guests commented, "What an address!" And what a difference from the very small hut we'd had on our first tour.

Following that tour I was sent to another Latin American country, as the COS, where the serving president was overthrown in a coup. Unlike everyone else, we called the coup before it happened. There were regions of the country populated by all forms of international terrorists, from old German Nazi true believers to Chinese gangs to Serbian assassins. We had a Wild West environment land in a target-rich environment.

At the end of that tour, I asked my LA boss for a tour outside the LA Division because I felt I needed to adjust my thinking. I was becoming too Latin American. He did not like the suggestion, and he threw me like Brer Rabbit into the briar bush of the newly formed Counternarcotics Center, where I was a branch chief in charge of everything except cocaine. Our branch's operations focused on money laundering, precursor chemical movement, drug transportation and smuggling issues, heroin trafficking issues worldwide, and some research and development projects.

We spent a good bit of time on liaison with U.S. law enforcement and jointly with the U.S. Drug Enforcement Administration set up the strategy to go after the drug kingpins of the major trafficking organizations. We also maintained liaison with foreign intelligence organizations involved in counternarcotics issues. I recruited a number of folks from all over the Directorate of Operations and the DI to work in this branch, and we had an unusual mix of very talented people.

Toward the end of this tour the branch was saddled with a Soviet expert named Rick Ames. I was told he had some baggage but was given no specifics. At that point he was already under investigation. I saw him as a drunkard who happened to write very well. Later, after I had left the group, Ames was given my old office, fully equipped by that time with video and audio to monitor him. When I heard of his arrest in February 1994, I couldn't help but have a sick feeling in my stomach.

I volunteered to go to another Latin American country to reorganize and set right a counternarcotics program that had run off the rails when that country's narcotics chief and one of our agency officers were involved in the actual and illegal transport of drugs into the United States. The flap that followed was serious and the entire program was in trouble. Following reorganization of that counternarcotics program, we conducted a major operation against a major narcotics cartel.

Upon return to Langley I had a short stint as the chief for a specific operational portion of the Haiti task force, and as such I joined the Counterterrorism Center (CTC). My small team on the Haiti task force was comprised of deputy chiefs of station from the Latin America Division who were brought to Washington on temporary duty to man this effort. I had some of the best and the brightest of the next generation of Latin America-based case officers.

At the CTC I was the deputy group chief for the training and counterterrorism group and co-leader of the Incident Response Team, a National Security Council–mandated team designed to quickly gather intelligence in a terrorist incident. We maintained a packed bag and had to be in the air on our way to an incident within four hours of the incident's initiation. At the same time I headed CTC's effort with a Middle Eastern terrorist group to promote their transformation from a terrorist group to a bunch of bureaucrats. It was at this time that I wrote an article about the team's efforts during a major terrorist event in Latin America. The piece, which was published in the agency's *Studies in Intelligence*, won the annual best article award. My flirtation with the DI continued with this effort. Imagine a knuckle dragger winning an award in a DI publication!

My last assignment was as Director of Central Intelligence George Tenet's representative to Marine Corps General Charles Wilhelm, commander of the Department of Defense Southern Command. There I had a small office and an assigned DI officer as my second-in-command.

I left the agency in 1998 during another period of downturn and recriminations. The agency was again under fire, and I felt fortunate, having achieved a position that was fairly political, to leave with my tail end intact. After being close to many sensitive operations during my career, the possibility of a politician wanting to further his career by throwing one of us under the bus seemed increasingly likely.

I received two medals of merit during my career and numerous—six or more—commendations with a bonus attached. I retired a long-in-the-tooth GS-15 step 10. I missed being promoted to the Senior Intelligence Service, probably because I thought each "attaboy" should be accompanied by at least one reprimand. After retirement I obtained a position handling international licensing for Cluett, Peabody and Company, Inc., a large U.S. corporation. I found that the skills I developed during my agency time were easily translated into the realm of private industry. For those who wonder, there is life after the agency and outside the Beltway.

14

Soldier, Sailor, Artist, Spy

CHIP BECK

I f you want to join the CIA, timing and luck are crucial. In 1969 I contacted the agency while an active duty twenty-four-year-old navy officer serving with the Third Marine Division in Vietnam. I was eligible for an "early out" when my combat tour was over, so I sent a letter and a brief résumé to the agency outlining my education and career. I had a degree in international relations and two years of service as a navy frogman, demolitions expert, and forward observer along the demilitarized zone separating North and South Vietnam. I indicated I would soon be on the job market.

Surprisingly, I received an immediate reply indicating that the agency had identified a position for me and wanted to talk to me after I got off active duty in early 1970. The Special Operations Division (SOD) was launching a new project for which they planned to recruit a new generation of college-educated, combat-experienced special operations officers who could fight America's covert wars during periods of Cold War conflict, and undertake traditional clandestine foreign intelligence operations (spying) in calmer times.

As it turned out, I became one of the first seven recruits for the new program, which launched in June 1970. Our group undertook extended and intensive training that included advanced special operations (denied area ops, survival-escape-evasion, large and small unit operations, weapons training, demolitions, parachute training, and other activities linked to Green Beret and SEAL training) and classical "tradecraft" and foreign intelligence operations (collection, recruitment, analysis, politics) at the agency's covert training site, popularly called The Farm.

The Cold War was still in full force during these years, with numerous hot conflicts that endured well into the 1990s. What most Americans did not know then, and still are not aware of, is that Western allies were combating the Soviets, Warsaw Pact countries, and the Chinese on various clandestine fronts and in conflicts around the world, at levels that were more direct than generally believed.

In the quarter-century that followed my return from Vietnam, I experienced numerous special operations and foreign intelligence engagements against the Russians, Cubans, Chinese, Pathet Lao, Khmer Rouge, North Vietnamese, Sandinistas, Marxist Angolans, Hezbollah, Iranians, Iraqis, Colombian drug cartels, and guerrilla groups of various stripes. Some of the conflicts involved direct combat; others were of the "cat-and-mouse," spy-versus-spy type.

My first assignment following training was to serve as a guerrilla battalion advisor in northern Laos from 1971 to 1973. One highlight was a fortuitous encounter with a disaffected Pathet Lao commando that developed into a friendship between us and led to the defection of nineteen of his comrades. Those men became a special "rallier" commando unit that ended up operating against their former Communist managers and allies. They proved their loyalty to me as their leader many times during patrols and operations, when they easily could have taken my Thai ops assistant and me captive and hauled us off to some POW camp. Instead, they continued to serve in unique clandestine operations even after the United States withdrew from Laos as a result of the Paris Peace Accords.

In Laos I had the honor of leading two emergency rapid action responses that rescued two Special Forces Green Berets and a fellow CIA paramilitary officer when they were either being pursued or surrounded by North Vietnamese army units. In those successful operations all bureaucratic obstacles were shoved aside or ignored and our field assets combined effectively to pluck our comrades from harm's way.

In other instances, two of my former roommates who joined SOD with me were killed in combat operations elsewhere in Laos. I had the unusual distinction of being shot point-blank in the face by an 1810 British flintlock musket fired by a suspected Pathet Lao double agent. Fortunately, during this Elmer Fudd–Daffy Duck shooting moment, the lead ball must have rolled out during the agent's journey to our meeting place, and all I got was a face full of rust, gunpowder, and flecks of metal.

After Laos, I was sent to a new mission in Cambodia, where I worked as an advisor to the Khmer National Armed Forces (FANK) Tenth and Eleventh Infantry Brigades in the Indochina Wars. During the first six months, I was the only American in a small town that was surrounded by brutal Khmer Rouge forces. Fortunately, the Cambodians I served with were the most courageous and professional soldiers in Asia, and we succeeded in winning major combat engagements against overwhelming odds during hand-to-hand or close-quarter combat that evoked the Alamo. At the end of the war, as politics won out and Cambodia fell to the Communist forces, I led two hundred men, women, and children across fifty miles of mountainous jungle to safety in Thailand. The oldest among those escapees was the mother of my Cambodian counterpart (who died on a special mission during the fall of Phnom Penh). She was sixty-five years old at the time. She turned 105 in Dallas, Texas, in September 2015, and I am proud to have provided her and the rest of my friend's family the opportunity to become outstanding American citizens.

Shortly after the collapse of Indochina in April 1975, I was dispatched as the lead advisor to the National Union for the Total Independence of Angola (UNITA) rebel forces in September, where I found myself in a new African battleground with Russian, Cuban, and Marxist People's Movement for the Liberation of Angola (MPLA) forces on one side and a handful of special operations officers, a contingent of South Africans, and our Angolan allies on the other. Against the odds, our forces turned the tide against the Soviet-backed MPLA and the Cubans, who were preparing their evacuation plans (as I was told in Havana twenty-five years later) just when the U.S. Congress stepped in to force the CIA to end its support. (South Africa, with the backing of Zambia, Senegal, Zaire, and Morocco continued to support UNITA, and the civil war dragged on for another twenty-two years).

After Angola I spent five years with the Africa Division, switching over to foreign intelligence roles as chief of station and deputy chief of station in Sahelien countries, with a smattering of single-agent operations in other parts of sub-Saharan Africa.

By mid-1980, I was back with SOD, and I embarked on several short-term assignments in Central America, including conflicts in El Salvador, Nicaragua, and Honduras, and supporting the anti-Soviet mujahideen in Afghanistan. Periodically I worked in Panama, drawing on my Navy Reserve experience, and eventually I was part of Operation Just Cause, which toppled Manuel Noriega.

During this period I embarked on a pleasant clandestine assignment, which required a small team of CIA and Drug Enforcement Administration agents to operate under cover as "yachtsmen" sailing a fifty-three-foot Bowman three-masted schooner through blue waters. During that operation, which I nicknamed "the Dixie Caper," we were confronted by modern-day pirates, nearly shipwrecked during gale-force winds, challenged by a foreign patrol boat, and infiltrated by a double agent. Despite those challenges, we spent most nights anchored in beautiful, out-of-the-way coves, diving for lobsters for dinner and sleeping under an incredible canopy of stars. In the end, the team's mission had an impact on a bit of Cold War history, and the double agent and his boss made counterintelligence history of their own two years later.

In 1982–83, SOD was turning its attention to the Middle East, where my good friend and comrade from Laos and Angola, Chief of Station/Beirut William F. Buckley, was heavily involved both before and after the bombings of the American embassy and the Marine Corps barracks in Lebanon. In 1984 Bill succeeded in getting the Near East Division to assign me as his special assistant for a three-month term in Beirut. I served alongside the U.S. Marines multinational force. My job largely consisted, as Bill directed, of going out to contested areas to see whether or not someone would shoot at me. I was in the streets the night West Beirut fell to the Muslim forces of Amal, and enlisted the support of a unit of masked Druze men to help rescue stranded Americans during an intense artillery barrage. Two days later the American embassy evacuated nonessential personnel, and the U.S. Marines withdrew from Lebanon as well. I stayed on with Bill as American civilians began to get kidnapped off the streets of West Beirut. At one point, in a tense standoff with gun drawn, I thwarted the first dry-run kidnap attempt against Bill near his apartment (see History Channel, *Tight Wire in Beirut*). Unfortunately, two days after I was ordered to end my temporary duty and return to headquarters, on March 16, 1984, Bill was kidnapped at the same location where we had been confronted before. This time Bill was alone (for an operational reason) and overpowered.

Although I volunteered to immediately return to Beirut and lead a search for Bill (and other hostages), internal politics took over and I was not allowed to go. Over the next fifteen months, Bill was subjected to torture and maltreatment, and he died in the Bekaa Valley on June 3, 1985. By then I had been searching for alternative ways to help the hostages and was unknowingly (at first) stepping on the toes of the so-called Iran-Contra, Arms-for-Hostages crowd. As I became a vocal internal critic of the lack of initiative and activity in support of Bill's rescue, the good-old-boy network took steps to isolate me and curtail my career progression, hoping to force me to resign.

After Bill's death was confirmed in late 1985, it took another six years to get the other hostages released. In 1991 the navy recalled me to active duty for nine months as its official combat artist for Operation Desert Storm. At the end of the war, I was able to use one of my own Middle Eastern contacts to find where Bill's body had been dumped and have the remains retrieved, and to arrange for the release of journalist Terry Anderson.

In the period 1984–93, I eventually outlasted the Iran-Contra cabal (several of whom were indicted and convicted of felonies, but later pardoned by President George H. W. Bush) and served in a variety of global black operations assignments, but I still had residual adversaries residing in senior Directorate of Operations positions who kept putting obstacles in my way.

Fortunately, by then I had met and married an FBI special agent, and I had a bit of protection from William Webster's senior aide after the judge left the FBI and came over to the CIA as director of central intelligence. I developed a couple of incredibly good recruitment prospects (that is, potential intelligence sources) during that period from among my hard target contacts in Washington, but I turned them over to my wife's FBI colleagues rather than go through the wringer within my own CIA-stymied channels. These candidates proved to be extremely valuable long-term assets, and I was proud to have served my country through our new self-styled FBI-CIA liaison, husband-and-wife team.

In 1993 the CIA followed the Department of Defense in offering early retirements as cost-cutting measures. By then I qualified for an agency retirement and decided to go back on active duty with the navy as a Naval Criminal Investigative Service agent and commanding officer until my service time expired in 1996. In 1995 I became a special investigator looking into the fates of American servicemen who had disappeared into the Soviet Gulag from 1918 through the end of the Vietnam War. After I retired from the navy, writer friend Tom Clancy gave me some walking-around money, which I used to go to East Berlin, Cuba, and elsewhere in Europe to talk to former East Bloc intelligence operatives about our unrepatriated POWs. What I learned will be the subject of a book called *John Bolo's Quagmire.*

I rejoined government service after September 11, 2001, serving another eight years with both the Department of Defense (as a defense fellow) and the Department of State (director of African peacekeeper training), spending fifteen months in Iraq and several years leading diplomatic and training missions throughout Africa. Then, in 2010, I retired from government for the third and final time.

In the five years since then, I have gone back to Africa on several occasions as a security expert in South Sudan, Somalia, Kenya, and South Africa and earned a doctoral degree in conflict resolution and organizational leadership. Most recently I spent a year in Haiti as program manager for a police advisory program that benefited from my experience and training in the United States Navy, the CIA, and the State Department.

Since my first deployment to Vietnam, I have traveled to 130 countries, experienced some twenty or more wars, revolutions, or conflict zones, and learned to speak a smattering of nine languages (two well; seven at an elementary level). Despite the unfortunate internal experiences after my Beirut mission, I consider my time with the CIA and the many outstanding colleagues I served with in war zones around the world to be among the best of times and friends.

In 1991, after I had returned from Operation Desert Storm, I was invited to speak to two hundred CIA summer interns in my capacity as a navy commander and the navy's combat artist (an official but limited occupation). The speaker before me advised the interns to master the "three s's"—substance, savvy, and style—if they came back for careers at the CIA. He said all three were needed to progress up the CIA ladder. Then he left the auditorium.

Before I initiated my Desert Storm presentation, I called on the interns to consider the (then) fifty-one stars on the CIA Memorial Wall and think about two more s's exemplified by the stars—service and sacrifice.

Careers in the CIA should not be simply defined by self-promoting progression, but by honorable service to one's country, humanitarian principles, and the global community. A person can be an honorable spy and warrior. That was my message in 1991, and it is the one I would convey to anyone thinking about joining the CIA today. Make a difference, not just a career.

15

Terminating an Asset

DOUG PATTESON

To the nonpractitioners in our line of work, particularly those who like to read the more salacious authors of the spy genre, "termination of an asset" carries a particularly nefarious connotation. It is assumed to mean the actual killing or otherwise disposing of an asset. But on the inside we know that sometimes a word is just a word, nothing more.

I was a first-tour officer—baby-faced, twenty-three years old, and newly certified from The Farm. I had been assigned to a country in Asia where I spoke only one of the common languages, and I looked nothing like a native. I was technically an adult and I was well trained, but I woke up every day hoping no one would realize they had made a terrible mistake hiring me as a case officer. Don't get me wrong: I was having a blast. I just couldn't believe I was getting paid to do this work.

As a new officer in a post with a wide range of targets and threats, I had a chance to pursue just about anything I wanted to do. Jumping out on the social circuit in search of developmentals (individuals who appeared to be promising sources of intelligence) was a natural starting point. I realized quickly, though, that the shotgun approach to spotting and assessing such sources was not very efficient; nor did it carry a high likelihood of a return. Fortunately, I had good senior officers who helped direct my efforts and temper my neophyte's enthusiasm. Oh, and I also learned that it was kind of like courting a beautiful woman. Sometimes the more you showed interest, the more the target pushed you away.

While fumbling around trying to find my first developmental, the station management made sure that I, like all new officers, was also given established assets to handle.

I'll never forget my first one. There was nothing "high speed" about him, but I didn't really know that yet. He worked on the periphery of one of the station's primary mission areas of focus. He seemed old to me at the time, but he was probably only in his late fifties.

On the night of the turnover, his handling officer drove on our surveillance detection route (SDR). It was my first time through this crowded Asian city, all the smells and sounds and sights overwhelming me as I tried to process how two white guys were going to prove they were clean in this environment. I was definitely not in northern Virginia anymore. I was excited, nervous, confident, and a thousand other conflicting emotions.

I don't remember much about the actual meeting with the asset. It was relatively uneventful as he had been an asset for a long time and had been handed over before, and his handler had transitioned other assets many times as well. The handler was a golden boy in the Directorate of Operations who later went on to the seventh floor (the most senior levels of the agency) and chief of station of multiple large stations in hard-target environments. I was the only one at the meeting who was new at this game, and I think the others were amused by my wide-eyed naïveté. The turnover was successful. I had my first case.

We met for about a year. I realize now that he was the perfect first asset. He knew what he was about but never overvalued what he did. He was careful with tradecraft, as the risk to his safety was real, and he expected me to be careful too. Much later it occurred to me that he was training me as much as or more than I was training him. I was able to apply the full spectrum of skills we had learned at The Farm—in particular, to task and collect intelligence, then draft and rewrite intel reports, and lather-rinse-repeat. It was a discipline that served me well for the rest of my time in the agency.

He provided some good intelligence but nothing stellar. It was on the periphery of our primary targets, but it never crossed into the real meat. At one time, he had had access and provided significant reporting, but no longer. We were also entering an era where interest in his primary areas of access was becoming less pertinent to analysts and policymakers. His work was one layer deeper than press reporting and just about as exciting.

At this time in the agency's history, we had no real hot wars, and eventually budgets came under scrutiny across the globe. In the end, his reporting was deemed to fall below our risk/budget/need trade-offs. My branch chief called me in and said I would need to terminate him (i.e., end our relationship).

I went back to the file and pulled his original agreement from his initial handling officer. According to his file, we had agreed to pay him one month's salary for each year of service as termination pay. As he had been an asset for almost twenty years, it was not an insignificant sum.

I drafted the termination plan, including the proposed termination payment in accordance with the agreement, submitted it to headquarters, and continued about my day-to-day responsibilities. A few uneventful days passed and I received my response. In no uncertain terms, my request to honor the terms of his recruitment was denied. I was only allowed to pay him five months' pay, not the twenty he had been promised.

To me, the biggest shock was that we as an organization would intentionally disregard our commitment to an asset—a promise we had made in exchange for his risk and the provision of intelligence, a risk that would continue long after the termination. Any exposure of his previous involvement with us would result in grave risk to his life. The difference in the amount of his pay wasn't really that much in Western terms, but it was huge in the developing world.

Wouldn't this—that we could, on a whim, renege on our promises—undermine every promise made to any asset we recruited?. Our reputation was all we had. We were the good guys; we didn't do this to our people.

I was mad. I went in to my branch chief's office and argued, yelled, and cajoled, trying everything I could to make my case. The branch chief and station management agreed that it was wrong but also said that we had no other choice. No room to maneuver. It was my job to sell the change to him, leaving him happy with us and the amount.

In the end, I did it. Or maybe he made it easy (continuing his own training of me as a case officer). Probably both. I sat there and watched his twinkling eyes and smiling face as he listened to my tortured logic about both the termination and the payment. I thanked him for his many years of service (this was the first time I had ever fired anybody) and said we just couldn't work together going forward. I even got him to sign the quit claim, acknowledging that we owed him nothing more. Then we parted ways.

We all lose a little of our hope when we see some of the shine of our agency dulled by decisions such as these. I guess I needed to grow up some. And I learned lessons I would apply throughout my time in the Directorate of Operations, chief among those not to make promises that I couldn't keep.

THREE

Cross-Directorate Careers

16

The Rocky but Interesting Road of Intelligence-Policy Relations

PAUL R. PILLAR

I came to Langley in the 1970s with a conventional notion of how a person with a skill set such as mine would contribute to the intelligence portion of U.S. national security. Because I was trained as a political scientist with a particular slant as an international relations theorist and I had a doctorate from Princeton, that notion involved elucidating for policymakers how the international system works, especially through profound analysis of big-picture questions. The unit to which I was initially assigned, the International Issues Division in the Office of Regional and Political Analysis, was about as well-suited as any could be to perpetuation of that notion, for a little while anyway. It was a division that addressed a mélange of global issues and was located within an office that otherwise mostly did political analysis specific to individual countries and regions. The atmosphere in that division was closer to academia than most any other place at the agency. One aspect of being productive was to come up with original ideas for analysis and to execute them without stepping too much on the toes and the turf of one's regional colleagues.

Even in that assignment, it soon became clear that any brilliant insights on the workings of the international system took second place to more immediate needs. I slid into topics related to arms control and got involved in some projects in which my role was less one of elucidation and more one of bureaucratic support. This support included backstopping ultimately unfruitful negotiations with the USSR on controlling trade in conventional armaments. It also included work on an interagency task force with the interesting mission of assessing whether declassification of satellite imagery—at a time when the public had not seen imagery any more detailed than clouds snapped by weather satellites—might bolster public confidence in our ability to monitor Soviet compliance with strategic arms control agreements.

Institutional needs trumped any individual ambitions during the rest of my intelligence career. Only once did I apply for a competitively filled position and get the job. For every other assignment I was given, I happened to be an available peg with a suitable shape for placing in a hole that needed to be filled. That is part of how bureaucracies need to operate, and it does not mean that assignments are any less interesting for having been filled that way. In my case it meant spending more than half my career outside my ostensible home base, the Directorate of Intelligence (DI).

While still a junior officer I became a charter member of what was initially called the analytic group at the National Intelligence Council, whose own identity as a council was also still fairly new. The group was intended to be a cadre of hired pens who drafted National Intelligence Estimates and other assessments conveying the views of the entire intelligence community. It was my first exposure to dealing intensively with the rest of the community. It also brought me a step closer to feeling the sensitivities and effects of strong policy preferences. These were the early years of the Reagan administration, when there was a propensity to see the hand of Moscow behind any bit of mayhem anywhere in the world. This atmosphere affected—mainly in the sense of slowing down—the handling of some papers I was assigned to draft, including an assessment of Soviet activities in the Third World. I had long moved on to other assignments, and the paper had gone through the hands of at least two other principal drafters before it finally became an approved and disseminated product a couple of years later.

After returning to the DI, I went from an analyst position to a series of managerial jobs at the branch and division level in the Office of Near Eastern and South Asian Analysis. This would become a pivotal shift in that today I am regarded as a Middle East wonk even though I cannot claim deep expertise on the region by virtue of field research or specialized academic training. But then again, countless others pontificate about policy questions on that region with less of a claim than I have, given my on-the-job training and my experience tapping the expertise of others in the course of my government assignments, so I don't worry about it. The events and problems addressed by units I led ranged from a coup in Sudan to the Iran-Iraq War to the euphemistically labeled "Middle East peace process." One major project on that last topic was put together mostly by John Brennan (who would later become director of the Central Intelligence Agency) when he was a senior analyst in a division where I was the deputy chief. John and I took a road trip to get comments on a draft paper from some eminent retired practitioners with views on the subject, including the late George Ball, the devil's advocate from Vietnam War days, who was still a sharp-minded critic in his advanced years.

In the late 1980s I moved to the seventh floor as executive assistant to the deputy director for intelligence. One of the regular duties of that job was to assemble weekly substantive briefings for the associate deputy director to present to the House Permanent Select Committee on Intelligence. The task involved deciding in consultation with the boss what topics were worthy of the committee's attention, and then obtaining talking points from the relevant analysts in the directorate. The committee's functioning in those days was far different from what it would become after getting paralyzed, as so many other things in Congress have been, by intensified partisanship. Back then it operated fairly well, with cooperation across party lines, and it certainly took its role seriously. The substantive weekly briefings about trouble spots around the world were a good example of how Congress can, and in my view should, be an active consumer of intelligence and not just an overseer of it.

Another major function of that job, one performed with the assistance of division-level managers who rotated through on a short-term basis, was ghost-reviewing draft research papers and intelligence assessments that came up from all the analytical offices in the DI. This seventh-floor review was the last chop such papers would get before any further necessary revision and then dissemination. The usual procedure was for me or my temporary colleague to provide our reactions to the draft paper to our bosses, mostly written on sticky notes placed throughout the paper, and then for either the deputy director or the assistant deputy director to adopt any of those comments and add their own, this time written in ink on the pages themselves. My part of this task provided a detailed immersion in the wide variety of analytical work being done throughout the directorate, as well as a sensitization to standards of quality and to what does and does not make sense in high-level review, bearing in mind the delays and bureaucratic costs each time an objection to a paper is raised.

I next moved down the corridor to become executive assistant to the director of central intelligence (DCI), William Webster, for more than half of his tenure as DCI. Judge Webster, as we called him, was an admirable boss, a man of the utmost integrity and the deliverer of what was expected of agency leadership in those post–Iran-Contra years. His experience as a federal district and appellate judge and as director of the FBI for nine years brought a wealth of fresh perspectives to the foreign intelligence mission that certainly broadened my own thinking about how that mission should be performed.

Working directly for the DCI meant exposure to the entire range of functions performed in the agency that he headed and, in a somewhat looser sense, in the broader intelligence community, which he also led. One of the principal observations I made from that perspective is that the time and attention of the person at the top is not apportioned in a way that corresponds to what one might expect by looking at organization charts. This is not because of the leader's choice but rather because of what is forced upon him. Most of the work at the agency is done in the directorates, without interference from above. For the most part this is good, in that it reflects people going about their jobs, with a clear concept of the mission they are performing, without major problems. The director's time, at least when I was on the seventh floor, was disproportionately consumed by matters involving public affairs, legal affairs, or congressional affairs, even though the direct support to him in these areas came from relatively small staffs. Those were the main areas where flaps could occur, and where there would be an outside expectation of some sort of response from the man at the top.

Those were interesting times because of outside events, especially the end of the Cold War. One of the foreign trips I took with the director was to Eastern Europe, the first visit by a U.S. intelligence chief since the collapse of Communist rule there. Some of the contrasts within the region were marked. Security services that had long been our adversaries slid quickly and seamlessly into the role of friends and partners.

After one more stint as a DI manager I spent most of the 1990s in the Counterterrorism Center (CTC), first as head of the analytic group there and then as deputy chief of the center. CTC was part of the Directorate of Operations, and I necessarily got involved in directorate management issues. But the center also was, even back then, a thoroughly integrated organization in terms of incorporating a range of personnel and functions not only from the rest of the agency but also other parts of the government that were involved in counterterrorism. The closest collaboration was with the FBI. When I was deputy chief I actually was one of two deputies, the other one being a senior FBI special agent. Our boss, the center's chief, was a CIA operations officer who had previously served as deputy of the international terrorism section of the FBI. None of this is reflected in the popular lore about U.S. counterterrorism before 9/11, according to which there supposedly was no interagency cooperation and the CIA and FBI were not talking to each other.

Also not reflected in the popular lore is how much of a focus there was back then on those who would become the perpetrators of 9/11. The center chief and I spent more of our time and attention on the problem of Osama bin Laden and his organization than on any other topic. That more was not done then to head off what would happen in September 2001 certainly was not due to any lack of understanding of, or U.S. government focus on, that particular threat. 9/11 itself would drastically change the American public's mood and the politics of counterterrorism, and thus it was only then that the gloves came off and there was political support for radically changed standards for how to respond to such a threat. I remember extensive interagency deliberations about capturing Bin Laden as early as 1996, when one of the main problems was the lack of a reliable legal case against him if he were to come into U.S. hands.

The CTC model of an integrated center worked well for the most part, but it had its own management problems. Chief among those was having to rely on personnel whose careers were controlled elsewhere. When I joined CTC the analysts who worked there were all on loan from DI offices. We thus were at the mercy of those offices—which naturally gave first priority to their own immediate needs—regarding whom we got and how long we could keep them. What may have been my most significant accomplishment as an intelligence manager was obtaining (working in alliance with similarly situated organizations such as the Crime and Narcotics Center) approval to establish for the first time a cadre of analysts whose career home would be CTC itself. That became the nucleus of what would later grow into a far larger force of intelligence officers whose primary specialty was counterterrorist analysis.

What was perhaps my most significant contribution to policy implementation came near the end of my tenure in CTC and spilled over into a couple of overseas trips I took on special assignment after leaving the center. After the Qaddafi regime in Libya, pressured by several years of international sanctions, turned over two suspects wanted for their role in the bombing of Pan Am Flight 103 in 1988, Libya contacted the United States through an intermediary and proposed turning over a new leaf and establishing a new relationship. This led to talks in the last part of the Clinton administration (very closely held at the time and only later revealed publicly) about the possibility of such a relationship, and specifically about our two governments' overlapping concerns about Islamist terrorists, some of whom had conducted operations in Libyan territory. My assessment was that the Libyans were serious about charting a new path for themselves. Follow-up negotiations eventually led to an agreement announced four years later that confirmed both Libya's turn away from international terrorism and the end of its unconventional weapons programs.

Upon leaving CTC I spent a year at the Brookings Institution as the first occupant of what became a seat that other CIA officers would occupy on a rotating basis. I used the year to write a book, *Terrorism and U.S. Foreign Policy*, drawing on insights from my CTC years. From there I went back to the National Intelligence Council for what would be my final government job: five years as the national intelligence officer (NIO) for the Near East and South Asia. NIOs were charged with managing and coordinating community-wide estimates and assessments on subjects in their areas of responsibility. After I left, the Near East and South Asia were split into two different NIO portfolios, as they probably should have been years earlier. But during my early months in the job, South Asia and especially Afghanistan, even before 9/11, occupied the majority of my attention.

And then came the march toward war in Iraq. That grand neocon experiment overshadowed and overwhelmed just about everything else for anyone in government who had responsibilities at all related to Iraq. Although the war, and more specifically the public campaign in support of it, was a suffocating reality, it did not mean a bigger role for intelligence officers doing analysis in that area. To the contrary—and as I described in detail in a book

I later wrote, *Intelligence and U.S. Foreign Policy: Iraq, 9/11, and Misguided Reform*—the decision to go to war was reached with almost no intelligence input, notwithstanding the war makers' selective use of intelligence-derived tidbits to help make their public case for the war. As the regional NIO I had responsibility for community-wide intelligence analysis on political and economic issues in the Middle East, and I received no requests from any policymakers in the Bush administration for any analysis about Iraq before the war.

I already was persona non grata among the war makers for some of the themes in my nonofficial writings, such as that terrorism and weapons proliferation are two separate issues that ought not to be carelessly conflated. More than once, leaked and garbled versions of comments I made to outside groups—such outside speaking being a normal part of what NIOs do—became fodder for polemicists such as the editorial writers at the *Wall Street Journal*. On one occasion, such a version was made into a column by Robert Novak, who wrote darkly about intelligence officers conducting an "insurgency" against the White House. A few days after that column appeared I was part of a group that briefed the Senate Select Committee on Intelligence on a different topic. The Republican members spent much of the time grilling me about the insurgency I supposedly was leading—a memorable way to spend an afternoon on Capitol Hill.

If maintaining good relations with important policymaking consumers is a part of an NIO's job (and I certainly believe it is), then my tenure in that job was in large part a failure. But I still am proud of what I did in that position, including what I did on Iraq and especially with regard to aspects of the job that were more under my control. I initiated two of the only three prewar community-wide assessments on Iraq (the third one being an infamous congressionally requested estimate on weapons programs). These two addressed the challenges that would be faced in Iraq after Saddam Hussein was ousted and the larger repercussions in the region. The papers made for grim reading. I wish for the sake of Iraq and for U.S. interests that the judgments in those papers had turned out to be wrong, but later events proved them largely correct.

My intelligence career was a long and sometimes uncomfortable lesson in how—notwithstanding the valuable policy-relevant work that is done day-in and day-out in the CIA and the rest of the intelligence community—the relationship between intelligence and policy in reality is quite different from the textbook model. It certainly is far removed from any application of international relations principles learned in graduate school to current policy problems. The differences between model and reality are partly a matter of politics. They are partly a matter of how the American experience has conditioned most Americans to see the world in ways an intelligence agency frequently has to push up against. That distinctly American perspective is the subject of another book I have written in retirement: *Why America Misunderstands the World: National Experience and Roots of Misperception.*

17

Cement, Speeches, Terrorism, and Stray Cats

SUSAN HASLER

I took a job at the CIA out of desperation. I had a master's degree in Slavic languages and literature from UC Berkeley. It was 1983, the economy was in recession, and no one was hiring literature majors. But the agency was looking for people with good language skills. I answered an ad, took a battery of tests, and waited months for my security clearances to go through. The polygraph examiner was obsessively interested in the two years I spent in Berkeley, living in an apartment complex where everyone had a pot plant growing in their window. I passed the poly after two attempts. I was assigned as a foreign documents officer at the Foreign Broadcast Information Service (FBIS), the part of the CIA that deals with open-source media. It was considered something of an agency backwater, but I didn't care. I wanted a job, not a career—a job that would allow me plenty of time to write fiction on the side. My plan was to work at the CIA no longer than four years, then move back to the West Coast.

Make plans and hear the universe laugh.

Thanks to a sudden cold November downpour, I reported to my first job sopping wet. The first thing I learned was the difference between concrete and cement. My new boss explained that I would be scanning Russian-language newspapers and journals to find items of value to intelligence. He said that I was now in charge of the construction materials account, a position that had been vacant for some time. He pointed to a desk covered in stacks of dusty journals. I read the first three titles: *Cement, Concrete,* and *Concrete and Reinforced Concrete.* I asked a stupid question: "Aren't these all the same?" He proceeded to deliver an extended lecture on the difference between cement and concrete, all the while puffing away on his noxious pipe (rumor had it that he was smoking Stalin's socks). By the time it was over, I was so depressed and nauseated I wanted to drown myself in the toilet.

The second thing I learned at the CIA? It's not that hard to move around. I cleared out the cement backlog and got a transfer to another branch. In even better news, the government banned smoking inside the buildings, so I no longer had to keep my trash-can at my knee in case of a sudden loss of lunch. I saved up and bought my first computer, an early Apple product that looked like a child's toy. I scanned newspapers during the day, wrote fiction at night, and drank boatloads of coffee. I also made friends in that job who would last me a lifetime.

Working at the CIA provided the occasional brush with infamy. At the time, FBIS was located in Rosslyn, Virginia. I frequented a nearby Chinese restaurant, where I would buy takeout hot-and-sour soup. Sometimes I would see the FBIS China Division there having lunch. They had a linguist who knew how to order deli-cious entrées not listed on the menu. His name was Larry Wu-Tai Chin. It was later discovered that he had been selling classified documents to the Chinese since the 1950s.

After two years at FBIS I took my first analytical job in the Directorate of Intelligence (DI). Despite my lack of an academic background in economics, I was hired as an economic analyst in the Office of Soviet Analysis. My new boss explained that most of the source materials I would need were in Russian. He said, "It's easier to teach a Russian linguist economics than it is to teach an economist Russian." I did well in that job. The lesson I took away was that in the DI, your background is less important than a fast pen and the ability to read into an account quickly—and the ability to read in the language of the country is invalu-able. My advice to people who want a job at the agency has always been the same: learn the hardest language you can handle and learn it well.

My advice for those embarking on a career in the DI: grow a thick skin. It's tough for an introvert to hold her own in an office full of opinionated, argumentative people, but I learned. Everything I wrote had to go through many layers of review. There were two people in our division—a senior analyst and a branch chief—who caused me exceptional pain. They took it upon themselves to cover every paper with red ink. They would sit me down and go over in excruciating detail everything I had done wrong, from the tiniest mistake in grammar to the biggest error in logic. At the time it was the worst thing in the world, but in later years I was immensely grateful for their time and attention. They taught me to write and think like an analyst.

In 1989 I married another analyst, Stephen White. All of our guests were agency friends. The biggest benefit of working in the agency was that I was surrounded with smart, committed people. The disadvantage was that my life outside the agency was shrinking. To keep some perspective, Steve and I bought a weekend place in the Shenandoah Valley, where I grew up. It was an 1861 farmhouse in dire need of renovation. I learned how to point up a crumbling stone foundation, rip out termite damage, and insulate. All of that was a great antidote to a week spent in front of a computer screen.

My job had somehow turned into a career, but I still wrote fiction on the side. At one point I was getting up at 4:45 in the morning to write before work. That was when I was still in my thirties. Finding the time and energy got harder each year. The hours at work got longer, and the commute to Langley from Reston slower.

The highlight of my time as a Soviet analyst was working the graveyard shift in the CIA Operations Center during the attempted Soviet coup of 1991. I loved the easy, off-hours commute, the silence of the dimly lit office, and the fascination of watching history play out across my screen. The experience demonstrated the real appeal of the CIA to people who love their subject matter. I couldn't imagine anywhere else I would rather be at that moment than watching information pour in from news media, intercepts, satellite imagery, experts in the field, and other sources. It was better than being a journalist or academic because we had access to so much. I wrote as quickly as I read conflicting accounts of Gorbachev's whereabouts, updates on the status of Soviet nuclear readiness, and reports on the fate of the coup plotters.

After the dissolution of the Soviet Union, it was clear that the Office of Soviet Analysis had far too many analysts, and I needed a break from straight analysis. Fortunately, a DI background prepares you for all sorts of work. I took a job in the CIA Office of Public Affairs as the junior speechwriter to the director of central intelligence (DCI). On my first day I had lunch with the deputy chief of public affairs and the CIA's spokesman in the agency cafeteria. They looked down in the mouth. The reason quickly became clear as they detailed all the stuff that was about to hit the fan. First there was the breaking case of Aldrich Ames, which would turn out to be one of the biggest betrayals in the history of the agency. In addition, a Harvard-educated human rights advocate named Jennifer Harbury was publicly taking on CIA activities in Guatemala. Also, a former employee of the Directorate of Operations was suing for gender discrimination in what would come to be called "the Jane Doe Thompson case." It blossomed into an enormous embarrassment and a huge class action suit that the agency lost. In many ways, my time in Public Affairs was like watching one train wreck after another, but I loved writing speeches.

The first director I wrote for was R. James Woolsey. His tenure at the agency was short and benighted. He was a small, feisty man known for picking losing battles with the oversight committees, having virtually no access to the president, and refusing to fire or demote anyone at the agency in the wake of the disastrous Aldrich Ames case. I remember sitting in his office with the other speechwriter and hearing him say that when he first heard about the Ames case, he thought it would be viewed by the public as a counterintelligence success. "Really?" I thought and tried to keep my face completely expressionless. The happiest I ever saw Woolsey was the day he resigned. He smiled nonstop.

The other speechwriter left with Woolsey, and I became the senior speechwriter to the new director, John Deutch. I liked working for Deutch, but he wasn't popular in the building. He brought over a handful of Department of Defense people to fill key positions and let it be known in the press that he preferred military personnel to intelligence officers. It was a culture clash that didn't have a happy ending.

Speechwriting was demanding, but I made a practice of working hard during the week to preserve weekends in the country. My husband and I had accidentally fallen into the cat rescue game. Our farmhouse was a magnet for stray cats. Moreover, my kind-hearted farmer father took to scooping up sick barn kittens for us to nurse back to health. We turned into "purveyors of fine fur." Making use of the bulletin boards all over CIA headquarters, we placed more than three hundred country cats into affluent northern Virginia homes over the span of two decades. Hungry kittens who drank manure-water from barnyard puddles grew into fat suburban cats with heated beds, filtered water fountains, and well-stocked toy baskets. Some of them traveled overseas with their owners. We bought a van just to accommodate all the cat carriers. Between the cats, the farmhouse renovations, the novel writing, and the speeches, I had a full plate, but life was good.

In January 1996 I was attending some sort of mandatory training when my husband pulled me out of the room to me tell my father had died of a heart attack. It hit me hard, but it was the busiest time of the year, with the Worldwide Threat Briefing coming up in February and a full roster of spring speeches. I didn't have the time or desire to think, so I just put my head down and worked. Deutch resigned in December of 1996. When he left he awarded me the Director's Medal. That's when my father's death hit me the hardest. I didn't have him to be proud of me. He would have loved attending the ceremony in the awards suite. My mother wasn't interested. She was still grieving too much to care.

Less than two weeks later, on Christmas Eve, my mother was diagnosed with pancreatic cancer. I left the Office of Public Affairs. I had too much going on outside of work to cope with the demands of speechwriting and adapting to a third DCI in as many years. I spent a lot of time on the road between my sister's home in Charlottesville and my home in Reston. I learned that a career in the DI does not prepare one to be a good nurse, and that the stress of doing a demanding job that you're good at pales in comparison to the stress of doing a demanding job for which you have no talent or inclination. On weekends I managed to unstop clogged feeding tubes, stay up all night administering medications at two-hour intervals, and help my mother use the restroom. My sister did that work during the week. Toward the end, I tapped into the agency's leave bank to be at the hospital full-time. My mother lived for seven months after her diagnosis. When she died in mid-summer 1996, I was emotionally drained, physically exhausted, and depressed.

A week later I was called back to the Office of Public Affairs to write speeches for DCI George Tenet. The agency's fiftieth anniversary was coming up in September and there was a backlog of speeches that had to be written in the next month. A huge backlog. I put off mourning until sometime in the future. I had to cut back severely on my coffee consumption because I didn't have time to go to the bathroom. I sat in my office and wrote nonstop. I wrote speeches, introductions, toasts, award citations, and thank-you notes. I dug into the agency's Historical Intelligence Collection for material. The speeches turned out well, and I got a nice performance award. Then one of my cats got sick and required veterinary care that took all but six dollars of that award.

I fled the Office of Public Affairs after the anniversary celebrations were over. I was just plain tired. I bounced around. I spent a year at the National Reconnaissance Office writing speeches and congressional testimony. I returned to the DI, where I spent a couple of years as executive editor of a monthly publication on the proliferation of weapons of mass destruction.

In the summer of 2000, I took my first management job as chief of the publications branch of the analysis group in the CIA Counterterrorism Center (CTC). During orientation an analyst broke into tears as he read a letter from the mother of one of the victims of the Khobar Towers bombing in Saudi Arabia. He felt like he had missed something that could have prevented the attack.

Over the next few years I found out just how easy it is to miss something in the world of counterterrorism. The volume of information coming into the center was extraordinary, especially in comparison to the volume of traffic I was accustomed to in previous DI accounts. It was not humanly possible for an analyst to read everything that landed in his or her inbox. Moreover, it was much harder to decipher the meaning of each report. In the typical political or economic account, much of what an analyst comes across is at least partially pre-digested. Embassy reporting, newspaper articles, and reports from clandestine sources tend to be well composed. They make sense. CTC information was much more fragmentary and hard to decipher. Intercepts caught bits of coded conversation. Analysts had to figure out who was speaking as well as what they were talking about. Every terrorist had a string of aliases. More than one terrorist might be using the same alias. Analyzing terrorists was a new discipline with a steep learning curve. It was painstaking work, nothing like the fantasies depicted on television. Whenever I hear someone say "just connect the dots," I know that they have no clue as to the nature or volume of data that counterterrorism analysts face every day. As one analyst used to say, "The page is black with dots."

The demographics in CTC were very different from what I was used to. The office had a preponderance of young analysts. They had a great attitude and work ethic. Those who had been there two years organized seminars for brand new analysts to ease their transition into the confusing world of counterterrorism. Senior analysts wrote handbooks to walk the new people through crisis situations. Unfortunately, it was a very small group of analysts, far too small to keep up with the volume of information flowing in. An estimated one hundred thousand jihadists had graduated from training camps in Afghanistan. How could a handful of analysts keep track of them?

The first terrorist event that happened while I was at the CTC was the bombing of the USS *Cole* in the Yemeni port of Aden on October 12, 2000. Almost immediately we began getting queries from the intelligence oversight committees on what had gone wrong. All the while, we worried that another, larger attack was coming.

The *Cole* attack was the work of al-Qaeda, a group I knew little about before coming to CTC. By 2000, CTC analysts had done a great deal of work on al-Qaeda, piecing together the structure of the organization and how it operated. The atmosphere at CTC grew increasingly tense as 2001 wore on. The al-Qaeda analysts were convinced that the group was planning a devastating terrorist event. They suspected it would be something along the lines of the 1998 African embassy bombings—simultaneous mass-casualty attacks.

I spent some of my time helping to pull together a briefing for my boss. She was using it to argue for six more analysts for the group. It's hard to believe how difficult it was then to persuade senior management to cough up six analysts for counterterrorism. Eventually, she succeeded. They arrived a few weeks before 9/11.

I remember well the famous August 6 memo entitled "Bin Laden Determined to Strike in US." One of my jobs as chief of the publications branch was to edit and archive everything that went upstairs for the President's Daily Brief. This memo was unusual because it mentioned the United States. CTC's job was to follow international terrorism abroad and threats to U.S. interests overseas. Monitoring terrorism in the United States was the job of the FBI. Condoleezza Rice later complained that the memo contained no specifics—well, those were all the specifics CTC could get from the FBI. Legal and institutional barriers hindered information sharing between intelligence and law enforcement agencies. These barriers—designed to prevent domestic spying—made it difficult to follow a networked terrorist group effectively.

On a Monday—September 10—I came into the office to find that Ahmad Shah Massoud, the head of the Northern Alliance in Afghanistan, had been assassinated by terrorists disguised as journalists. The bomb was hidden in their camera. The feeling in the office was that this was a prelude to something. It turned out to be a gift that Bin Laden gave to his host, Afghan Taliban leader Mullah Omar, because he knew that the United States would soon invade the country.

The next morning I was sitting in my office with the door open when I saw an analyst running between the cubicles toward my boss's office, which was next to mine. I heard him say, "A plane hit the World Trade Center and it's bad." I watched the second plane hit the south tower on live TV. The phone rang and the secretary handed it to our boss with a scared look on her face. "It's the president," she whispered. My boss mouthed an obscenity as she took the phone.

We got word that the Pentagon was burning and another plane was headed toward Washington. I called my husband, whose office was on the fifth floor of the side of the building facing the Potomac—the likely place for a plane to hit, I thought. I told him, "Get out of the building now. Go to your doctor's appointment. You won't be able to get out in few minutes because everyone will be leaving." Shortly after that, the DCI ordered headquarters to be evacuated, except for CTC and emergency teams. We stayed in the office while workmen began laying cables for an operations center in the conference room.

The next few days run together in my memory. I started working the graveyard shift. One morning my boss came into my office and unrolled a huge sheet of paper. It was the wiring diagram for a much larger counterterrorism effort. "Which branch do you want?" she said. I looked at the sheet. I really didn't like being in management. I pointed to the new Strategic Analysis Branch and told her I would rather be a senior analyst there. Later that day I found out that my husband and his entire branch had been moved into CTC, along with quite a few other branches from other parts of the DI. Overnight, the former analysis group of CTC had grown several-fold.

The few analysts who were veterans of the analysis group now had the task of training all the new analysts, as well as briefing senior officials, writing situation updates every few hours, and trying to keep up with the thousands of cables that came in every hour, twenty-four hours a day. In addition, new counterterrorism units were being set up all over the place, and their new managers were calling us with questions. Expertise was spread thin. The people around me seemed to age overnight.

The queries from the Bush administration on Iraq began almost immediately after 9/11. Even though the intelligence case against al-Qaeda was overwhelming, they were eager to connect Saddam Hussein to the tragedy.

It was my opinion that invading Iraq was the worst thing the United States could have done after 9/11. It caused friction with allies who were critical to our counterterrorism efforts. It diverted resources from Afghanistan at the worst possible time. It created a new terrorist cause and a new training ground in Iraq. Analysts should stay politically neutral at work. That had never been a problem for me, but the invasion of Iraq angered me in a way that no other foreign policy had done.

The Strategic Analysis Branch had some terrific analysts. I got to work with Cindy Storer and Barbara Sude, who were among CTC's original al-Qaeda experts. They had been working on al-Qaeda since the 1990s. At the time, nearly all of the people working on al-Qaeda were women. They were known as "the sisterhood" and they were warning about Bin Laden long before anyone higher up was willing to pay attention. Cindy, Barbara, and I appeared in a 2013 documentary, *Manhunt: The Search for Bin Laden*, which focused on the sisterhood. Since then I have had to correct a lot of people who mistakenly thought I was a member of the sisterhood. I wasn't. I was in the documentary largely because the producer had read my 2010 novel, *Intelligence*, and wanted a writer's perspective on the 9/11 era.

I decided to leave the agency when my husband reached retirement age, even though I was a decade away from my earliest retirement date. My parents had died in their mid-sixties. I figured if I wanted to be a full-time writer, I'd better not put it off any longer. I gave the CIA over a year's notice, but my bosses still seemed surprised that I was actually going to leave. In August of 2004 the cats and I moved down to the weekend place and lived there while my husband got our Reston house ready for sale.

I started writing fiction full-time. I had already published a few short stories in literary journals. Now my goal was to get a novel published. I wrote three novels set in the Shenandoah Valley and got a literary agent. I didn't sell a novel, however, until I wrote one about the CIA. I wrote the first draft of *Intelligence* in three months. Everything that had been milling around in my head about counterterrorism and the political response to terrorist attacks came out in that novel. It was published by Thomas Dunne Books in 2010. I was thrilled to get good reviews, including a big one in the *Washington Post*. I've since written two more novels about the CIA. *Project HALFSHEEP* is set in the 1950s and deals with experiments with mind control drugs along the lines of the CIA's Project MKUltra and Project BLUEBIRD. *The Flat Bureaucrat*, the sequel to *Intelligence*, is about a terrorist attack on CIA headquarters. My next novel will probably also be about the CIA. I haven't run out of material yet.

18

Rock Star or CIA Officer

KATHY THOMAS

I never intended to work for the CIA, or anywhere else in the government. I wanted to go into broadcasting or, less realistically, become a rock star. I had just completed my first semester at Shenandoah University and was majoring in communications. I was at my father's house for Christmas, and he encouraged/forced me to apply for one of the student programs the CIA offered. I filled out the application and secretly hoped not to be accepted. Fast forward to spring and there was my letter of acceptance. By that point I figured it was either wait tables at the pizza restaurant in my tiny Virginia town (go Northern Neck!) or work at the CIA for the summer before my sophomore year. The CIA won. That was over twenty years ago, and I'm still running around the intelligence community.

I will never forget my first day, when I laid eyes on the compound after I made it through the gate. Little small-town, tiny high school, small-college me was staring at the massive buildings with a rising panic and feeling of complete dread. I knew I'd spend the entire summer lost in that facility. There was a reason why I'd chosen a small college. I knew I was in over my head.

I started out working in finance in CIA's travel office. I had no idea why they put me there, but I liked it and ended up working there for three years. I even transferred to George Mason University so I could work part-time while I went to school full-time. It was exhausting managing school and work, but I realized how lucky I was when my graduating friends were looking for jobs and I already had a "real" one. I was also lucky that I could apply for new positions whenever I was ready and not have to change employers. This flexibility helped me learn early on what I liked and didn't like when it came to work.

I learned that I absolutely loved event planning (who knew?) and communications work (my degree was not a waste!). I also learned that I liked concrete deadlines and that the long-term strategic stuff was just not for me. My goal from nearly day one was to work in the CIA Office of Public Affairs (OPA), and five years after I started with the agency, my wish came true. OPA's work consisted of internal communications, public communications, and media relations, and they even had a liaison to Hollywood. I was selected as an officer in OPA's Public Communications Branch. My job included giving tours to select academic and professional groups (the CIA does not give public tours); responding to letters, faxes, and—eventually—emails; and answering the phone when people called the number listed on the CIA's website.

As you can imagine, I talked to a lot of crazy people. I also saw many, many photos and drawings of naked people, because apparently it's popular to send those to the CIA. I was apprehensive to answer the phone for the first time because you just didn't know what you were going to get. Would it be a student asking how to get a job? Someone who wanted to do business with the CIA? Or a crazy person? Well, my first call was both crazy and not. About halfway into our conversation, when he was naming one of my co-workers and talking about upsetting Tiger Woods (and I had NO IDEA what was he was talking about), he stopped and asked, "You're new, aren't you?" Um, yes . . .

Perhaps my favorite exchange occurred when a woman called and said she wanted to report a missing person and then explained that she was that person and had been missing for twenty-plus years. I explained that the CIA didn't handle missing-persons cases. She remained undeterred and I was busy, so I told her that she could contact the FBI. A few hours later my office received a phone call from some rather annoyed FBI agents. Apparently the "missing" woman was in Washington DC that day and showed up at FBI headquarters and told them I sent her there. Oops! We had a good laugh after I explained what had happened (and apologized A LOT).

A lady once mailed us a newspaper clipping of a police report that she thought we would find amusing. A man apparently called the police to complain about the "sleek, well-groomed" raccoons the CIA had trained to spy on him. We thought the article was hilarious and hung it up in our office, but I still eye any stylish raccoons I come across with suspicion.

It took me years to realize one of the most important things that job gave me: I learned not to react when baited. A frustrated boss of mine once told me that no matter what he said, he couldn't get a reaction out of me and he couldn't read me. Answering those phones trained me to be prepared for ANYTHING someone says to me, and it's served me well in a variety of situations, including job interviews, ever since. It was also uplifting to hear from people who wanted to volunteer their time to help and those who called just to say thank you. They knew we couldn't often publicize our successes because they were classified. I also loved getting letters from kids who wanted to grow up to be spies and told us how hard they were working to make that happen.

I left the job in the Public Communications Branch because I received a more senior position within OPA. I was in my twenties and had a large office on the top floor (the seventh floor, as it's known) of CIA headquarters. I had arrived. I got to plan a joint CIA/CBS premiere of a new TV show about the agency—named, appropriately enough, *The Agency*. I was doing my beloved event planning with executives from CBS, and the invitee list was a who's who of senior CBS executives and Washington political figures.

It was a beautiful morning on the East Coast, complete with gorgeous skies and fall air. I was excited to be responsible for the event and thrilled to be a part of the premiere itself. We were one week away from the premiere, and I was finalizing the details. It was the day RSVPs were due from those invited. The date was September 11, 2001.

This was the day I learned how rapidly a communicator's job could change. Like the rest of the nation, we were saddened and confused when the first plane hit the World Trade Center; we were in shock when the second plane hit. We did not know what was happening any more than anyone else did, and the ten or so of us in the front office that day realized at varying speeds that these were indeed acts of terrorism. I still remember a colleague staring at the TV in disbelief and commenting that it was a sunny day. "How can two planes accidentally fly into buildings?" he asked. The realization had not yet dawned on him.

The phones started ringing with reporters wanting to know what was going on. Shortly after, a plane destroyed a wing of the Pentagon. There were false reports on the news of missing planes and of car bombs in Washington DC. An administrative assistant was responsible for answering calls, and I can still hear her pinched and terrified voice as she told us her brother was in the Pentagon. We scrambled to answer phone calls from the media and try to calm our colleague, while fully expecting one of those missing planes to fly right into us.

We all, including the administrative assistant, escaped personal tragedy that day, and I returned to work the next day to a completely different job. We canceled the premiere; and inquiries from the media, employees, and the public flooded into a staff much too small to handle them all. I went from planning an exciting television premiere to writing crisis communications.

I came in on weekends to help my former branch try to keep up with the massive number of emails and can't begin to describe the patriotism and pride I felt in my country after reading those messages. At the same time, my role in post-9/11 communications provided no escape from the nightmare and pure evil of the day. I didn't have the maturity to deal with the magnitude of the tragedy and I cried a lot. I suspect my reaction wouldn't be much different today.

I remember responding to one particular email, and the writer replied almost immediately. He thanked me even though, he said, he knew he'd received an automated message, and I fired back that if the message had been automated, I wouldn't be at work on a Saturday (see lack of maturity above). He thanked me again and said he'd buy me a beer when this was all over. I haven't received that beer yet, but I also know that "this" still isn't over.

As a communications professional, I recognize the significance of having worked for the CIA's communications arm on 9/11. It took me many years to fully understand it, but I am honored to have performed that work at such an historic time in our nation's history. As an American, I will never forget the lives lost that day or the reason why we're fighting. As a communications professional, I realize that I will likely never have another experience like the one I had on 9/11 and the days following, and I sure don't want to.

Since that September morning, I've had so many exciting moments and opportunities, and I've worked for three different agencies within the intelligence community: the CIA, the Office of the Director of National Intelligence, and the National Reconnaissance Office. Highlights include the time President Clinton waved to me and the time President Bush shook my hand. I have been an extra on a TV show (*The Agency*), attended a movie premiere for *Enemy of the State*, and met Hollywood stars, including Jon Voight, Gil Bellows, and Jake Busey. I've planned events for a thousand people or more and communicated with thousands of people at a time. I've done video work and voiceovers, making my dream of being in broadcasting come true, if only for a few days here and there. I've even been a rock star, having the opportunity to sing at agency-wide events.

I eventually made the move to the contract world to have access to more communications positions so I could always pursue what I love. But you know what? No matter where I work, the CIA is and will remain my home. I have zero regrets regarding my career path, even with the bumps and periodic confusion. Where else could I possibly work with a mission like the CIA's? My vote is nowhere, and you can't convince me otherwise. Thank you, Dad, for interfering.

19

An Accidental Career of Consequence

JEFF J. JOHNSON

I didn't plan on a career with the Central Intelligence Agency. I became involved in electoral politics at an early age, and my work on political campaigns continued when I attended the University of Minnesota, where I majored in political science. I was one of a handful of young people in the state selected by my political party to be groomed for future political office. My life was on a well-defined trajectory.

As I neared graduation, I started to have second thoughts. There were discussions with political operatives about attending law school or moving to Washington DC for a few years to work for a senator from Minnesota. The more I thought about it, the more the idea of living in the public eye and in an environment of constant compromise was unattractive to me.

On a whim, I checked into the interviews being conducted on campus and signed up to meet with a CIA recruiter, which led to taking the Professional Applicant Test Battery. Several months later I was asked to go to Washington DC for interviews and more testing, including a polygraph and psychological examination. During the polygraph I was asked if there was anything misleading in my résumé, and I confessed that I had never applied to graduate from the university, so while I had completed all of the requirements I wasn't technically a graduate. A few weeks later I was offered a position with the agency, pending receipt of my diploma.

I started work at the agency in July of 1985, literally in the mailroom. The agency was quite adept at gathering information, and it was a challenge to make sure it reached the correct analysts and policymakers. Officers in the Dissemination Branch reviewed all incoming intelligence and routed it to the correct personnel. I spent close to a year memorizing all of the agency units and their particular subject interests. The work was tedious at times, but it provided a great introduction to the agency, and it was my first introduction to information management, a theme that would recur throughout my career.

My early years there were training-intensive. In addition to learning about the agency in great detail, I attended the Foreign Service Institute and began several years of Russian language training. My focus during college had been on political behavior and political institutions, so I took night classes at American University and George Washington University to learn more about international affairs. I was also given the opportunity to study nuclear proliferation issues in-depth, which included making visits to the Los Alamos and Oak Ridge national laboratories. I was in class at the Department of Energy, next door to NASA headquarters, the day the space shuttle Challenger exploded during launch.

I remember one funny anecdote from this first assignment, which speaks to the myths surrounding the work of the CIA. When an insurance agent called the office one day, a colleague of mine at answered, "Dissemination Branch, this is Joe." After a long pause, finally the caller asked, "Did you say Assassination Branch?"

My next assignment immersed me in the worlds of collection and analysis. Within the Visual Media Branch in the Directorate of Intelligence, television broadcasts were recorded by a team of engineers, reviewed by analysts, and archived if deemed of value. This was a major effort. The 1980s saw the rise of cable television and the development of the twenty-four-hour news cycle, and our engineers worked around the clock with their collection activities. This was before the digital video age, and the bulk of recording and archiving was done on three-quarter-inch videotape. It wasn't practical or financially feasible to archive every-thing that was recorded, so if a news story was identified for retention, it was edited and transferred to an appropriate subject tape: foreign leaders, military hardware, or drug trafficking, for example (this also made it easier for analysts to view video clips on their specific areas of interest). A diligent effort was made to purchase the rights to all of the video segments or programs that were selected for retention.

The agency holds an annual family day in which employees can bring their spouses and children to headquarters to learn more about their work. Each component is given the option to open their space for visitors. I was surprised that my colleagues chose not to open up the Visual Media Branch and asked one of my fellow analysts why he was opposed to bringing his family into our space. He replied, "It's not a good idea to let my children know that watching television is a viable career choice."

The Visual Media Branch also operated a video distribution system at headquarters—essentially functioning as an in-house cable provider. The major broadcast and cable networks were available on the cable grid, as were occasional live broadcasts of events in the headquarters auditorium. We also had selected foreign television broadcasts available on the cable grid, includ-ing live Soviet television. While traditionally a propaganda tool, under the President Gorbachev's leadership and policy of glas-nost (openness), Soviet television was becoming interesting. The agency's director of Soviet analysis asked that we begin looking at Soviet television more aggressively, and because I had been studying the Russian language, I was asked to lead the effort.

This was one of the most interesting projects of my agency career. Working with a contractor, I essentially recreated with Soviet television the work we performed with domestic television. We recorded Soviet broadcasts around the clock, and a team of analysts proficient in the Russian language reviewed the broad-casts for clips that were relevant to our intelligence analysts. The clips were then assembled onto subject tapes with dual audio tracks—the original Russian audio and an English translation—and disseminated to the appropriate agency consumers.

The Soviet television subject tapes were an immediate hit, supporting many analytical assessments of the Soviet Union. Rarely did a week go by when Soviet television wasn't referenced in agency publications, often augmented by still photographs taken from the broadcasts. The Soviet military reliably showed off their latest hardware on Soviet newscasts. The rise and fall—as well as the health—of leaders could be assessed by the frequency of their appearances on television. President Gorbachev once gave a speech that seemed to indicate a return to a more Stalinist mindset, but by viewing the live broadcast it was apparent from his long pauses and disgusted expression that he hadn't written the speech and that he disagreed with what he was asked to read.

We benefited from applying additional scrutiny to some news broadcasts. *Vremya*—the Soviet nightly newscast—once aired a story about the new automated control center in Moscow for their railroad network, including footage of one of the workers showing off his new personal computer. This gave me an opportunity to try out some emerging technology used by our National Photographic Interpretation Center. We captured still frames of the computer screens, enlarged them, and enhanced them using cutting-edge digital tools. To our surprise we discovered the center in Moscow was using a shareware version of the same communication program in use at the CIA. On a whim, we applied the same technology to the view outside a window in the background, after which analysts were able to pinpoint the location of the center in Moscow based on visible landmarks.

We once discovered footage of one of the CIA's senior leaders on Soviet television. It didn't appear on a newscast; rather, it was within a music video. The video showed an attractive woman sitting at a sidewalk cafe anxiously awaiting her man of mystery. The footage then shifted to our senior leader quickly walking down the street, allegedly for a rendezvous with his mistress.

Our best guess was that this was KGB surveillance footage that was being reused by Soviet television. I had an interesting visit with our man of mystery to show him his Soviet television debut.

As much as I enjoyed my work with the Visual Media Branch, it came time to look for a new assignment. CIA officers are encouraged to move every two to three years for their career growth. My work as an analyst had included interaction with personnel in the Directorate of Operations, who approached me about coming aboard as a case officer. I was intrigued about the opportunity and accepted. The skill sets of analysts and case officers are very different, and at that time it was somewhat rare for officers to move between directorates (in fact, rotations were suspended for several years following my move—I tried not to take it personally!). Today, interactions between directorates are more valued and you see more movement between them.

Typically, when a case officer is first hired, they go through several years of training before they reach full performance. The skills of foreign intelligence collection and espionage are not taught in college. I received an accelerated version of this training, an intense three weeks of indoctrination into a new line of business. On top of this, I needed to acclimate to a new working environment—each of the agency directorates had their own personnel policies, operating procedures, and even computer networks. My head was spinning at the end of the day.

The agency is fiercely protective of its foreign recruits, known as "assets." In many cases these assets are putting their reputations, their careers, or even their lives at risk to aid the United States. The agency takes great care to hide their identities, restricting access to the information they provide lest it be used to expose the source. In many cases the motive of these assets is simple greed—they are in it for the money—but in other cases it is more complicated. In the 1960s the agency had a high-value asset in place who provided intelligence for many years until his retirement. At some point, once his work with the agency had ended, he told his son about the work he had performed on our behalf.

Years later the agency approached his son to become an asset, which he eagerly accepted due to his pride in his father's work. I was assigned as his case officer and was impressed by his motivation. We went to dinner one evening and ran into his father with a large group of their friends. I could tell his father was scrutinizing me carefully, but he gave no indication that I was anything but a friend of his son. I was equally careful not to do anything to cause suspicion of either my asset or his father, either at that moment or at any time in the future.

I was fortunate to work in the Directorate of Operations at an exciting time in history: during my tenure I witnessed both the First Gulf War and the collapse of the Soviet Union. The latter was a tumultuous time for the agency. The CIA was largely created to battle the scourge of communism, and most of the agency's resources—analytical but especially operational—were directed at this goal. Many agency officers had spent their entire careers focused on the Soviet Union, and while the collapse of communism was celebrated, it did lead to a bit of floundering as the agency shifted focus to the emerging transnational threats facing the United States.

After more than two years as a case officer, I made the difficult decision to leave Operations and take a new assignment. My work had been fascinating and quite gratifying, but I was ready to get married, buy a house, and settle down. The work of a case officer entails long hours and unexpected absences, neither of which is conducive to a relationship. I have the utmost respect for those officers (and their families) who make a career out of Operations and rarely receive any recognition for their sacrifices.

As a case officer I had observed with fascination the advances in digital technology that were taking place, and I was eager to see if these advances could be applied to the agency's work with video. During my time in the Directorate of Operations, the agency reorganized, and my former component had moved from the Directorate of Intelligence to the Foreign Broadcast Information Service, part of the Directorate of Science and Technology. As a consequence, I ended up accepting an assignment in my third of the four agency directorates.

While the focus of the Directorate of Operations was on gathering intelligence from human assets, the Directorate of Science and Technology focused on technical collection of intelligence. Tangential to this was the delivery of intelligence to the appropriate analysts and policymakers, as well as devising effective methods of data storage and retrieval. Increasingly, this data was electronic, including text, audio, and video files. It was the video files that captured my attention. Video was still a cumbersome medium for the analysts to work with, but at the same time it was developing into an incredible resource: the advent of twenty-four-hour news channels and the growing availability of foreign television broadcasts at the agency made the work almost overwhelming. I wanted to tackle this challenge, but first I needed to develop the necessary skills.

The agency sponsored me to attend a part-time graduate program in interactive multimedia development at George Washington University. I worked in the office in the morning and attended classes in the afternoons. While my focus was on digital video production, I also took classes in web development and coding. I was able to work with HTML and design some rudimentary websites, but the field was undergoing such rapid change in the mid-1990s that my skills were almost obsolete even as I was learning them (for example, at the time I graduated, we heard about something new called "Java"). Nevertheless, I graduated with an understanding of the fundamental concepts behind digital media, and my final project was a proof of concept that provided agency analysts with foreign television broadcasts in an easily digestible form.

Back at the agency I put forward a successful proposal to purchase a high-end digital video editing suite for my component. Our video production team was already using this suite of tools, but I wanted to show that it would also be an effective tool for our media analysts, and possibly for all-source analysts (those who develop insights from all different sources of intelligence—human, photographic, open, signals, and so on) in the future. Several of our analysts received training on the tools and found effective uses for them, but the project was deemed too expensive for expansion. This is astonishing to imagine today, when smartphone users have more advanced video editing tools than we did at the agency in 2000.

My digital video skills led to my involvement in early efforts to enhance the President's Daily Brief (PDB). The PDB is the signature output of the intelligence analysis process, and significant resources are used to create the daily publication. During the 1990s this was still a tightly controlled hard copy publication, but a few nascent efforts were under way to produce and deliver it in a multimedia format. I was asked to contribute my digital video expertise to these efforts. While several pilots were conceived and created, the technology was deemed too immature, and production of the PDB continued in hard copy for many years thereafter. My work on these projects did lead to my next assignment, however.

The digital revolution had accelerated the agency's collection capabilities during the 1990s, and each of the directorates had efforts under way to process and work with the resulting tidal wave of information. Each of the directorates built their own computer network to serve the needs of their own officers, and each created their own support infrastructure for information technology. This quickly grew untenable. The agency created an Office of Information Technology to tackle the infrastructure issues and an Office of Advanced Analytic Tools (AAT) to find solutions to our data challenges.

Due to my interest in using information technology to solve our data challenges, I was one of the first officers recruited for the new Office of Advanced Analytic Tools. AAT was unique in that it was a hybrid component shared by the Directorate of Intelligence and the Directorate of Science and Technology. It was also the first entirely new component in the history of the agency—

there had been plenty of reorganizations and name changes in the past, but never before had a new group been created with personnel "stolen" from elsewhere in the agency, creating the need for a new career service. Those of us who joined AAT did so as an act of faith that we hadn't sacrificed our careers for the new component. As it turned out, I was the first member of AAT to receive a promotion, which reassured everyone else that they still had a career.

Our first challenge was to develop a program plan for the fledgling office. Where would we focus our limited resources? Where could we make the biggest impact the quickest? We met with senior managers and thought leaders from throughout the agency. We brought in vendors to demonstrate tools that might be useful in our workplace. We inventoried existing tools to look ways to reuse them. My past experiences as an analyst, a case officer, and a technical collection specialist all came in handy as we immersed ourselves in technologies such as data mining, data visualization, information sharing, storage and retrieval, and collaboration.

Using technology to support and encourage collaboration was an interesting challenge. An interagency group of senior managers focusing on one of the U.S. government's hard targets asked if technology could be leveraged not only to support their efforts at collaboration, but to include the hundreds of other analysts from throughout government who were focused on the issue as well. We succeeded in building an interagency network, and with input from the analysts, we designed an application that would encourage information-sharing and, hopefully, collaboration. But we realized early on that our real challenge was changing the culture of the analysts. If the organization valued analysts for their expertise, what incentive did they have to share their knowledge? We struggled with this issue as we delivered more target-specific networks, but it took several years before we found technical and management methods that recognized analysts for their collaboration with colleagues.

It didn't take long to identify the need for a technology demonstration center at CIA headquarters. We needed a facility to market the applications we were building and to train users on the new technology. There was a political angle as well: we needed to defend the agency's investment in information technology. A demonstration center would highlight our accomplishments. I was assigned to the team that designed the center and later operated the facility. It seems quaint now, but the flat-screen monitors in the demonstration stations, along with the floor-to-ceiling projection capability in the open area, were pretty advanced for the late 1990s. Accordingly, the demonstration center became a frequent destination for outside visitors to the agency. We became accustomed to supporting briefings for members of Congress and visiting celebrities, who often had little or no interest in our technology. CIA Director George Tenet was such a frequent visitor that he learned where we stashed our snacks and made a beeline for the cabinet whenever he was onsite.

I eventually spent twenty years working as an IT project manager, and during that time I saw our initial program plan go from concept to realization. As the mission of the agency evolved, new IT challenges were identified and tackled. Our small team in the Office of Advanced Analytic Tools grew to hundreds of engineers and project managers. The office itself underwent numerous name changes and administrative reorganizations. For a time we were put under the purview of the Directorate of Administration (thereby making me a veteran of all four CIA directorates). Finally, a chief information officer was established under the CIA director and our component followed.

After the 9/11 attacks drove home the need for greater collaboration between the agencies of the intelligence community, the director of national intelligence (DNI) was chartered, and I was asked to take over an existing project intended to support interagency collaboration. This turned into one of my most gratifying assignments as well as one of the longest: eventually I spent seven years on the effort. In the end, the application we created became the tool that made secure collaboration and communication within the intelligence community possible.

My work at the Office of the DNI was one of several assignments that involved interaction with IT teams at other government agencies. It was readily apparent that we at the CIA were far ahead of our colleagues with respect to IT infrastructure and the tools we had available for use. I was particularly disturbed by the technology (or lack thereof) in use at the FBI. Due to a lack of investment, they were several years behind the rest of the government, which made efforts to include them in our interagency IT efforts a real challenge. In 2010 I attended a large government IT conference, which included a keynote address by the chief information officer of the FBI. He began his address to the several thousand of us in attendance with "I'd like to start by apologizing to Jeff Johnson if he is in the audience." I was taken aback by this—I thought I had been pretty circumspect with my disdain for the FBI! The truth was more innocuous. His name was also Jeff Johnson, and when he registered at the conference he had been given my credentials by mistake (and apparently I was given his credentials—which explained the VIP gift baskets that appeared in my hotel room every day). This was not the only occasion when our career paths intersected. Jeff and I were both advocates and early adopters of Agile project management methodologies at our respective agencies (which in his case served to transform and modernize the FBI IT infrastructure).

One of my regrets is that I never returned to work specifically on digital video. I observed progress from afar, however, and was successful in making the business case for the purchase of the agency's first digital video server. This in turn sparked a revolution in how video was managed and leveraged as an analytic resource at the CIA. I like to think I played an early role in making this happen.

I feel very fortunate that during my thirty years with the CIA I held substantive assignments in all four agency directorates, as well as under the CIA director and the DNI, and had interactions with over thirty other government agencies. The experience has given me a greater understanding, as well as appreciation, of the work of our intelligence community. My first decade at the CIA gave me firsthand knowledge of how the agency operates, which I then put to use in helping harness the IT revolution of the past twenty years. There is no longer a Dissemination Branch charged with hand-delivering hard copy intelligence to the analysts. My assignments and projects helped end the Cold War, were credited with saving lives during the First Gulf War, and have impacted the work of my colleagues throughout government. While joining the CIA may have been accidental, I will never regret my tenure and look forward to further accomplishments in the future.

20

Developing a Better Understanding of the Personal Dimensions of Working at the CIA

HECTOR J. ESCOBAR III

Overview

To many observers, the work of the CIA is shrouded in mystery. Film, television, and novels are often the leading sources of information giving the public insight into the "spy world." These often inaccurate depictions not only cause the agency to be misunderstood, but also create false perceptions of the CIA's employees. Those interested in pursuing a career with the agency are not given an accurate view of the motives, experiences, and costs related to working at the CIA. To help individuals interested in pursuing a career at the CIA, this study examines information on the agency's official website, determines what information may be lacking, and attempts to provide a better depiction of the personal dimensions of working at the CIA through a variety of firsthand accounts by former employees. This information will enable prospective employees to weigh the costs and benefits of working at the CIA and make an informed decision regarding their career path, reducing the possibility of cultural mismatch and turnover.

Introduction

Because the agency must maintain high levels of security and secrecy, the information it provides to the general public, specifically to those interested in pursuing a career at the CIA, remains limited. Most modern job searches happen online, and the CIA can benefit from this tremendously. Film and television sensationalize CIA employees. Fictionalized versions of CIA employees, such as Tom Clancy's Jack Ryan, the analyst-turned-action-hero, or Robert Ludlum's rogue agent Jason Bourne, looking to take down corrupt CIA officers, do not represent CIA culture accurately. The news media often only focus on controversial events or the agency's mistakes. We are not often made aware of CIA successes, partly due to the clandestine nature of agency operations. Regardless of the source of public information, there seems to be a common theme: whatever is said often is not confirmed by the CIA. Today, all of these sources can be accessed via the internet, a source of both fact and fiction—and little credibility checking. To respond to this, the CIA, through its official website, can give needed insight into the agency's culture.

This chapter aims to bridge the gap between the information that is currently available to potential employees and what they might learn from the testimonies of former intelligence officers. The interviews with seven formers officers give a broader understanding of life within the CIA. They show that the CIA can offer potential employees a more in-depth look inside the agency's culture by providing the testimonies of former officers on its website, without endangering the CIA or national security. Potential employees will be able to better understand the personal dimensions of working at the CIA before applying, which may save time and money for both the potential employee and the CIA.

Background

Organizational Socialization

In *Analytic Culture in the US Intelligence Community: An Ethnographic Study*, Rob Johnston and Stephen H. Konya state:

> Every organization has a unique culture that is defined partly by its individual members and partly by its structure, history, and policies. For that culture to endure, it must be transmitted from current members to new members. This process, known as organizational

socialization, is especially important in organizations with strong, insular cultures, as those with weak cultures have less to transmit and will tend to experience culture changes as members come and go.[1]

Simply put, organizational socialization is the process by which a potential employee transitions from being a nonmember of an organization to being a member. To explain the process, Johnston and Konya present Daniel Feldman's three stages of organizational socialization: "getting in (or anticipatory socialization), breaking in (or accommodation), and settling in (often referred to as role management)."[2] This chapter focuses entirely on the first stage—anticipatory socialization, or the getting-in stage. According to Johnston and Konya, "During the getting-in stage, potential employees try to acquire information about an organization from available sources, such as websites, professional journals, and corporate annual reports."[3] The chapter compares the information the CIA provides to potential employees with the information supplied by former employees of the CIA through interviews.

When you google "CIA" the first link that turns up is the one to the official CIA website. Following the official website is the CIA *Wikipedia* page, then the official *Twitter* page, a *WikiLeaks* page, and six magazine and/or newspaper pages with articles pertaining to topics such as Iran, drone strikes, and enhanced interrogation. Only two of the first ten links are to official CIA sites. Of these two websites, only one is meant to aid potential employees.

Throughout the getting-in stage, potential employees develop expectations about working at the CIA. It is important for these individuals to have a realistic understanding of what a career at the CIA entails so that if they are hired, they will be more likely to remain satisfied with their job. "What a person has heard about working for a particular organization, such as an intelligence agency," Johnston and Konya say, "provides an idea of what to expect if hired. Conversely, individuals who do not believe they will fit in may decide not to apply."[4]

CIA *Recruitment Sources versus Independent Sources*

Company-dependent sources such as advertising are part of the organization's recruitment activities and can be directly controlled to communicate a positive message to potential applicants. Conversely, company-independent sources such as word-of-mouth can be influenced only indirectly through other recruitment activities and can contain positive as well as negative information.[5]

Because there is no way to control what most independent sources state about the CIA and its employees, the organization should put out an almost equal amount of information about the institution and its employees. This would combat the information provided by inaccurate sources. The amount of information on the official CIA website pertaining to the agency was sufficient; the website covered everything from purpose and mission to leadership and history. Looking at it the mindset of a potential applicant, however, the website does not present enough information about the individuals who make up the agency.

Because there are fewer former CIA officers than there are former employees in other professions—and these individuals have the choice to disclose whether or not they were previously employed by the agency—it is difficult for potential employees to have a sit-down conversation to discuss daily work life at CIA. Potential employees who are not able to speak with a former CIA officer have to rely on either independent sources or the CIA website for firsthand accounts. The CIA could use the "Employee Profiles" section of the website to present a variety of in-depth testimonials by former CIA officers. "Potential applicants are more attracted when testimonials provide more information about individual employees than about the organization."[6] Therefore,

Using employee testimonials in recruitment advertising might help to address the problem by combining the advantages of company-dependent recruitment sources that can be directly controlled to promote a favorable image, with the characteristics of word-of-mouth as an interpersonal information source. In fact, employee testimonials can be seen as company-controlled imitations of word-of-mouth.[7]

Sampling and Methods

Analysis of Current CIA Website

According to CIA.gov:

> The CIA is separated into five basic components: the Directorate of Operations, the Directorate of Analysis, the Directorate of Science & Technology, the Directorate of Support, and the Directorate of Digital Innovation. They carry out "the intelligence cycle," the process of collecting, analyzing, and disseminating intelligence information to top US government officials.[8]

The CIA's official website provides information that can aid potential employees in determining whether the CIA is the right career path for them, as well as which directorate they are best suited for. The "Careers and Internships" portion contains ten subsections:

- Career Opportunities
- Student Opportunities
- Application Process
- Life at CIA
- Benefits
- Diversity
- Military Transition
- Tools and Challenges
- FAQs
- Video Center

The "Careers and Internships" section gives insight into career paths within the CIA's five directorates. Each position has a detailed description, which includes the job description, location, salary, minimum requirements, and additional application requirements. The website also provides information that could benefit more specific types of applicants, such as former/ current military employees looking to transition to the CIA and interested students.

LIFE AT THE CIA

Within the "Careers and Internships" section, "Life at CIA" deals with the personal dimensions of life as a CIA officer. Life at CIA is described as follows:

> The CIA offers exciting career opportunities and a dynamic environment. We're on the forefront of world-altering events—as they happen. So working here isn't just a job, it's a mindset and a lifestyle.
>
> You'll find a supportive environment to help you grow and excel both professionally and personally. And a culture that expects you to do your personal best every day. Explore our world and imagine yourself working for the nation, in the center of intelligence.[9]

The subsections under "Life at CIA" include:

- Top 10 Reasons for Working at the CIA
- Why Choose the CIA?
- Our Culture
- Benefits
- Employee Profiles
- Discover The Washington, D.C. Area

These subsections all portray a positive outlook on employment at the CIA, which one would expected given that the website is a recruitment tool. But can this be a disservice to the CIA? When deciding whether to apply for a job at the CIA, potential applicants more than likely know the benefits of working at the CIA. The answers given by the individuals interviewed provided both praise of the work and mission, but also critique of the everyday general aspects allowing for a more holistic representation of life with the CIA. According to a comparative study on the effects of positive and negative information on job seekers, "positive information has relatively little impact on job seekers' attraction immediately after exposure, suggesting it is less relevant to them at this stage of the recruitment and job search process."[10] In contrast, it is the negative information about the employer that potential employees remember and recall before and during the application process. Therefore, positive information provided by employers (i.e., the CIA website) is moot. Even neutral information tends to have less of an impact on a job seeker's decision than negative information. "Job seekers who were exposed to negative information were much less attracted to the organization compared to participants who were only exposed to neutral information, suggesting it was particularly salient to job seekers."[11] Therefore, if the CIA website provided a narrative about their officers' time of employment that described the CIA from a personal perspective, with both positive and negative information, job seekers could better weigh the CIA as a potential place of employment. On the CIA website, a testimonial from one employee recalls, "I came across the CIA at a career fair. I thought I would give it a shot for a year, but as soon as I got there, I loved it. I have a double major in nuclear engineering and history, and I write analytic papers on nuclear issues, so my career is a great fit. I get to look into some incredible issues and give briefings to senior policymakers. It's very exciting to see our Government up close, influence policy and see decisions get made."[12]

The above quotation does mention the importance of "job fit," but it only acknowledges the positive aspects of employment at the CIA. It doesn't address any issues with the job, so if someone wanted a more in-depth look at what employment is like, they would have to seek outside sources of information.

RETENTION IN THE AGENCY

Because the CIA website provides solely a positive description of life at the CIA and because potential employees weight negative information more heavily than either positive or neutral information, information about the more negative aspects of

CIA employment could prove useful. A 2010 report by the CIA's Office of Inspector General contains data pertaining to retention and turnover at the agency. The report looks at both retirees (individuals who are fifty-five to fifty-seven years old or who have twenty-plus years of service) and resignees (individuals who have left the CIA of their own volition before retirement).[13] The top ten reasons for leaving the CIA in 2009 were as follows:

1. Lack of advancement opportunities

2. Poor management at office or National Clandestine Service-division level

3. Lack of communication about things that affect my work

4. Desire to do something different

5. Lack of appropriate recognition for my contributions

6. Poor management at first-line supervisor level

7. Lack of management support for prudent risk taking

8. Make better use of my skills and knowledge

9. Poor management at directorate level

10. Lack of promotions.

Other reasons resignees cited as reasons for leaving the CIA included the following:

- Opportunity issues, including a lack of interesting and/or challenging assignments (45 percent of resignees compared with 28 percent of retirees) and a lack of opportunities for field assignments (41 percent of resignees compared with 20 percent of retirees)[14]
- Expectation issues, including that the work was not what they expected when they joined CIA (45 percent of resignees compared with 11 percent of retirees), a poor onboarding experience (34 percent of resignees compared with 9 percent of retirees), or that they never intended to stay with CIA for a

full career (18 percent of resignees compared with 4 percent of retirees)[15]

- Discrimination on the basis of race/ethnicity and racial harassment (significantly more likely to be cited by black, Asian, and Hispanic employees as reasons than by white employees)[16]
- Unfair performance appraisals and unfair assignment processes (more frequently cited by Asian, Hispanic, and black employees than by white employees)[17]

With access to this information or more recent reports, potential employees can better weigh the negative and positive aspects of working at the CIA—and, in some cases, may choose to look elsewhere. Providing this information would make the CIA, which has no shortage of applicants, appear more open and committed to good job fit.

Finding the Middle Ground

The CIA could also provide the general public and potential employees with the testimonials of former CIA officers within the "Employee Profiles" subsection of their website. By combining CIA-dependent recruitment sources (CIA.gov) and testimonials from former CIA officers that detail the pros and cons of working at the CIA, the organization would give a more balanced and complete picture. Potential applicants would better understand the CIA's mission and duties on a personal level. The next section shows how former CIA officers can provide a detailed narrative of life at the CIA without divulging sensitive information.

Developing a Set of Questions

To get a broader understanding of life at the CIA, I developed a set of open-ended questions meant to induce a narrative. These questions were as follows:

1. What is your academic background?

2. What is your CIA career background?

3. Why did you join the CIA?

4. What difficulties did you encounter while employed at the CIA?

5. What surprised you about working at the CIA?

6. Was it difficult to balance the CIA with your regular life?

7. What did you find most rewarding about working at the CIA?

8. What is life like after the CIA?

9. What advice do you have for potential employees?

10. What areas of interest should potential employees focus on with regard to national security?

After acquiring approval from the University of Texas at El Paso's Institutional Review Board (IRB) and completing the Collaborative Institutional Training Initiative Program's course for social and behavioral researchers, I set out to recruit potential interviewees, focusing on two positions in particular:

- Intelligence officers or analysts in the Directorate of Analysis (formerly the Directorate of Intelligence)
- Operations officers in the Directorate of Operations (formerly the National Clandestine Service)

I chose these positions for the following reasons: (1) They are the more commonly known directorates at the CIA and have the bulk of the institution's employees, as well as the most desired positions. (2) They entail the two core functions of the CIA—analysis and operations. (3) They are the more commonly misinterpreted CIA positions because they are misrepresented in popular culture. As one former CIA officer explained:

Intelligence is providing analyzed information to the right customer at the right time. Covert action is actually doing something. It's (covert action) got something in it, it's not providing information—it's implementing policy. Covert action is a policy tool like diplomacy or military action, it's not intelligence (collection). Only if you look at intelligence as an institutional definition rather than a functional definition can you include covert action. There are things you do when implementing policy that you don't do when you're collecting information.

Recruitment

Through an advertisement in the Association of Former Intelligence Officers weekly newsletter and individuals recommended by a professor, I found seven CIA alumni willing to take part in an interview. I told them that they would remain anonymous and that, per IRB requirements, any documentation collected would be destroyed after the study. Other precautionary measures were taken to ensure that the identities of these individuals remained undisclosed. The interviewees had held the following positions at the CIA:

In the Directorate of Analysis (DA):

- Interviewee 1: Four years at the CIA
- Interviewee 2: Thirty-three years at the CIA
- Interviewee 3: Ten years at the CIA

From the Directorate of Operations (DO):

- Interviewee 1: Eight years at the CIA
- Interviewee 2: Thirty-five years at the CIA
- Interviewee 3: Thirty years at the CIA

Served in both Directorates:

- Analysis and Operations Interviewee 1: Thirty years total at the CIA

Interviews

Because the interviewees lived all over the United States, I conducted six interviews by phone and one by email and also conducted follow-up interviewees over the phone and by email. Each interview ran for approximately an hour (not including the follow-ups), during which the individuals answered questions and offered additional information. The interviewees reserved the right to not answer any questions they did not feel comfortable discussing. I told them they were being recorded for the purposes of reference and recall only, under the supervision of a faculty advisor. The quotes in the sections below are all from the 2015 interviews.

Findings

Q1: *Academic Background*

All interviewees possessed a bachelor's degree; some possessed master's degrees and doctoral degrees. Their fields included political science, foreign affairs, foreign service (international economics), economics, engineering, history, modern European history (Central Europe), and philosophy.

Q2: CIA *Background (Offices and Divisions)*

Within the Directorate of Analysis (DA), the analytic branch of the CIA, officers had experience working in the following offices and/or on the following issues: Near East, South Asia, and Africa; Soviet military and defense economic issues, Europe (including Bosnia), Director of Central Intelligence Analytic Support Team, Crime and Narcotics Center, transnational issues, science and technology, weapons issues, terrorism, and psychological profiling (of world leaders).

Within the DO, the operations/actions branch of the CIA, which includes covert action and human intelligence collection, officers had experience working in the following: Europe, Latin America, Soviet, and East Asia divisions, and on issues such as counterterrorism, counternarcotics, counterproliferation of WMDs, counterintelligence, and rogue nations.

Q3: *Why did you join the CIA?*

One of the interviewees' reasons for joining the CIA was their drive to serve and protect their country by supporting the United

States and its efforts in a meaningful way. The majority of interviewees felt the need for a purpose that transcended themselves. Four interviewees came from families with a long line of military service or who were government employees. All interviewees were drawn into the CIA because of its mystique, culture, and reputation. The opportunity to travel and live and work overseas played a role for several individuals. Interviewees were also very interested in working on international affairs, not merely studying or writing about U.S. dynamics with other countries, but also helping develop them. Six interviewees were impressed by the high levels of expertise within the agency. They saw the CIA as an information hub and appreciated having access to the vast amount of data to develop answers while working with other highly intellectual individuals.

The CIA prides itself on its diversity and recruits from all walks of life. It sees the importance of having employees who can provide different perspectives because of their unique backgrounds. Every officer has a unique story about how they ended up working at the CIA. Two stories I found particularly interesting because they speak to the diverse personnel are summarized below:

In the early 1990s, I had dropped out of college and wasn't sure what to do. I thought about a variety of "protect and serve" jobs. I took a couple of criminal justice courses at the local community college and talked to an army recruiter. But those jobs weren't quite right. And then I read the Tom Clancy books and decided that what Jack Ryan did sounded like it would be fun to do. He was an analyst, but was involved in all these adventures. After transferring to a four-year university, I took as many courses as possible on issues like international relations, international ethics, international economics, American foreign policy, national security, and so on. There was a course taught on intelligence there at the time, so I took that, too. And then I wrote my senior thesis on the cause of intelligence failure, and my honors thesis on the post–Cold War roles and missions of the intelligence community. I ended up graduating magna cum laude, with honors in political science, elected to Phi Beta Kappa, etc. Basically, college worked out well for me when the motivation was there to put in the effort. When my university's career services center organized the opportunity to speak with a CIA recruiter, I put in an application and that's how it all started. Protect and serve, but in a thinking way.

No career planning, it was a generational thing. Married into the CIA. Worked in the foreign service as a staff officer, met my spouse while working who worked for the CIA. [My spouse] died suddenly three years after marriage and the CIA offered me a job. The CIA is very good at taking care of its family. My spouse worked in operations and since they were the ones to offer me a job, that's how I began my career in operations.

Q4: What, if any, difficulties did you encounter while employed at the CIA?

Officers serving overseas encounter different challenges than those serving stateside, and these challenges differ further across countries of assignment. One participant stated: "Having diarrhea in a foreign country that you don't know the language . . . [getting] to a pharmacy and try to get medicine for it. Simple circumstances turned very difficult. It's part of the job." Stateside analysts generally have an 8:00 a.m. to 5:00 p.m. workday and a five-day work week. This will vary if the officer is on an account with a crisis associated with it. In that case, late nights and early mornings can be common for the duration of the crisis. One interviewee recalled: "I never had a 9:00 a.m. to 5:00 p.m. workday. For me on average it was a twelve-hour weekday and half-days on the weekend." The majority of the other DA interviewees maintained a "regular work schedule." But DO officers, and many officers from other directorates, have a 24/7 job if they are stationed abroad. Because they are working in a foreign country, they must always be alert, constantly watching their surroundings and maintaining their cover—this is essential tradecraft. A former officer pointed out: "You have to always remember you are living your cover. You also have to always be aware of your surroundings. Even today I can still remember at least twelve license plate numbers and the description of the vehicles. These things are learned, but can be difficult at times."

Within the DA, work also varies. For instance, three interviewees stated that junior analysts are usually asked to do simple things until they master the basics. As they progress throughout their career, they are tasked with more difficult things. The CIA has a probationary period to assess the capabilities of new employees. Within the DO, every member of a team, whether seasoned or novice, is in the same situation and is held to the same standard of operation. All but one individual stated that they encountered difficulties while employed at the CIA, but as one interviewee noted, "The difficulties at the CIA aren't specifically CIA issues; it's a job with issues that can relate to any other job ... for the most part." One participant stated that "at times it felt like management was oblivious, and policymakers need to be better versed in intelligence and how to use it, but those things are manageable."

Q5: Was it difficult to balance life at the CIA with life outside of the CIA?

All interviewees felt that balancing work with their personal lives was as complicated as in any other job, just in a different sense. Most jobs require a give-and-take between work and a person's personal life and family. Some other jobs require secrecy the same way the CIA does; the difference is that the secrecy pertaining to the agency is of national importance. Working at the CIA can be stressful, but for the most part—because CIA officers are dealing with privileged or classified information—there is very little (if any) take-home paperwork. When you are working with classified information, you do not take it home to work on over the weekend. You may be at home thinking about your account, but you cannot go further than conceptualizing the information in your mind. Two interviewees expressed the dynamic as follows:

It's useful early on to tell your family roughly what you are doing, so they understand that at times you can't make it home for dinner, or that you have to travel for a "while" and won't be there. A strong family relationship mitigates problems that may arise, and every job can cause issues. I'm not persuaded that because one has a challenging job at the agency—that it is the sole cause for your divorce. You need good communication between you. As far as children, there is a time for your child to hear what you do, till then they do not care what you do for a living. Your family will get used to hearing "I can't talk about it."

I had a cover story, that's often the difference between the DA and the DO—being overt and covert. The agency guides you on whom to tell the truth. I did not tell my family (parents and sibling) the truth. They were given the cover story. My spouse worked for the government as well so I never found it difficult to speak with h**. My spouse understood that there were some things I couldn't talk about. When leaving the agency, I told my family the truth. They never suspected that I worked for the CIA, but it was easier to hide it from them because they lived in other areas of the country. It was easier to maintain cover. You have to always remember you are living your cover.

Q6: What surprised you about working at the CIA?

The surprises discussed by the interviewees dealt with many topics, including how wrong the public and the media are about what the CIA is and does. "There's no James Bond stuff here; in fact, James Bond wouldn't last five minutes at the CIA . . . he's too flashy." Some interviewees experienced a cultural mismatch or disconnect because of their expectations or preconceptions—partly because they formed opinions based on how the CIA appears from the outside, and partly because they didn't fully understand going into the job what their job would actually entail. As one former analyst noted: "The initial job was to produce leadership profiles, which involved a lot of research and copying/

pasting, but not a whole lot of analysis. A lot of CIA's analysis is a lot more like journalism than it is political science. As someone who enjoys trying to figure out what is going on, I found this lack of emphasis on thinking to be challenging."

But not all revelations were negative. Two interviewees found the level of sophistication and expertise impressive and more abundant than they expected. Four interviewees stated that working at the CIA didn't feel like any other agency or any other office environment. Several interviewees mentioned the unique atmosphere. One stated that "CIA headquarters doesn't feel like a government agency; it has a special feel to it." Former CIA officers said that when working in the CIA you can always feel the energy of the people there, which is fueled by CIA officers' purpose. The esprit de corps is real at the CIA because of a shared sense of purpose. Officers develop and maintain a real sense of family with the people they work with. "Everyone looks out for everyone," said one interviewee. "When you go see one of the CIA's doctors before you travel abroad, they make sure you are good to go. They do what they can to keep you safe. You can truly feel like they are not only looking out for the success of the mission but you as an individual."

Q7: What did you find most rewarding about working at the CIA?

"While recruiting from different colleges I would ask audience members, 'If you were to write your memoirs, would people be interested in reading them?' Working at the CIA, the answer is yes they would, and your record of accomplishments will outlive you."

One of the themes was the importance of getting critical intelligence to the policymakers who need to make the hard decisions. Members of both the DO and the DA noted that keeping fellow members of the CIA safe overseas and having the sense that what you are doing contributes to the security of the country (in a major or minor way) was rewarding as well. "I (personally) made a difference in U.S. foreign policy decisions. Information or intelligence I gathered made a difference in the Gulf War." One interviewee noted the rewarding nature of being part of the intelligence process and affecting policy: "I like to do analysis. I like to manage analysis. I like to read analysis. This was the perfect job for me. I was excited to go to work every morning. I loved listening to the news and hearing them talk about things that I'd be working on that very day. It doesn't get much better than that." Preventing attacks targeting the United States, disrupting drug trafficking organizations operations, and eliminating foreign adversaries were all considered rewards of the job. The one sentiment found across all interviewees was this: in a sense, they were making history.

"I thought I was making a difference, you know? Avoiding a nuclear holocaust . . . that's pretty important."

Q8: What is life like after the CIA?

"I know people who left the CIA and pursued very different career paths. Because so many members are PhDs and a lot of what we do is closely related to research done in academia, people tend to transition to teaching at universities."

Many former employees pursue jobs within academia or transition to privately owned security firms where their jobs mimic their CIA careers. Others become attorneys, writers, advisors, public speakers, politicians, political aides, and even brew masters.

After leaving CIA, I really enjoyed being an analyst at the U.S. Government Accountability Office. This is an arm of Congress that conducts program reviews of executive branch agencies. In my case—working in their Defense Capabilities and Management team—that reviewed Defense Department programs. Most of the things that didn't work for me with CIA analysis worked with GAO analysis. There was more thinking and more conceptualizing . . . the projects were built on a PhD dissertation design framework. There was more primary source information acquisition. There was more working in teams, and collaboration. The projects took longer so we could think through issues more carefully. And we had the opportunity to write recommendations on what Congress could do to fix problems. For me, that was a much better fit in terms of analysis.

Q9: What advice do you have for individuals interested in pursuing a career at the CIA?

The following statements contained the most detailed advice for individuals pursuing a career within the CIA's DA and DO. These statements provide potential applicants with questions to consider before applying to the CIA.

First think carefully about what you like to do and are good at. Do something related to that. If that means be an intelligence officer, then do that. But find out what the job entails first. More important than the job title is to enjoy what you do . . . that is most important. But if you enjoy the requirements of the intelligence analyst—research, reading, thinking, writing, and speaking—then expose yourself to a variety of ways of doing each of these. Get as much breadth and depth as possible, because after you start working full-time you won't have much time to learn new and different ways to do the job.

The CIA looks for a strong technical background—hard science (chemistry, mathematical statistics, physics, engineering) . . . or very strong area studies (master's or PhDs) and language capability. People who get a degree in intelligence—that isn't the best preparation for work in intelligence. Get your substantive foundation first. You need to be really expert in either a functional area like economics or statistics or cyber or a geographic area. You want to have that in place before you walk in the door.

It's easier to go in single; bypass the decision on whom to tell. You have to be career-oriented. If you want to make a change (leave the CIA), the skill set isn't directly relevant to a lot of civilian careers, and you may have restrictions on what you can say about what you did. That lack of information makes it harder to show that you are a qualified individual.

Part of the job is a sense of adventure; you cannot live in fear. Experience the cultures. You'll never be a native, nor does the CIA want you to be, but you need to understand the cultures. Go into it as a career. This is not a job hop. In operations it takes about ten years before you get the real sense of what's going on. Within operations it's important to understand the business. Within the CIA there are other opportunities. Even if you don't want to continue doing the same job, the CIA has many other jobs to choose from. And speak truth to power—it doesn't matter if the president is a Republican or a Democrat; politics should not determine your effectiveness within the agency.

Figure out what you would like to do first; don't come up with an image of what a CIA person does. The agency needs every kind of person; go be *you* first. If you intend to be James Bond—know that he wouldn't last five minutes at the CIA; he's too flashy. Things are done in teams; you can't care about who will get credit.

Q10: *What areas of interest should potential employees focus on?*

This list includes possible areas of interest that the interviewees felt would be of concern to the United States and national security. If the CIA website provided this information, potential employees could choose an area of interest to focus on. It was also suggested that potential employees review the annual Worldwide Threat Assessment.

- Cyber security
- Terrorism
- Proliferation of WMDs
- Iran
- North Korea
- Extremist groups (amorphous groups and religiously motivated violence)

- Russia
- China
- India
- Pakistan
- Counternarcotics
- Latin America (Mexico, Brazil, Colombia)
- The Balkans
- Power concerns throughout the world
- Fragility of economic systems and how they interrelate across the world
- The clash over various resources (water, land)

Limitations of the Study

Because of IRB requirements, I interviewed only seven individuals. A larger sample would have been preferable, but finding potential candidates was challenging. One cannot simply look in a phonebook for former CIA officers.

I chose to leave out certain details about the individuals because I felt they could be used as identifiers. If the CIA were to add former employees' testimonies to its website, it might be able to provide these details.

I would have been interested in hearing what potential employees would like to know about life at the CIA. The retention report was published in 2010; access to more current numbers would have allowed updated figures related to retention. The CIA could also release a yearly "retention in the agency" report that could also be available through the CIA's website.

Future research could include the testimonies of spouses or children of former CIA officers to convey their perspectives on how their lives were affected during and after the spouse's or parent's employment at the CIA. Developing testimonies for other employees within the other three directorates at the CIA would also be useful to potential applicants.

Finally, it would also be helpful to develop a set of questions that potential applicants would be interested in having answered and a mechanism for feedback from them (applicants) as to whether or not the information was useful and whether it positively and/or negatively affected their decision to apply. The CIA website could have a section for suggesting a question to be answered, and those questions could be used to create a set of open-ended questions for former employees to answer when providing their narratives.

Conclusion

Most of the general public doesn't have an understanding of what the intelligence community (IC) is in general. Matter of civics, it's good for Americans to have a better understanding of the CIA and its role in the IC, to gain a more objective understanding without being privy to secret information. Americans must trust their government. Secrecy is needed to function in the global environment to protect the U.S. . . . Distrust comes from a lack of information. The only things you hear about are the failures or shortcomings of the agency. You never hear the good stories or successes. The agency does make mistakes, officers can break the law, or there can be a scandal, but the agency is made of people who [sometimes] make mistakes.

Because the CIA must maintain security through secrecy, the amount of information it can provide to potential applicants remains limited. Potential employees need to receive as much information as possible before they apply. Today most research pertaining to the job search process is conducted online. If the information online doesn't provide a realistic view of employment within the CIA, it is crucial that the CIA itself provides information to fill the gap. Former CIA officers who can write about their personal experiences within the CIA provide the type of insight the CIA should give to potential employees. If potential employees have an unrealistic picture of employment at the CIA, low morale and a low work ethic could develop after they are hired and lead to greater issues with their effectiveness. With unbiased, unscripted testimonies on the CIA website, potential employees will have a better understanding of who works at the CIA and what CIA life is like. This will help both the employer and the employee avoid a cultural mismatch, aiding job fit and employee retention. It is possible to allow an in-depth look at what working at the CIA is like without divulging any sensitive information that could damage the CIA or national security. Former officers' testimonies could be vetted before they are posted on the CIA website to ensure that no sensitive information is divulged to the public.

Acknowledgments

I would like to thank the former CIA officers (who will remain anonymous) for their time and participation in the study. Without them this study would not have been possible. I would also like to thank the individuals at the Association of Former Intelligence Officers who were kind enough to post an "Interviewees Wanted" ad in their newsletter. Dr. Michael Landon-Murray was a tremendous help throughout the process and offered sound guidance. Finally, I would like to thank all officers (former and current) of the CIA for their service and commitment to our country. We might not hear about your successes as frequently as we hear about the failures, but we know that you are serving the United States honorably.

Notes

1. Rob, Johnston, and Stephen H. Konya, "Organizational Culture: Anticipatory Socialization and Intelligence Analysts," in *Analytic Culture in the US Intelligence Community: An Ethnographic Study* (Washington DC: Center for the Study of Intelligence, 2005), 97, https://www.cia.gov/library/center-for-the-study-of-intelligence/csi-publications/books-and-monographs/analytic-culture-in-the-u-s-intelligence-community/analytic_culture_report.pdf.

2. Johnston and Konya, "Organizational Culture," 98.

3. Johnston and Konya, "Organizational Culture," 98.

4. Johnston and Konya, "Organizational Culture," 99.

5. Greet Van Hoye and Filip Lievens, "Investigating Web-Based Recruitment Sources: Employee Testimonials vs Word-of-Mouth," *International Journal of Selection and Assessment* 4:15 (December 2003): 373.

6. Van Hoye and Lievens, "Investigating Web-Based Recruitment," 372.

7. Van Hoye and Lievens, "Investigating Web-Based Recruitment," 373–74.

8. Central Intelligence Agency, "Today's CIA," CIA.gov, https://www.cia.gov/about-cia/todays-cia.

9. Central Intelligence Agency, "Today's CIA."

10. Adam M. Kanar, Christopher J. Collins, and Bradford S. Bell, "A Comparison of the Effects of Positive and Negative Information on Job Seekers' Organizational Attraction and Attribute Recall," *Human Performance* 3:23 (2010), 193–212.

11. Kanar, Collins, and Bell, "Comparison of Effects," 20.

12. Central Intelligence Agency, "Frederick: Analyst," CIA.gov, https://www.cia.gov/careers/life-at-cia/employee-profiles/employee-profile-transcripts/frederick-analyst.html.

13. Central Intelligence Agency, Office of Inspector General, *Report of Follow-Up Inspection: Retention in the Agency*, (Washington DC: CIA), 13, 19, 23, s3.documentcloud.org/documents/741885/cia-employee-retention-report.pdf.

14. CIA Office of Inspector General, *Report of Follow-Up*, 19.

15. CIA Office of Inspector General, *Report of Follow-Up*, 19.

16. CIA Office of Inspector General, *Report of Follow-Up*, 23.

17. CIA Office of Inspector General, *Report of Follow-Up*, 23.

21

Beginnings

LESTER PALDY

My first experience with nuclear weapons took place when I was serving as a young infantry officer with a marine battalion assigned to the Sixth Fleet in the Mediterranean in 1957. We were supported by an artillery unit that had an image of a golden bullet painted on its vehicles. When I asked what the image represented, I was told that the weapons could fire nuclear artillery shells that were stored aboard ship in a compartment under twenty-four-hour guard. I understood the nuclear physics involved but had no opportunity then to learn more. After leaving the U.S. Marines to attend college, and after I later became a physics instructor, I always remembered that brief but intriguing experience, and I began to get involved in arms control issues, focusing particularly on nuclear weapons testing.

My experiences providing technical support for the delegation meeting with the Soviets in Geneva began in 1988 when a CIA officer whom I had met at an arms control conference suggested that I apply for a leave of absence from my university position and spend a year at the agency. The assignment gave me an opportunity to observe the liberation of Eastern Europe and the efforts of the first Bush administration to deal with the collapse of the Soviet system. It also gave me a chance to watch the evolution of the U.S. national security community from one that had to deal with a single major adversary to one forced to confront global threats of arms proliferation and terrorism.

Early in 1989, six months after applying for the position, I was accepted and participated in a week-long orientation at CIA headquarters. Looking back, I think it was useful to go through an orientation week with others who would work in various job capacities. It gave us all some background information and gave me a chance to take the measure of the organization where I would serve first as a staff officer and later as an independent contractor. The orientation served some of the same purposes as the Marine Corps boot camp and officer candidate programs I had passed through four decades earlier. By the end of the week I knew the rules well enough to get by without making serious mistakes, knew where to find the things I would need, and knew where to go if I needed help or advice. I was eager to begin.

Entry on Duty

I walked into my new government office for my first full week of work and learned that Jay Castillo, the office head who had approved my appointment, was leaving to go to another unit. The man I thought I would work with was leaving on the day I arrived! I learned abruptly that CIA job rotations were routine and that people had to learn new skills to function in different settings every few years. I would have to get used to the style, pace, and culture of an organization that was very different from that of a university, where people spent their entire careers in the same job. Who would be my new boss? Would he even know what a middle-aged academic was doing in his office? How would he react when he learned that he had a staff member who, unlike the rest of his veteran staff, had no experience in the civilian national security community? It was going to be an interesting beginning.

Since I had no specific assignment I began by reading material about chemical and biological weapons from the office literature collection. Some of my previous views proved untenable. I had thought that the 1979 outbreak of anthrax at Sverdlovsk in the Soviet Union could not be attributed to a biological weapons accident with any degree of certainty. Biological weapons are prohibited by treaty and a Soviet violation would be a serious matter.

The Soviets said that anthrax was endemic in the area and that persons who contracted it had eaten contaminated meat from infected cattle. One of the pieces of evidence I'd found persuasive when the outbreak was first reported was an account by a U.S. scientist in Sverdlovsk at that time. He said that there had been no public alarm sounded. Surely, I thought, a release of an anthrax-bearing aerosol, even from a clandestine weapons laboratory, would have generated a public warning. After we learned about the initial cover-up of the Chernobyl accident, I was not so sure. Now I read a description of powerful evidence, acquired with the help of Yale University DNA pioneer Matthew Meselson, that the Sverdlosk facility had released an aerosolized anthrax powder that was almost certainly designed for offensive biological weapons.

At my first staff meeting I observed our new office head, Douglas MacEachin, in action. As a former marine infantry officer, he would be well suited to take part in the infighting that, as I was learning quickly, was common in the interagency arms control group. One of my office colleagues said the Soviets were easier to deal with than our Department of Defense because the Soviets were rational. I would soon come to realize that the new George H. W. Bush administration still had no arms control agenda to drive policy agencies toward a common goal.

For an information addict, working at CIA headquarters is like being the proverbial kid in a candy store. I read everything I could find on weapons of mass destruction. For example, one day I read a report on the Soviet SS-24 rail-mobile missile that made a great impression on me. The location of these weapons was tracked closely with all the devices at the disposal of the intelligence community. The Soviets tried to hide them, concealing them in rail tunnels during the day and moving them at night. Somewhere out on the vast Russian steppes, many warheads were aimed at us. It was a sobering thought with which to begin the day. When it was my turn to report on my activity at the weekly staff meeting, I said I was reading background material to get up to speed. Nobody paid much attention; I was a novice, and it was going to take time before I had much to contribute. My cubicle in a crowded office was not much larger than a phone booth.

What would I work on? When MacEachin learned that I was interested in nuclear weapons testing issues, he proposed that I work with the interagency group supporting the Geneva delegation to negotiate the verification protocol for the unratified Threshold Test Ban Treaty (TTBT) that had been signed by the United States and the Soviet Union in 1974. U.S. and Soviet nuclear tests in the atmosphere ended in 1963, but both sides continued underground tests. The TTBT would limit the explosive yields of underground tests to 150 kilotons (of TNT equivalent). Seen in perspective, this was an inconsequential limit since the explosions that destroyed Hiroshima and Nagasaki were about 15 kilotons.

The underground tests conducted at the Nevada test site about seventy-five miles northwest of Las Vegas from 1963 until all tests ended in 1992 mainly involved the testing of "primaries." These were usually plutonium or uranium fission "triggers"—explosive devices used to trigger thermonuclear "secondaries" requiring the radiation and energy of the primary explosion to fuse lighter elements in what are usually called hydrogen bombs. Most of these primary explosive tests generated yields much less than 150 kilotons, so the TTBT did not limit the ability of the United States to develop improved weapons.

The political backstory of the TTBT in the United States involved placating the burgeoning antinuclear movement of the 1970s and 1980s with a nuclear treaty that did not hamper the development of new nuclear weapons or efforts to improve the reliability of older ones. The danger, from the perspective of U.S. policymakers and lobbyists who sought improved nuclear weapons, was that the TTBT might pressure the United States into entering negotiations for a treaty that would ban all nuclear tests, something U.S. military and national laboratory leaderships opposed. Give them this one, they argued, but don't agree to anything that might lead to further limitations or a complete ban on testing.

The TTBT verification protocol would specify the inspection requirements and related details for the treaty to ensure compliance by both sides. However, many U.S. policymakers and intelligence officials assumed the Soviets would try to cheat and test explosives with yields greater than 150 kilotons. Conversely, the Soviets seemed to believe the United States would use inspections to conduct espionage. The CIA role in developing the protocol was to ensure that it included measures that would detect or prevent the Soviets from cheating. My responsibility would be to present and defend the technical recommendations from the CIA's Office of Scientific and Weapons Research in the interagency forum that would inform and support the U.S. negotiating delegation in Geneva.

Routines and Recollections

I started using my lunch hour to work out in the gym in the basement of the CIA Original Headquarters Building where I worked. A group of about twenty people usually crowded into the small room at lunchtime, working out on the Nautilus equipment and exercise bicycles. The locker rooms were very small and one sometimes had to wait for a shower. The newer headquarters building on the opposite side of the compound had a more modern and better-equipped gym. but I liked the atmosphere in the old one.

Most of the men working out seemed very fit. They went through their workouts with few words and wasted little time. I once noticed a man working out next to me, perhaps in his late forties, who had burn scars covering nearly 50 percent of his body that I guessed were from burns from an aviation fuel fire. Later I would learn that he was a heroic figure at the agency; he survived a plane crash and made his way to safety alone through the African bush.

I tried not to stare at the scars and found my thoughts drifting back to Jack Raisler, who was killed when his AD-2 attack plane crashed on takeoff at the K-3 marine airbase near Pohang, South Korea, in 1955. The plane had reached about three hundred feet over the end of the runway when its piston engine started backfiring and smoking. I was standing near the flight line when the sounds riveted my attention. As I watched, the plane lost altitude and disappeared beneath the edge of the runway plateau, about a quarter mile away. I grabbed a fire extinguisher and ran toward it. When I reached the site, breathless, I saw that the plane seemed relatively undamaged and there was no fire. The pilot was slumped, motionless, in his seat.

The crash crew reached into the cockpit and eased the pilot out. They cradled his head, face up, still wearing his gold-colored flight helmet, and gently lowered him to the ground. I recognized Jack and thought he was unconscious. As we crowded around, one of the crash crew turned to us and shook his head silently. Jack was dead, his neck probably broken by the impact of the crash. At least there was no fire and probably no suffering. His eyes were closed and he looked Christ-like, lying on the ground in his flight suit with his arms extended. All those memories came back to me when I saw the man in the gym that day.

After several weeks on the job, I was beginning to think that the CIA was an efficient bureaucracy. It seemed far superior in every respect to the National Science Foundation, where I had spent two Washington tours a decade earlier. Some of my reactions might be dismissed by salty veterans as a new recruit's naïveté, but my first impression was uniformly excellent. Everything seemed to work. The people were smart and worked hard. Morale was high.

I was still soaking up background material and reading interesting arms control reports. Once our new management was fully in place and the reorganization of our unit was complete, I hoped to do some useful work. Meanwhile, I thought they were trying to figure out where I could fit in best and what kind of person I was. I made it a point to ask a lot of questions and listen carefully to answers.

Working Group Assignment

My work on the interagency group began with MacEachin giving me a stack of cables and a hundred-page draft. The document contained outlines of inspection and monitoring procedures that the United States and Soviets would have to agree to implement to verify that underground nuclear weapon tests did not exceed 150 kilotons of explosive yield. I needed to get up to speed quickly. My first task would be to try to understand the issues well enough to ask questions and participate fully in interagency meetings. I learned soon enough that these meetings were scrums.

An office veteran and I attended my first interagency meeting of a group that included representatives from the State Department, the Defense Department, the Department of Energy, the Arms Control and Disarmament Agency (ACDA), the Joint Chiefs of Staff (JCS), and the CIA. The committee spent two hours on a page-by-page review of an arms control document, with one member proposing a replacement paragraph that sounded to some of us like a piece of flimflam. The group rejected it, choosing less tendentious language. I was surprised by the sharp tone of the discussion in this interagency forum but was soon to learn that it was typical. When I asked if the group ever used game theory in its analyses, the eye-rolling response was immediate: "This isn't gaming; this is hard-ball interagency politics." I retreated into my academic shell and never mentioned game theory again.

Several days later I attended the second of what would be many working group meetings usually held at the State Department. About fifteen people attended, representing the Secretary of Defense (OSD), the JCS, the ACDA, the Defense Intelligence Agency, the State Department, and the Energy Department. MacEachin introduced me and said I would be working with them, eliciting a few good-natured comments about university professors leaving the soft life for the real world. I made it a point never to wear my tweed jacket.

Most of these meetings dealt with procedural matters. We met at least twice a week to prepare for the reconvening of the Geneva negotiations. Some members of the group believed that President Bush and the National Security Council might not support the decision to reconvene, but our working group had to assume that things would take place on schedule. I paid careful attention to what was going on, hoping that as I gained experience and learned the implicit rules I would be able to meet my responsibilities. I was also learning that it was important to be prepared for these meetings and come with a sense of humor. There was plenty of good-natured kidding among members, one of whom suggested to me that if you wanted to avoid being the target of barbed remarks, you should never be the last to arrive.

I learned quickly that the CIA opposed having the (since dissolved) ACDA become involved in intelligence processes. The agency position was that as a policy body, ACDA was excluded by statute from the intelligence community and the preparation of intelligence products. The CIA's fear was that a policy agency would slant the intelligence to suit its own policy goals. I was beginning to understand the CIA's arms control group's mission. It brokered requests from the policy community for intelligence support on arms control issues, tasking its production offices with preparing the necessary briefings and analyses, and distributed these intelligence products. It also prepared reports on foreign nations' compliance with arms agreements, using the intelligence resources at its disposal. It could commission and manage studies by various intelligence community offices to assess our government's ability to monitor treaties. Its staff served as intelligence community representatives at interagency meetings dealing with arms control policy.

Interagency working group environments are competitive. We used most of our time considering alternative wording for issues raised by the participating agencies. I spent much of my energy making sure I understood the words and context and found it difficult to take notes and consider the merits of the alternatives at the same time. Our task was to pass our recommendations on to a more senior policy coordinating committee that would then deliver the result to the National Security Council. There were eighteen of us at one working group meeting, including a new member from OSD who had once been a CIA officer. Another member characterized the new person from OSD as very smart, ultra-hawkish, and extremely dangerous. I thought at the time that this was not a bad reputation to have in this arena, and I expected him to rise quickly in the OSD hierarchy.

My notes for the meeting were scrawled; changes in my notes and changes to the changes quickly overwhelmed me. As the pages in my notebook filled with barely decipherable handwriting, I became worried about keeping track of the information. I knew it was easy to get trapped into following details and lose focus on where the discussion was leading. I felt like the high school valedictorian who goes to Harvard and finds himself in the lower part of the freshman class; I was in with the fast crowd.

Don Phillips, a navy commander representing JCS, was a naval aviator with a Texas drawl who had also served on the Geneva negotiating team. While we were waiting in a Pentagon corridor for a conference room to clear, he said that he had concluded that everyone in Washington is a failure. "Look," he said, "people are having fun herding cattle and doing other useful work, and here we are, spending hours a day in traffic, attending one meeting after another, and arguing about syntax." I thought he might have a point.

With our working group now meeting several times each week at the State Department, I was learning how these forums produce options. Each agency comes to the meeting with a set agenda. There was relatively little real give-and-take. Representatives rarely changed their positions because of anything that was said. The Energy Department focused primarily on maintaining its role in the manufacture and testing of nuclear weapons. JCS focused on testing to improve the quality of the existing nuclear stockpile and introducing more sophisticated weapons.

The intelligence community wanted to maintain and enhance its collection and analytic capabilities while guarding its flanks to repel incursions from policy agencies who were trying to get into the intelligence game to argue that their positions were supported by intelligence. When the agencies couldn't agree, the issue was just bumped up to a higher group.

One of our meetings at the Pentagon was held in the Garand Room, named after the designer of the M1 rifle, standard issue during World War II and the Korean War. The room contained a plaque and a mounted M1, and I could not resist walking over to it and sliding the bolt back and releasing it by inserting my thumb into the clip chamber, enjoying its reassuring metallic click. "How did you know how to do that?" asked someone sitting at the table. He didn't know that I must have done this a thousand times as a marine.

Nuclear Technology

After a month of grueling meetings, our office head told me I needed to become more familiar with nuclear weapons technology. While I understood the physics, the closest I had ever been to a nuclear weapon was with a marine infantry battalion supported by nuclear artillery. He wanted me to visit the nuclear weapons laboratories and the Nevada test site to observe an underground nuclear test, the Rocky Flats plutonium facility not far from Denver, and the Pantex site in Texas to see how weapons were assembled and disassembled. That all sounded very exciting to me.

At night most of my building was quiet. Its long corridors receded into the distance like a piece of surrealist art. I often found myself working late into the night to keep up with cable traffic and prepare for working group meetings. On one of those late nights I was working at my computer when I sensed someone standing behind me. Security officers who noticed that the room was not secured had entered quietly and were checking up.

One of my office friends asked if I would be interested in visiting the CIA Operations Center to see its night operations. I eagerly accepted. The operations center is busy all night receiving incoming traffic and preparing and processing incoming information for the National Intelligence Daily and the President's Daily Brief for early morning delivery to the White House.

It is the nation's early warning center and maintains continuous contact with the White House situation room. It occupies a large complex, high in the headquarters building. On the night I visited, lightning flashes from an approaching thunderstorm provided a dramatic backdrop to the work in progress. The commanding element in the room was the desk of the senior duty officer who sat at a console with analysts' desks arranged in a semicircle around him. Video monitors and world clocks lined the walls. It was an impressive facility and I left feeling that the nation was being well served by the men and women working there. One of the young women who briefed me that evening would later rise to the top of the agency's Directorate of Intelligence.

Over the next few months, I traveled to Los Alamos National Laboratory, the Rocky Flats plutonium machining plant, and the Nevada test site, where I observed an underground nuclear test. I was developing the insights I needed. Back at headquarters we watched a film narrated by Charlton Heston. It was reasonably informative, but it had a tone that reminded me of the corny anti-communist films of the mid-1950s, and for unfathomable reasons it was classified. The actors playing the parts of Soviet agents were disguised as cleaning women and always seemed to be dusting something with feather mops as they eavesdropped on conversations; perhaps the mops are KGB standard issue. Another briefing dealt with the way in which the new U.S. embassy building in Moscow had been extensively bugged.

One of my most interesting tasks during this period was briefing senior officials and national laboratory directors on the outcome of the last negotiating round in Geneva. It was held at a downtown building in Washington, not far from the White House. The panel included Edward Teller (the father of the hydrogen bomb), the directors of the Los Alamos, Lawrence Livermore, and

Sandia weapons laboratories, and other senior figures from the nuclear weapons community. Teller reminded me of my father in his last years, with his baggy eyes and jowls. He appeared to sleep for a good part of the meeting, his head slumped over on the table. I thought this posture might have been a clever ruse designed to disarm people since he raised questions from time to time in his richly accented and resonant voice. When I mentioned that one of the senior Soviet negotiators, Victor Mikhailov, had been a student of the great Russian theoretical physicist Lev Landau, Teller perked right up, saying that he had written a paper with Landau.

At the break Teller asked me to sit with him on a bench in the State Department corridor, and he asked me why I thought the Soviets wanted a nuclear test ban. I said I thought they believed they could not keep up with us in the continuing weapons competition. He chortled and said, "That's right! We're ahead of them!" Later in the session he asked questions about our ability to detect Soviet cheating on test limits. "Could we detect an underground nuclear test if it was conducted in a large cave filled with ice?" I did a quick calculation of how much ice it would take to absorb the energy of a small nuclear weapon, and I remember scribbling a note to the person next to me saying that the old physicist still had what it took. He replied that he had been thinking the same thing. The opportunity to talk to this legendary figure made it a memorable session for me. (Writing this, I realize that I am older now than he was then.)

When working group meetings focused on potential Soviet cheating scenarios designed to make nuclear explosive yields appear smaller than they were, I could sometimes weigh in with rough calculations involving little more than arithmetic. One of the most frequently discussed cheating scenarios involved exploding the nuclear device in a cavity that would absorb some of the shockwave and reduce its seismic signature.

I drew a picture of a cavity one hundred meters in diameter and tried to estimate whether the Soviets could construct it without us knowing about it. Making a cavity that large would not be easy, for it would have to be reinforced with steel to keep it from collapsing and killing its miners. The miners would have to dig side galleries and get the steel inside and get the steel to the site without being detected by satellite reconnaissance or agent reports. The presence of steel at an otherwise innocuous mining site would be a tip-off that something unusual was going on.

The Soviets would also have to hide the material excavated from the cavity without detection. A cavity of that size would produce one million cubic meters of soil or rock. That would generate about twenty-five thousand dump truck loads. Those trucks would wear deep ruts in roads or tracks in snow. It would not be impossible to hide them from satellites but it would be difficult. Later I estimated that even a cavity twenty meters in radius would pose daunting construction problems. The cavity must contain the explosion underground to avoid detection. Containment and cavity size considerations work against each other. One has to go deep underground to contain the explosion, but that increases the overburden pressure on the cavity. If you go too deep, the cavity collapses.

The Soviets might try to create a cavity in a salt deposit by pumping water into the salt bed, dissolving it, and pumping the brine solution up. Solution mining in salt is easy enough, but it might be difficult to dispose of the hot brine without detection. Anyone who has ever tried to dissolve salt in hot water knows it requires a lot more water than salt. Suppose it took ten times as much. That would generate a pond that would be one kilometer square and ten meters deep. Could you inject that into some subsurface region? Maybe. Evaporate it? Then you would have to hide the resulting crystallized salt from prying eyes and satellite sensors. The Soviets might try to divert the hot brine into a nearby river, but that would change the river's temperature. An infrared-detecting satellite would detect that change. People relying on the river for irrigation or drinking water would also notice it.

To reinforce the analysis I suggested that we invite Lynn Sykes of Columbia University, a leading authority on Russian salt formations, to brief us, but my immediate boss declined, saying that Sykes did not have a security clearance. I argued that Sykes would do the talking and that we would be listening, but that rationale did not prevail. The agency's insular culture sometimes works against it.

Don Phillips, the gregarious navy commander serving on our working group, had a fine sense of humor and often told us stories about his time on the Geneva delegation. One described a reception at the Soviet mission where there was some discussion about the possibility of each side bringing a nuclear weapon to the other's nuclear test site for a demonstration test that would be useful for yield calibration, since soil and rock properties affected the seismic detection of underground tests. The proposal was a nonstarter because of the technical and political problems involved, but a Soviet asked the commander what he thought of the idea. Don reminded the Soviet that he was an attack pilot in the U.S. Navy and said that he would be glad to deliver a nuclear weapon to the Soviet Union. As his response was translated, the commander said he could see the wave of consternation and confusion sweep over the Soviets' faces as they digested the ambiguities in his response. Afterward, Don, who did not hide his dislike of the Soviets, said that it was one of the best exchanges he had ever had with them.

Between our biweekly working group meetings, I reviewed and forwarded cables to Geneva from Washington containing the latest technical updates related to issues being negotiated by the two delegations. I would try to digest and condense all the information to make it absorbable. The Geneva talks were stalled. With no pressure from the White House, it was easy for policy representatives to raise obstacles to proposed treaty language and insist on inspection provisions they knew the Soviets would not accept. I contributed to the working group technical discussion when I had something to offer.

We would get interesting feedback from Geneva delegation members coming back to Washington for short visits to brief the working group. Every U.S. mission must have a set of common procedures, but each also has organizational quirks, as we were to see, tragically, in Benghazi many years later.

Geneva had not been the target of terrorist activity. We had heard rumors that the Swiss had an informal agreement with groups like Hamas allowing them to use Geneva as an international repository for their bank accounts and business transactions as long as they did not carry out any violent actions there. When a delegation member suggested that the bus taking the U.S. delegation between the U.S. and Soviet missions should vary its route and departure times, U.S. mission security officers dismissed such a plan as unnecessary. When our man said that mission security should publish an assessment of the fire safety of Geneva hotels housing our delegations, the mission security officer said that the suggestion was unreasonable because most European hotels did not meet U.S. standards for smoke alarms and sprinkler systems. Our man persisted and said that mission security could at least let delegates know that it would be a good idea to bring smoke alarms with them and that the mission might also have a supply on hand to make available for loan. Mission security's main goal appeared to be to avoid extra work.

The negotiation in Geneva ground on through December and into early January 1990 without making much progress until Secretary of State Baker and Soviet Foreign Minister Shevardnadze reached an agreement (at Baker's ranch) on getting the deal done. President Bush wanted an agreement to sign at the June summit meeting with President Gorbachev. With that message from Washington, the working group environment changed; the Geneva delegation was instructed to work six days a week to reach agreement on the language of the treaty's verification protocol.

One cable from Geneva reported on one of the more pleasant meetings at the Soviet mission, which took place on Red Army Day, a Soviet holiday. General Sergei Zelentsov hosted the session for the Soviet side, noting the occasion and offering glasses of vodka to all the delegates. Tom Dowling, our State Department senior representative, was very fast on his feet, offering an impromptu toast: "Today we honor the valiant past achievements of the Red Army. Let us hope that they do not have to be repeated." General Zelentsov beamed and gave the U.S. delegation member Red Army medallions that the members promptly fastened to their jackets. We learned from Geneva that working relationships with the Soviets were usually excellent. Meetings were businesslike and cordial with handshakes before and afterward. There was no posturing or anything else that would make one think that the negotiations involved anything more than a business transaction.

One of the funnier incidents during the negotiation apparently occurred when the senior Soviet representative, physicist Victor Mikhailov from the Arzamas-16 nuclear weapons laboratory, gave an illustrated presentation describing the Soviet nuclear test site on the Arctic island of Novaya Zemlya. He pointed out that because of the threat posed by polar bears, site personnel could only travel outside the compound if they were attended by armed guards. When one of our members observed that the site reminded him of Alaska, Mikhailov replied grimly, "Never again will we sell part of the motherland."

Once, when a delegation member commented on the fears of Scandinavian countries concerned about radioactive fallout from Novaya Zemlya nuclear tests, Mikhailov said, "We only test when the wind is blowing toward Russia." Later, when asked about how the citizens of Tomsk felt about the tentative Soviet plan to build a plutonium storage facility there, he said, "We don't care what the citizens of Tomsk think." Hearing about this exchange I remembered that the United States had not hesitated to build the Rocky Flats plutonium manufacturing facility dangerously close to Denver without much consultation with local citizens. That risk became apparent when a plant fire spread radioactivity and led the United States to close and bulldoze the site. When I also remembered how marine infantry were made to advance through fallout from atmospheric nuclear tests at the Nevada test site in the 1950s, I realized that we were not beyond reproach.

Another exchange with the Soviets involved the type of aircraft that would be used in transporting inspection teams to each other's countries. We were told that General Zelentsov, who was responsible for the Soviet units transporting nuclear weapons, was bothered by the prospect of using anything other than regular commercial flights. He asked our Geneva delegation, "What if we decide to send our team to the United States in a Backfire bomber?" Don Phillips, our relentless navy commander, quickly responded, "In that case, General, we will escort it with an F-14." Zelentsov absorbed the translation and said, "If you send a B-1 to Russia, we will escort it with a MIG-29." Phillips then said, "General, when you visit my home I'm going to give you one of my purebred puppies." When I heard this story, I sent a note to Phillips saying, "It's lucky for you that the interpreter did not say that you were going to turn your dogs on the general if he ever comes to your house." With throttles eased back and the engagement broken off, the delegation returned to its routine, businesslike discussions about ways to limit the explosive yields of weapons that would destroy entire cities and kill one hundred million or so people with blast, heat, and radiation.

End Game

Under pressure from Washington and Moscow, the Geneva delegation reached a final agreement with the Soviets early in the morning of May 20, 1990, after a day and night of meetings. The two sides had quit at eight o'clock the previous evening when the U.S. delegation got a call from the Soviets saying they wanted to reconvene at midnight. Our men and women were tired but decided they should not let the Soviets think they were weak. They freshened up and met the Soviets at the front door of the U.S. mission for the obligatory handshakes with a great show of bravado. The document was done and ready for review by our Washington working group and the lawyers.

All of us on the Washington working group and Geneva delegation hoped to attend the treaty signing by Presidents Bush and Gorbachev. However, the East Room of the White House was not large enough to accommodate our delegation and other guests whose treaties were considered more important than ours. Only the delegation ambassador, Paul Robinson, and the delegation senior State Department representative, Tom Dowling, could attend. The rest of us watched it on the news that night. Later that week I found the obscurely located State Department treaty storage room and persuaded its elderly custodian to find the red, white, and blue ribbon–bound document and make a copy of the signature page for me.

In September 1990 the U.S. Senate and the Supreme Soviet ratified the treaties limiting the size of underground nuclear explosions. By June 1991 both sides planned inspections of each other's tests. The Soviets planned to shift their test site from Semipalatinsk in Kazakhstan to the Arctic island of Novaya Zemlya. This generated a flurry of protests from Scandinavian countries that felt threatened by the prospects of any release of radioactivity relatively close to their borders. By 1992 the United States and Russia concluded that nuclear tests were expensive and unnecessary. Testing ended and the nuclear testing moratorium was still in place as of early 2020.

By 1992 I had spent my entire adult life in a Cold War environment. My service in the Marine Corps was my first and most immediate experience with the clash of ideologies and cultures that characterized this grim period. My education was paid for by the GI Bill. I chose to study physics at least in part because of the value society placed on a discipline with obvious implications for the development of powerful weapons. Now, with the increase in tensions between Russia and the West, it remains to be seen whether the international community can use its resources and energy to maintain the peace and improve the lives of people everywhere on the planet. Little will be gained if we merely change the conflict from one of competing ideologies and systems to one of wealthy nations against poorer ones clamoring for a share of the world's resources. If U.S. support for NATO and our Asian allies falters, other nations may decide to develop nuclear weapons.

When I returned to the university in the fall of 1990, I began to teach arms control courses again. My service in Washington gave me deep insights into arms control issues that I would never have acquired otherwise. I will always regard it as a privilege and one of the great experiences of my life to have been associated with the fine men and women at the CIA and the interagency group with whom I worked during that intense period.

FOUR

The Directorate of Support

22

My Career as a CIA Logistics Professional, 1986–2013

JAMES R. PASQUALINI

I was born in Pittsburgh, Pennsylvania, in December 1962. I had a typical childhood growing up in a working class, blue collar family. In 1980, at seventeen years old, I graduated from South Park High School and joined the U.S. Army as an infantry private. I completed my associate's degree in general studies while on active duty by going to class in the evenings and on weekends. I left active duty after a few years. I transferred to the National Guard as an infantryman and later went to the Army Reserve as a field artillery noncommissioned officer. I also attended Gannon University in Erie, Pennsylvania, as a full-time student to complete my bachelor's degree in political science. In my last semester at Gannon I met a CIA recruiter at one of the career fairs. Although I wasn't focused on a career with the agency, I was exploring several opportunities with local, state, and federal government organizations. In addition to completing my degree, I also completed officer candidate school at Fort Benning, Georgia, and was commissioned as a second lieutenant in the U.S. Army Reserve Corps of Engineers. I continued to process my application with the CIA while simultaneously exploring other options, including the Pennsylvania state police. The agency recruiter explained to me that the hiring process could take several months, and it did indeed take close to a full year from start to finish. When the final CIA interview was scheduled, I was informed that several offices wanted to meet with me during my trip to Washington. I met with the Directorate of Intelligence (predecessor to the current Directorate of Analysis) to discuss imagery analyst positions and the Directorate of Administration (predecessor to the current Directorate of Support) to discuss security and logistics positions. A few weeks after I returned home to Pennsylvania, I received an offer from the Office of Logistics for a GS-7 position in the supply officer trainee (SOT) program. I accepted and my career with the Central Intelligence Agency began. On my "entrance on duty" day, the most memorable event was swearing in and citing the oath of office: "to uphold and defend the Constitution of the United States of America, against all enemies." It was an oath that I was very familiar with from my time in the U.S. Army, and an oath that I was very proud to take again to begin my civilian career.

I had two objectives when I graduated from college and began to search for a career. The first, of course, was to find a personally rewarding position that would enable me to make a salary and benefits to provide a suitable life for my family (I was married and had three children at that point). The second but equally important goal was to find a position that would enable me to continue to serve my country. My career with the agency exceeded my expectations on both objectives.

I moved with my family from Pennsylvania to Sterling, Virginia. It took some time to adjust to the major differences, such as the high cost of living and traffic congestion in the Washington DC area, but eventually Sterling became our new home. I joined the Sterling Volunteer Fire Department and transferred to the Army Reserve unit at Fort Belvoir. On a personal note, our fourth child was born not long after we moved to Virginia.

The SOT program was approximately one year long. It was intended to identify officers with potential, then provide them with training and work experiences to accelerate their career growth. The program provided noncompetitive promotions at minimum time in grade through GS-12. My first year in the SOT program was spent in training courses and short, interim on-the-job-training work assignments. Although the CIA had several major covert action programs under way in the late 1980s, I was not directly assigned to support them. After completing my first year in SOT training, I was assigned to my first regular assignment as a GS-9 logistics officer based at CIA headquarters, supporting a traditional area division responsible for Europe in the Directorate of Operations (DO). The scope of my duties as a junior logistics officer were diverse—from completing local procurements to ordering material through the agency's procurement system, to maintaining records for accountable property and vehicles to arranging for transportation of material to overseas stations to ad hoc duties as assigned. The motto of the Office of Logistics was simple—"can do"—anything that needed to be done, anywhere in the world, at any time. At the lower grade, many of the duties were routine in nature, but all my effort played a key role in supporting the greater mission. Solid logistics—getting the right material to the right place at the right time—is essential for a successful operation.

I was then selected for an agency-wide, year-long career trainee (CT) program, which was similar in nature to the SOT program. What the SOT program was for the Office of Logistics, the CT program was for the CIA. The major differences between the two were that the SOT program consisted only of logistics officers while the CT program included officers from all of directorates. The CT program enhanced the building of relationships throughout the agency, and the training/interim assignments focused on developing agency officers into the best career intelligence officers. The cornerstone of training for the CT program was a several-weeks-long paramilitary training course at The Farm. Sharing these unique field experiences as a class greatly enhanced the bonds between the students. The CT program developed students' knowledge of the functioning of the CIA and the intelligence community and broadened their understanding of how their individual contributions, regardless of career service, affected the overall success of the agency's mission. During these interim assignments I became involved in supporting several major covert action programs.

By the time I completed the CT program it was the early 1990s and I was entering the mid-grade (GS-11) logistics officer range. My duties began to transition from transactional work to project management. I was assigned to an office responsible for leasing properties in the Washington area, and my duties were completely different from those expected of a traditional logistics officer. This was the first of my nontraditional assignments, and I found it both very interesting and very challenging.

The next phase of my career included several significant changes. It was my first permanent-change-of-station overseas assignment and it was also my first supervisory position. I was assigned as the chief of logistics for a small logistics office at a base in Asia. I also served as the deputy chief of support for the base. The base had regional responsibilities, so in addition to managing the logistics for the base, I was also responsible for coordinating all logistics requirements for operations in Asia. The regional duties required me to be on temporary duty (TDY) to CIA stations and bases throughout Asia. I assisted with property inventories, helped establish logistics policies and procedures, coordinated transportation and procurement, and assisted with the implementation of a new automated property accountability system. My duties at the base included managing housing for base personnel, coordinating with other U.S. government agencies on support-related issues, completing local procurements, managing the base warehouse and store room, controlling accountable property, managing transportation, managing contract procurement though headquarters, directly supervising two logistics officers, and assisting in the management of all base support personnel and all support issues (finance, communication, personnel, security, and so on). This assignment gave me the opportunity to travel and to experience diverse cultures in the Far East and work environments. It also provided a fantastic opportunity to continue to grow and develop skills such as supervision and management. On a personal note, it was during this assignment that my wife and I divorced. Living overseas far away from family and friends can put a strain on a relationship, and it was very difficult to deal with serious marital issues and life-changing events while living so far from home.

I returned to headquarters as a GS-13 and went into my second nontraditional assignment. My responsibilities included project management for the unique/specialized acquisition and transportation of goods and services that were required to support CIA operations. One of my most interesting projects was the acquisition of large industrial machinery overseas. I built relationships with local businessmen and was able to successfully negotiate a multimillion-dollar contract and sea shipment of the material. This project was nothing like what I expected to be doing when I accepted the position of a logistics officer with the CIA. It was very challenging, and this was as close to the duties of an operations officer as I had ever personally experienced. One of my favorite stories during the trip was when I met with a group of local businessmen for lunch. Another American (who was a CIA officer under cover like myself) was meeting them for the first time. During the lunch, one of the foreign businessmen said to my colleague, "I think you might be CIA." After a few seconds of awkward silence, I spoke up and said, "What about me? Don't I remind you of James Bond?" Everyone laughed. The tension was broken and nothing more was mentioned about the CIA. I learned a valuable lesson: that you must be comfortable living your cover and not panic when the CIA is mentioned. The project itself was a major success. This is only one example of the many nontraditional projects I worked on during this assignment.

After several years in this position, I applied for and was accepted into a new program call the admin cadre. Under this program, officers remained assigned in their specialty home career service (in my case, logistics) but would be available to fill worldwide general support positions as required. I was assigned to my next nontraditional position as the support officer for a counterterrorism center station. This position broadened my experience beyond logistics into other areas of support. The responsibilities were heavy in budget and finance. In addition, since I was responsible for opening a new station, I spent much of my time on facilities and security-related issues.

As an admin cadre member, I was also called upon for other special projects. One such project required that I be on TDY to Africa for an extended period to support the relocation of the CIA station from one city to another. Once again, logistics was not my primary focus; instead, my focus was on facilities, security, and secure communication requirements. I had to work with other government agency officials to identify, lease, and make ready a new chief of station residence. I also had to ensure that the station's secure office space was up and running as quickly as possible. I found that acquiring new, diverse experiences was extremely beneficial to my overall career growth as a CIA support officer.

The Office of Logistics then selected me to attend a senior U.S. military school, the Logistics Executive Development Course at Fort Lee, Virginia. The students were officers (from captain to colonel) from the U.S. Army and allied militaries, which provided another wonderful opportunity to build relationships. Although logistics in the military and the CIA differ in many ways, there are some similarities and overlaps. The course also provided graduate credits, which sparked my interest in pursuing a graduate degree. The agency provided me with many opportunities for internal and external training during my career. The courses helped me develop technical skills to build proficiency in my field of expertise and career development skills to facilitate my continued growth in leadership and management.

Upon completion of this course in the late 1990s, I returned to headquarters as a GS-14 officer and became deputy chief of a large logistics office that supported the agency's paramilitary operations. In addition to the duties I had performed in my previous assignments, a new responsibility was added—expeditionary logistics. I went on temporary duty overseas to harsh, austere locations in the Balkans and the Middle East as a member of the first CIA team on the ground. My role was to work closely with my DO counterparts to survey the local environment, develop a support plan of action, and then implement the plan to establish a forward operating base (FOB) from which the agency could conduct field operations. Speed was far more important than perfection, and field expediency was the key to success. This was also the first time in my agency career that I was armed for self-defense in the performance of my duties. Once again I found that I learned much in this assignment that I could draw on in my future assignments. Many of the skills I acquired during my career in the U.S. Army proved useful (e.g., the ability to improvise, adapt, and overcome obstacles) in this environment. One memorable example was when, after being on the ground for about a week at a FOB, the chief of base operations officer asked me to walk with him for a few minutes. We walked out a few hundred yards from the base and he asked me to turn around. What had been an empty field only a few days earlier was now a fully functioning FOB, complete with tents, pods, generators, latrine, communication center, and all required security/life support. He said to me, "You did this. All of your hard work and long hours did this." I remember looking back and reflecting on the flurry of activity that had occurred over the previous few days. It all had to fall into place for things to work. The keys to this success were anticipating common requirements (ordering material you think you will need before you need it), utilizing local resources (reducing the logistics pipeline by acquiring material such as local fuel, water, and food as close to where you intend to use it as possible), and partnering with local liaisons for local services and material. This was also my first experience working very closely with local liaison services.

At this point in my career I began to think about moving into supporting the agency beyond the logistics specialty. The Directorate of Administration support officer (DASO) program was created as a replacement for the admin cadre program. Unlike the admin cadre, DASO officers would transfer out of their specialty fields to a new career service and become a "support generalist." I applied, was accepted, left the Office of Logistics, and transferred into the DASO program (the DASO was the predecessor to the current support integration officer in the Office of Mission Integration).

My first assignment was with the DASO front office in a staff position. I was responsible for review of new policies, managing the approval process for director of CIA (DCIA) special authorities, and other duties as assigned. In this assignment, I felt far removed from supporting the actual mission of the CIA, but it was a valuable learning experience. I was exposed to the inner workings of the highest level of the organization, and the staff assignment afforded me the opportunity to complete my master's degree in public administration. I attended classes through Central Michigan University after work hours and on weekends at U.S. military installations in the Washington DC area. Although the agency did not sponsor my graduate degree, I was able to justify most of the classes I took as related to my job, so most of the expenses were covered. The other benefit of being in a staff position was that it was easy for DASO management to redirect me to higher-priority requirements. I was in this position on September 11, 2001, and that historic day was my last day in that position.

It began just like any other day. I sat in commuting traffic from Sterling to headquarters. I heard on the radio that a plane had hit the World Trade Center in New York City, but not much information was known. Within minutes after I arrived at headquarters, more information began pouring in. Time seemed to move in slow motion as the reality of the horrific terrorist attack started to sink in. The CIA and the rest of the federal government began a full-scale evacuation. Headquarters emptied out quickly, and I was tasked with coordinating support for the emergency personnel who remained on the compound, including the DCIA. The first task was to relocate the DCIA out of his office on the seventh floor to a safe location in case headquarters came under attack. Within hours we had the DCIA on a line with the president in the basement of one of the buildings on the compound. The next task was to account for all remaining personnel to ensure full accountability in the event of an attack. Of course, the life support required for the many essential officers who remained at work also had to be addressed. I had the headquarters cafeteria unlocked so we could provide food and the gyms unlocked so the officers could shower. Areas were set up so that people could take a break and take a nap. It was a long day. I arrived home at approximately 2:00 on the morning of September 12, after all the necessary support for headquarters was in place.

I remember gathering my children that morning when I got home to cry and pray. I didn't know what to expect next. I told my ex-wife Kelley that although we had our differences in the past, I needed her help. I asked for her full support in taking care of our children so that I could focus on whatever was needed of me. I didn't know where I would be sent, or for how long, but I knew that this was what I had prepared for my entire life. She assured me of her total cooperation and said that it was her way to support the country during this time of crisis. She would take care of the children and I would do whatever I needed to do for work. When I returned to headquarters after a few hours of sleep I was asked if I could immediately go on TDY to New York City. Of course I said yes. I took the train to New York on September 13, passing the still-smoking Pentagon on my way to the train station in Washington. I remember looking out of the train window as we pulled into New York and seeing a skyline that was very different from what I was used to seeing in pictures. Where the Twin Towers once stood there were now only plumes of smoke rising into the sky. The world had changed.

My job in New York was to do whatever was needed to support U.S. government operations. One of my tasks was to set up a joint CIA-FBI command center at Ground Zero. Simple tasks such as acquiring material (e.g., tents and generators) were not so simple, given the high demand for emergency items and the complete shutdown of lower Manhattan. Somehow things fell into place through arduous work and the ability to improvise, adapt, and overcome obstacles.

This was my first visit to New York City. The sites I saw reminded me more of a movie than real life:

National Guardsmen sitting in Starbucks drinking coffee with their M-16s next to them

A temporary U.S. military base set up in Battery Park with the Statue of Liberty in the background

U.S. military checkpoints stopping all vehicles

No vehicle traffic in lower Manhattan, except for government and emergency vehicles, for days

Supporters lining the streets with signs of support and then coming up to the emergency vehicles to shake our hands and thank us

After several weeks of nearly twenty-hour workdays, one night I was walking back to my room to get a few hours of sleep when I passed a local corner bar and decided to stop in for a beer. I was by myself, but I wanted to catch my breath and let what had happened over the last few weeks sink in. I ordered my beer and began to talk with the New Yorkers in the bar. It was like we were all old friends. All we could talk about was the horrific attack. The firefighter funerals had begun for those killed in the line of duty. Every fire station in Manhattan suffered heavy losses, and every fire house had piles of flowers in front of it. As a volunteer firefighter for eight years, I was hard hit by the loss of life in the fire departments and all the other feelings of horrific loss. I could never fully capture my emotions and feelings after the September 11 attacks, but the bottom line was that work still needed to get done, and that was where I focused my attention. In late November 2001, when I felt that things were falling into place and I was no longer needed in New York, I caught the train back to Washington.

Upon my return to headquarters, I was asked to take on managing support for CIA operations in Afghanistan. Again, I of course said yes. The logistics pipeline to get material and personnel into Afghanistan was very limited for a variety of reasons, including political alliances. It wasn't long before I was on a plane heading to places that I had never heard of a few weeks earlier. I was on an extended TDY to serve as the chief of support for the forward support base. My first task was to build the support base, while simultaneously beginning to move material and personnel forward to Afghanistan as the base was being built. Although the support base would be collocated on an existing U.S. government facility, standard processes would not suffice. Operations had already begun. CIA officers were in the field and required immediate support. The CIA presence at the base swelled from very small to very large (over ten times larger in the number of personnel) within a matter of weeks. Speed was of the essence. Planes, helicopters, people, material, and cash were already moving. The support base began functioning immediately while continuous improvements were being made. As one example, we went from a handful of available classified workstations to five times that number. Within a few months the support base was at full operating capability.

Around that time, it was decided that I should go further downrange to begin planning for a more suitable support base closer to the front lines and which would provide additional capacity. I recall a memorable experience from this survey trip. I was sitting with a group of locals in a border town. Most likely this was their first exposure to an American. With the assistance of a translator I was asked to make a toast. I raised my glass and presented my toast as an official representative of the U.S. government. I explained that as a representative of the president of the United States, I was there to seek their assistance in defeating the evil of terrorism lying on the other side of their border, and that with our two great nations working together, there was no doubt that we would succeed! There was a loud cheer and everyone drank. The trip was a complete success. However, Kabul fell under U.S. control much sooner than anticipated so the new support base wasn't required. The best laid support plans must always adapt to changing operational mission requirements. We began establishing support capabilities in Afghanistan and the original support base began to transfer responsibilities. I finished my TDY with a trip to Kabul to discuss the best ways to facilitate the transfer.

After several months, I returned to headquarters to see what was in store for me next. I was asked to take the temporary position of chief of support for a large new program until a permanent officer could be identified. I eagerly accepted and hit the ground running. The new program was just starting to wind up. I did not look at my role as that of a caretaker. I decided that I would do the job to the best of my ability until I was replaced. Within a few days the operations chief of the program decided that I was the right officer to be his permanent chief of support.

As with any new position or job, you're never quite sure what is in store. This assignment would become my most professionally rewarding job and my favorite assignment of my thirty-plus years with the U.S. government. I managed all aspects of worldwide support for this major program, and I felt completely connected to the mission and directly involved in its overall success or failure. Early in this assignment I was also promoted to GS-15.

I had the full trust and confidence of the DO managers of the program, and I quickly formed a close bond and strong partnership with the chief of the program. He made it known that I was responsible for ensuring that resources were in place where and when they were needed to support operational mission objectives. He allowed me total responsibility for all support and asked only that I keep him informed. He also told me that he intended to hold me fully accountable. He included me in all meetings to ensure that I had the entire picture so I could create the best support plan to complement the operational plan. He included me in all high-level briefings for the DCIA and Congress during the preparation phase of the program. When he was told that I would not be able to attend some of the meetings, because only very senior officers would be invited, his response was that he would not attend without me because I was the architect of the support plan and was in the best position to answer questions. I was included in all meetings, not to "backbench" but rather with a seat at the table, to take ownership of all support and to fully participate in the meetings. I traveled throughout the Middle East and took the necessary actions to ensure that all support preparations were in place. I had the chief's full confidence as he informed me to take any necessary actions on the spot and he would fully back any decision that I made.

Time was of the essence. This agency program was a key component of a much larger U.S. government response, which included military action. It was essential that the CIA lead the way in both foreign intelligence collection and covert action program goals to prepare the battlefield and minimize the loss of U.S. lives. Much work was required in a very short period of time. Several forward operating bases had to be identified and built; large amounts of material (including ordnance and vehicles) had to be purchased and transported by plane and ship; supply chains had to be developed and then implemented; personnel had to be prepared and then deployed; an aircraft fleet had to be purchased, transported, and then put into service; and all other aspects of support (including finance, security, logistics, contracts, medical, communications, human resources, facilities, and general support/integration) related to these tasks had to be completed. The accomplishments of the support team in less than twenty-four months from initiation to completion of the program were remarkable. I was awarded the Distinguished Intelligence Medal for my contributions in leading a team of hundreds of support professionals based all over the world.

However, not everything went perfectly. The following are examples of three situations where I was not able to overcome obstacles. First, one of our partner nations refused to allow the United States to use their territory as a staging ground. We believed that ultimately they would allow us, but time passed and they did not. I finally had to make the decision to redirect the supply chain via a completely different route, which had a negative impact on support but did enable the mission to continue to move forward. I learned that some things are out of my control, regardless of the amount of effort I apply to overcome them. When I flew to this country and met directly with their most senior leadership to make one final attempt to secure their cooperation, their response was that "your problems are not our problems."

The second example was when a U.S. government contractor oversold his capability to deliver time-critical cargo to a very difficult end destination. Since my options were limited and the delivery was critical to the success of the mission, I approved the contract. But the contractor was unable to deliver. My boss had to brief the president on the failure. I informed my boss that I accepted full responsibility. His response to me was that even though this part of the plan was unsuccessful, he understood why I had to try this risky option since we only had very limited options available. Overall, we were still able to achieve mission success. I learned that although partnership with contractors is essential, unfortunately some contractors focus more on making a profit than on patriotism.

The last example was when a senior support officer volunteered to be the first support officer in a hostile country and to coordinate all support on the ground. When the time came and he was called to cross the border, he refused to go. After I had several direct conversations with him, he finally did go. But after only one day, he was sent out of the country because of his behavior, which was deemed a liability to the team and inappropriate for a war zone. His actions put the lives of his team members at risk. I was reminded that not all agency officers have the same strengths and abilities. Although this officer was successful in a standard station environment, he was not cut out for a dangerous environment. In my last conversation with him I said, "The worst thing that would happen to you is that you could die. People die in war. What did you think you were volunteering for?" From this experience, I learned the importance of selecting the right officer for extremely challenging assignments. Grabbing whomever is available does not always work out well.

I have never felt so well suited for an assignment. My previous assignments and training with the agency had provided me with knowledge, skills, and abilities I needed to be successful. I was also able to refer to my assignments with the Army in the infantry, field artillery, engineering, and military intelligence. Surprisingly, I even drew on my experience as a volunteer firefighter to purchase a fire engine and establish a firefighting unit at a forward operating base where airfield operations were being conducted.

For the final phase of this assignment, I went on TDY to a newly liberated capital city to establish a new CIA station. I served as the temporary chief of support until the permanent replacement arrived. The work day was twenty hours per day, seven days a week. We had no running water, very limited food, no toilets or showers, regular rocket and mortar attacks, and extreme heat (normally over a hundred degrees Fahrenheit). Survival was a daily challenge. Every night at eleven o'clock I held a meeting with the branch chiefs from each support section. The purpose of the meeting was tactical—to prioritize what support actions needed to be accomplished in the next twenty-four hours to keep the agency's mission moving forward. We covered questions such as these: How many agency officers were onsite and how would we feed and house them? How would we keep the generators running to keep communications working and the station on line? Our goals were simple—keep our officers as safe and comfortable as possible, support mission requirements, and try every day to make things a little better than the day before. It was challenging but also extremely rewarding. On a personal note, my eldest son

James was in theater serving with the army. I was able to arrange a trip into the area where his unit was operating to spend some time with him. I reached his regimental headquarters base, but unfortunately he was out on patrol with his troop in the desert and I was not able to link up with him. After I left the country my son was injured in a firefight and medevacked back to the capital city. Because I was no longer in the country, I called my replacement on the secure phone and asked if someone from the station could check on my son. In no time our station medic had picked up my son from the army hospital and I was able to talk with him and hear from him directly that he was alright. This is an example of how agency officers go the extra mile to take care of each other and each other's families.

My next assignment was completely different. I went to the agency's largest traditional station, located in Europe, as chief of support. Living in Europe provided an exceptional quality of life. The housing was fantastic, and the schools were great. My son Joseph graduated from the American International School during this assignment. My responsibilities were to be a key member of the station management team, to manage routine support tasks, and to be a key member of the support infrastructure. My staff consisted of specialists in security, budget and finance, logistics, information technology, communications, and general administrative support. We supported all the major agency missions, including operations, science and technology, analytics, and the Open Source Center. My responsibilities also included housing, hiring staff, and other duties as a member of the management staff for the combined U.S. government team. The station served as a regional secure training/conference facility for the agency, and we routinely had large numbers of agency staff on TDY. In addition, due to its strategic location, the station also hosted many senior U.S. government officials, including the president of the United States, congressional delegations, and the DCIA. I served two years in this assignment and then returned to Washington.

My next assignment was as chief of support for an area division in the DO. This was my first assignment at the Senior Intelligence Service (SIS) level. I managed all support for the division at headquarters and overseas stations, including all routine support functions and the support staff. One of my first duties was to coordinate follow-up activities after the death of Rachael Dean, a support officer killed in the line of duty in a tragic accident overseas. My work included the repatriation of the deceased's remains at Dulles Airport, where I met with the next of kin to explain the circumstances of the accident. I also assisted with arrangements for Rachel's funeral and burial, which were attended by the DCIA and honor guard. I advised the DCIA on preparation of the speech he would make at the graveside memorial.

Another example of my many unique responsibilities in this position was the opening of a new station in a newly independent country within the division's area of operations. I went on TDY to the capital city to work with the chief of station and other senior U.S. government officials to establish a safe and secure government presence as quickly as possible.

During this time, I retired from the U.S. Army Reserve as a lieutenant colonel with more than thirty years of military service.

During this assignment I had the only negative experience of my career. Although I met daily with the DO managers of the division, apparently there was a breakdown in communication, as I was unaware that they were not satisfied with my performance. After two years in the position I was informed that they wanted me to move to a different position so that they could replace me. In thirty years of service with the federal government, this was the only time I was basically relieved of my duties. I was completely taken by surprise and my pride was badly damaged. I pointed out all of the division's support-related successes that my staff and I were responsible for, including a balanced budget for the first time in years, a major reorganization of headquarters office space, substantial cost savings in facilities and the vehicle fleet, to name just a few. I asked the division leadership to provide examples of where I failed to meet their expectations. Their response was that they did not feel I was the right person for the job. With that explanation, I felt there was nothing tangible in my performance that I could or should change, so I agreed to leave the position.

When I became unexpectedly available, I was asked to take an assignment in a new program office to study and make recommendations for the agency's supply chain management. The goal of the program office was to baseline the agency's current worldwide supply chain, evaluate the supply chains of other government agencies and the private sector, and identify best practices that could enhance the agency's supply chain. I stayed in the program office for eighteen months until we completed our objectives.

I applied for several senior SIS positions and was selected as chief of support for the Counterintelligence Center. This position managed support for a headquarters-based component. My job focused on budget and financial resources, staffing and human resources, and office space at headquarters, which was at a premium. I remained in this position for eighteen months until I was confronted with a personal tragedy: my two sons, Joseph and Edward, were walking home in January 2009 when they were hit by a drunk driver.

Edward sustained relatively minor injuries and was released from the hospital the same day. However, Joseph sustained life-threatening injuries that left him permanently disabled. The outpouring of support from my agency family was phenomenal! I took an extended leave to provide care for Joseph. Once I exhausted all of my annual and sick leave, the workforce was asked to donate leave to the emergency leave bank for my use. Within hours they donated the maximum amount of leave allowable. I also received anonymous financial contributions on top of prayers and emotional support from the agency community. Eventually, Joseph became medically stable and continued to show slow but continuous improvement.

Once I was able, I returned to work in another SIS position as the deputy chief of support for the DO area division responsible for the Middle East, including several war zones. The chief of support and I managed a large support staff and all support functions for the division, both at headquarters and at overseas locations. In this assignment there were unique requirements associated with supporting the agency's mission in war zones and hostile environments. As an example, we were responsible for the emergency evacuation of numerous stations. To accomplish this, we maintained a robust relationship with the State Department. I was also responsible for managing support for several major agency paramilitary operations, including supporting agency covert action programs and expeditionary team deployments. I received the Intelligence Commendation Medal for managing support for one of these programs, which reinforced my reputation as one of the agency's leading experts on supporting covert action and expeditionary operations. I traveled extensively throughout the Middle East and worked closely with junior officers as a mentor and a coach. In 2011, while I was in this assignment, I was promoted to the SIS grade.

My next assignment was as deputy of logistics for the CIA. I worked in partnership with the chief of logistics to manage the logistics career service, the working capital fund business enterprises, and the logistics depots. We also ensured that the logistics requirements for supporting the agency's mission were met and that the strategic vision for the agency's supply chain was implemented. After eighteen months in this assignment, I made the difficult decision to retire to have more time at home providing care for my son.

I began my career with the agency as a junior logistics officer, and twenty-seven years later I retired as the agency's second-most senior logistics officer. My career was filled with many highs and a few lows, but overall I found it to be rewarding and fulfilling. In recognition of my accomplishments, I was awarded the Career Intelligence Medal. Looking back, I am very pleased that a large part of my life was spent in a career with the Central Intelligence Agency.

Where am I now?

After I retired I moved back to Pennsylvania to the small town of Slippery Rock, just north of Pittsburgh, where I enjoy the family time with my five children and ten grandchildren. Unfortunately, Joseph succumbed to his serious injuries. He fought bravely and tirelessly for nearly eight years after his injury, but he passed away in December 2016. Losing a child was the worst experience of my life, but somehow I will go on living until I join him in heaven when my time comes.

I am exploring several business opportunities, including opening a third-party logistics company. I have a wonderful girlfriend, Karen Benson, whom I have been with since I retired. My hobbies include watching the Pittsburgh sports teams, golfing, hunting, and traveling. I am making the most of my retirement and trying to get by without my son Joey.

I still miss my friends and colleagues at the agency. Since my retirement, the agency has hired me as a part-time independent contractor, which enables me to contribute to developing the next generation of support officers. I was tasked with developing and conducting a new training program that will better prepare officers to support the unique requirements of expeditionary and covert action operations. I am pleased to be able to continue to contribute and serve my country.

23

Black Programs and Services

ROBERT M. BLANSFIELD

There is no history without the factors of production: land, labor, and capital. What does this mean? Every organization needs at least one each of these factors, and successful organizations bring them together in the kinds and quantities needed to optimize the production of either a service or a product, or both. The government, however, produces no products—not even the mythical widget. It therefore turns to private industry when it needs something, and this is where people like me, contract auditors, come in.

After my enlistment in the U.S. Army, where I served first with the Eighty-Second Airborne Division at Fort Bragg, North Carolina, and then with the Eleventh Airborne Division in Germany, I went to college. I graduated from California State University Northridge in 1972 with a degree in accounting. Upon graduating I became an internal auditor for private industry, where I had the opportunity to perform audits covering corporate compliance, insurance fraud, and, on occasion, actual losses from robberies. Since I had prior government service I decided in 1979 to go back to work for the federal government. I went to work for the Defense Contract Audit Agency (DCAA), a premier audit organization, where I became a certified cost analyst. In 1984, while working for the DCAA, I earned a master's degree in business administration from Pepperdine University, and the following year I moved to the Central Intelligence Agency (CIA). In January 1985 an organization looking for contract auditors with experience offered me a position with their Commercial Systems Audit Division (CSAD), which I accepted in September of that year.

Contract Audit Responsibilities

Like DCAA, CSAD audited proposals and final contract claims on "black programs"—top-secret programs about which only briefed personnel know what is being purchased and from whom. All audits of both open and black programs were performed in accordance with the GAGAS (the Generally Accepted Government Auditing Standards, or Yellow Book), GAAP (Generally Accepted Accounting Principles), GAAS (Generally Accepted Auditing Standards), FAR (Federal Acquisition Regulations), CAS (Cost Accounting Standards), NISP (National Industrial Security Program), and, where applicable, federal statutes such as 18 USC 1001 (False Statements), 18 USC 287 (False Claim–Criminal), 18 USC 3729 (False Claim–Civil), 18 USC 1371 (Conspiracy to Defraud), 15 USC 78 (Foreign Corrupt Practices Act), and 18 USC 1961 (Racketeer Influenced and Corrupt Organization, or RICO, Act). We also provided instruction to members of CSAD and contracting officers in the form of a forty-hour course called "Introduction to Contract Audit" and an eight-hour course called "Fraud, Waste, and Abuse." In addition, the Deputy Director of Administration called on us to assist in the implementation of activity-based costing, which is a more accurate measure of the cost of a product than one can obtain through conventional cost accounting.

We also assisted contracting officers in compiling solicitations for fixed price, cost, or time-and-material contracts to be sent out for bid. When proposals came into our office, they would be assigned to an auditor who in turn contacted the contractor for an entrance conference and subsequent audit of the basis of estimate for the proposal. If there was any defective pricing involved, it was usually in the proposal's basis of estimate.

Exactly what is defective pricing? Essentially, the government is entitled to "truth in negotiations" when negotiating for the services of a contractor. If a contractor deliberately withholds information from the government that affects negotiations in terms of the quality or price of a product or service, the undisclosed information constitutes defective pricing and allows the government to recover costs and interest as a consequence of the deception. If the defective pricing is significant, the contractor may be disbarred from future work with the government.

In addition to proposals and audits of contract costs, CSAD also performed "floor checks." A floor check is a surprise audit to determine the accuracy of labor charges on contracts. Sometimes a floor check discloses false labor charges. When this happens the examination becomes a fraud audit and the findings are submitted to the inspector general for follow-up legal action. Floor checks may also uncover uncompensated overtime. Exempt employees receive an annual salary immaterial of the number of hours they work in a year. If the exempt person works more than the deliverable man-years, the direct labor rate must be reduced to agree with the actual hours delivered. When this happens, actual labor costs have to be reconciled to contract costs, which usually results in lower contract costs for the government. Failure to adjust the labor rate produces a windfall for the contractor. This is one of the major reasons for floor checks.

Another practice employed to manage contract costs is earned value management, which is designed to measure actual achievement against a detailed performance plan to predict the final costs of a project. This practice is useful in managing contract costs; it produces early signs of a possible cost overrun, thereby preventing a violation of the Antideficiency Act.

A Specific Case

In the late 1980s I worked on an audit for the agency's introduction and purchase of unmanned aerial vehicles (UAVs). Upon learning about these vehicles, the agency entered into a contract to purchase two of them. The contractor had to demonstrate proof of concept. The contractor did this by flying the UAV from an undisclosed place to a landing strip off the coast of California and back. However, during contract performance, the buyer, by means of the government contracting officer's technical representative (COTR), embellished the UAV requirements, which produced a significant cost overrun. In other words, the COTR and the buyer were obligating the government to pay costs in excess of the authorized and appropriated funds, which produced a violation of the Antideficiency Act. I don't know how this was ultimately resolved because this aspect of the contract fell to the government contracting officer and the contractor. However, under the Antideficiency Act, the contractor can be forced to accept the loss, even though the government may ultimately benefit.

Other Services

While working for the agency, I had the opportunity to work nights as a member of the surveillance detection course. This program was designed to teach new officers how to detect surveillance while driving in a foreign country. With my background in business, I found this challenging; it revealed how to perform vehicle surveillance and detection. It was our team's job to pursue trainees (new officers) and prepare them to spot vehicle surveillance while driving in a foreign country.

After retiring from the agency in October 1997 I established Business Systems Associates, a management consulting firm. I was able to apply my education in business management and accounting and my years of experience and knowledge as a contractor to other agency operations such as proprietaries (government-owned businesses used for cover) and the U.S. Standard General Ledger. The Office of Management and Budget had mandated that all government agencies adopt the Standard General Ledger, which required all agencies to book like transactions to a specific account for comparison across agencies. This made evaluating like transactions across government agencies possible. However, at the time I worked on this project, the agency was unable to comply, resulting in a negative opinion from the auditors. A negative opinion precludes reliability on the financial statements for business decisions. I have not heard the outcome of this problem.

Proprietaries, also known as "props," presented their own unique challenges. These were operations designed to look like businesses while at the same time conducting espionage in a foreign country. A couple of the ones I worked on revealed defects that, if examined closely by a foreign tax authority, would have attracted attention and possibly exposed their true purpose. When I was first introduced to a particular prop the first question I asked was, "Is this a drug operation?" The most significant question was where the business got its initial millions of dollars of equity. At the time there was no explanation or documentation to address such a question. If a tax agency audited such a business, the business would not only have had to close down, it also would have been reported to an investigating agency. Had the country where the prop was located investigated the business, they might have discovered that it was not a legitimate business, and the consequences for those running the prop could have been catastrophic. My concern over the weaknesses in some props encouraged me to submit a proposal I believed would address many of these deficiencies. Today it appears the agency has recognized these weaknesses and brought in consultants to address them.

Another opportunity I received after retiring was to work on the new human records system. The objective was to create a current application program that could access legacy records based on the level of clearance of the person authorized to see and use such information. The subcontractor I worked for saw significant difficulties in bridging the gap between the legacy data and the new application program. However, the prime contractor that created the application program insisted that it worked and was ready to be shrink-wrapped. We agreed that a test would be performed to determine how significant the gap was before the application program was ready. We created a subpopulation of 2,500 records that represented a cross-section of all types of records. A sample of two hundred records from the 2,500 revealed that only fifty records were correct. This meant that the bridge between the application program and the legacy data was grossly inadequate and the application program was not ready to go. Much more work was required.

I also had the opportunity to work in the Counterterrorism Center. Our objective was to follow money that moved among banks, ultimately winding up in the hands of terrorists. When we discovered funds going to a terrorist we reported this by means of a cable to those able to surveil and capture both the terrorist and the money.

Conclusion

No organization can exist without the kinds and quantities of each of the factors of production needed to be efficient, effective, and economical. In my more than thirty years of experience in business I have found that the most important of these factors is labor. The loss of competent and effective managers can bring an organization to a halt. For an organization to remain successful, succession planning and implementation is vital.

FIVE

Remembering Our Fallen Colleagues

24

The CIA Book of Honor

DOUG PATTESON

Editor's note: Some agency officers did not live long enough to write their memoirs. Their colleagues offered to memorialize the contributions of the fallen to our country in this book.

Y ou've seen it on countless TV shows and movies. The glass doors push open and you're walking into a marble foyer reminiscent of a national monument or a mausoleum. Displayed on the floor in front of you is the logo of the CIA, a mosaic in shades of marble gray in the lobby of the Original Headquarters Building. The lobby is spare, a security officer and a couple of turnstiles the only sign of permanent activity, the officer eyeing you as you make your way toward him.

Turning your head to the left, you see a memorial to the men and women of the World War II–era predecessor of the CIA, the Office of Strategic Services (OSS), their sacrifice collectively recognized by one large star chiseled into the marble. Above the star is an inscription: *IN HONOR OF THOSE MEMBERS OF THE OFFICE OF STRATEGIC SERVICES WHO GAVE THEIR LIVES IN THE SERVICE OF THEIR COUNTRY.* The American flag and a statue of General "Wild Bill" Donovan in bronze frame the OSS Book of Honor, containing the names of the 116 OSS officers—out of the 7,500 who served overseas—who fell in the line of duty.

Across the lobby on the north wall is another memorial and another Book of Honor. This one is flanked by both the American flag and the agency flag. Above the book is another inscription: *IN HONOR OF THOSE MEMBERS OF THE CENTRAL INTELLIGENCE*

AGENCY WHO GAVE THEIR LIVES IN THE SERVICE OF THEIR COUN-TRY. And this time 113 stars (as of this writing) represent the men and women of the CIA who have given their lives while in the service of our nation. The memorial was built in 1974, after agency officers made a request to honor those who had died in Southeast Asia. Initially the wall contained thirty-one stars, recognizing the sacrifice of officers from 1950 through the early 1970s.

The Book of Honor itself is compelling. You draw your eyes downward to its gold stars and names in calligraphy. But equally compelling are the stars without names. Those stars honor the officers who remain anonymous heroes even in death, their stories known only to the few who served with them, and maybe their families. Only eighty of the 113 stars have names next to them, the majority of those from 1950 to late 1970s. The other names may well be added later, when their operations are declassified and their stories can be told.

When I headed overseas, there were seventy-one stars on the Memorial Wall, of which thirty-five were named. As a newly minted operations officer (we were called case officers then), I would walk past the wall and wonder about the stories of the men and women represented there. The losses made very real the risks that my new career posed.

The earliest of those stories is that of Douglas Mackiernan, represented by the first star on the wall. His death in April 1950 was marked only by a star until his name was added in 2006, six years after the agency publicly acknowledged his death in service. Mackiernan was shot by Tibetan border guards while crossing the Chinese border into Tibet.

Another compelling story is that of Lawrence "Gus" Freedman, also known as "SuperJew," who was killed in 1992 in Somalia when the jeep he was riding in hit a land mine. Having already had a distinguished military career as a Special Forces soldier in Vietnam and as an early member of Delta Force, Gus joined the agency only six months after I did. I met him first at The Farm and then in the hallways of the Africa Division, although I was never fortunate enough to work with him directly. Men like Gus held us new career trainees in thrall with stories of adventure. He hated headquarters and was ill suited for it, his ponytail and Delta experience a contrast to the "cold warriors" who filled headquarters hallways. The field was his natural environment. Several months after his death, another officer, who had been with Gus that day and was wounded himself, shared with me the story of Gus's sacrifice. Gus spent just over two years at the agency, but his flamboyant personality had an outsized impact on the Special Activities Division, where he had found his home. Already the bearer of a couple of Bronze Stars and the Purple Heart from his time in Vietnam, Gus was posthumously awarded the CIA's Intelligence Star.

Other stars on the wall represented stories—like those of William Buckley and Richard Welch, both active chiefs of station and the victims of the Beirut embassy bombing—that were used as cautionary tales and object lessons to those of us being trained for assignments in hazardous locations. By learning their stories, we would be better prepared for our assignments.

When I left the agency a decade later, six more stars had been added to the wall, for a total of seventy-seven, and still only thirty-five names were represented in the Book of Honor. While more stars have been added since, many tragically as a result of the war on terror, some of the previously unnamed heroes in the Book of Honor have been revealed, including Barry Castiglione, Matthew Gannon, Freddie Woodruff, Jackie Van Landingham, and Molly Hardy.

25

Camp Chapman

DOUG PATTESON

nglorious Amateurs is a website run by former CIA officers to illuminate the intelligence world for the average American. One ongoing goal here is to honor the memory of those who have given their lives in the performance of their duties serving the Central Intelligence Agency. Here we remember and honor the seven Americans killed at Camp Chapman on December 30, 2009:

- Jennifer Lynne Matthews, CIA officer
- Scott Michael Roberson, CIA officer
- Darren LaBonte, CIA officer
- Elizabeth Hanson, CIA officer
- Harold Brown, CIA officer
- Dane Clark Paresi, CIA security contractor
- Jeremy Wise, CIA security contractor

On that day, Humam Khalil Abu-Mulal al-Balawi, a Jordanian doctor and al-Qaeda triple agent, detonated a suicide vest at forward operating base Chapman near Khōst, Afghanistan. The detonation killed seven Americans—a mix of contractors and CIA officers—a Jordanian intelligence officer and an Afghan contractor. Six other CIA officers were seriously wounded in the attack. The attack caused the single largest loss of life for the CIA since the 1983 bombing of the U.S. embassy in Lebanon and carried a severe emotional toll within the agency and the broader U.S. intelligence community.

Al-Balawi had been arrested earlier in the year in Jordan and reportedly had been turned as an agent against al-Qaeda. After several months of sharing information on al-Qaeda, he requested a meeting to share information about a senior al-Qaeda leader. That meeting was set to take place at Camp Chapman and would have been the first time the CIA had interacted directly with al-Balawi. Shortly after arrival at Camp Chapman, according to *Washington Post* reporter Job Warrick in his book *Triple Agent*, after passing through three separate security checkpoints without being searched, al-Balawi's vehicle arrived in the middle of the base and stopped. As he exited the vehicle, some of the waiting American officers approached to search him. He detonated the bomb he was carrying before they reached him.

Much has been written about the lead-up to the attack, the attack itself, and the various decisions made by those onsite. I'll not go into those here, except to say two things: First, it is easy to play Monday morning quarterback for an operation gone wrong when you were not there and with the information that becomes available after the fact. It is much harder to know whether you would have made different decisions onsite in the same time-frame with access to the same information. Second, after-action reports, especially in cases like this, can be invaluable as learning tools to help protect our people in the future. That process, though, need not be a public dissection of the folks involved and their decisions. That serves no legitimate public benefit. The public only needs to know that the community is committed to learning from its mistakes and failed operations, and that such operations will always carry a significant risk to our officers, a risk they themselves choose to bear in order to do the difficult job America asks of them.

At the time of initial writing, we focused our attention on two officers based on access to the information that was available at the time. Their lives are described below.

Jennifer Matthews was the forty-five-year-old chief of base for the CIA's location in Khōst. She was a long-time CIA officer with significant experience working on the al-Qaeda target. She was also a wife and the mother of three young children, an incredibly difficult balancing act for anyone in the agency, much less someone devoted to chasing al-Qaeda in war zones. Jennifer had been married to her college sweetheart, Gary Anderson, since 1987.

Jennifer joined the agency as an intelligence analyst the same year I did, 1989, although we only knew each other in passing. Friends who worked with her spoke very fondly of her. She was both the perfect candidate and an unlikely candidate for work at the CIA. She had degrees in political science and journalism from a small Christian college in Ohio—definitely not the stereotypical Ivy Leaguer recruited by the Office of Strategic Services while serving as an adjunct professor.

A colleague who worked with her in her early role as an imagery analyst said, "Jennifer was a sharp, witty, and incredibly strong-willed woman who was a natural leader in our branch. I remember fondly our daily morning meetings with Jennifer at the forefront of discussions about the overnight intelligence or the latest cable traffic. Her insights were invaluable to our team and she pushed us all to be better analysts. Passionate in her beliefs, she was especially driven by the challenges faced in protecting our national security. Most importantly, Jennifer was a good person who was devoted to her family and faith."

Jennifer had been committed to the al-Qaeda target since the 1990s. She worked for Mike Scheuer and later was one of the first members of Alec Station, working in various capacities of increasing responsibility. The bombings of the U.S. embassies in Africa in 1998 intensified her efforts to chase down the al-Qaeda threat. By the late 1990s she had become one of the agency's most knowledgeable experts on al-Qaeda. When she learned about the 9/11 attacks while on vacation in Europe, her zeal for chasing down al-Qaeda was redoubled. Nada Bakos, an al-Qaeda targeting officer, described Jennifer as "dedicated to her job, focused on finding Bin Laden, and adamant that she would stay on the team until it was done." Another counterterrorism analyst who worked with Jennifer, Cindy Storer, called her "very intense, very focused, passionate from the beginning."

Jennifer's experience was firmly rooted in analysis and helping teams connect the dots in the al-Qaeda networks worldwide. She had experience overseeing operations from a distance or through foreign liaison contacts, but she had little direct operational experience herself. She has been described by coworkers as a "passionate analyst," very bright with an "agile mind" and aggressive in her pursuit of terrorists.

Coming off a relatively comfortable assignment in Europe, Jennifer sought and was selected for the Khōst assignment, an unaccompanied tour in a war zone. One likely motivation might have been the agency requirement that to be promoted to the senior leadership, one had to go on operational tours in a war zone.

Less than six months after getting the assignment, Jennifer Matthews was mortally wounded. She died in a medevac helicopter en route to a hospital.

At the time of his death, **Dane Clark Paresi** was a security contractor working at Camp Chapman. In 2009 he had retired from a twenty-seven-year career in the U.S. Army. After twelve years in the regular Army, Dane made the jump over to Army Special Forces, spending the rest of his career (almost sixteen years) in assignments in First and then Third Special Forces Group, deploying multiple times to Europe, Asia, Africa, and the Middle East. He received the Bronze Star and Meritorious Service Medals as well as the Combat Infantryman Badge.

After retiring from the Army, Dane joined XE, a private military contractor, formerly known as Blackwater. Dane loved the Army and his family, as well as his home in the Pacific Northwest. His long experience in the Army Special Forces gave him skills well suited to supporting agency operations in a war zone.

His colleague Isaac, who served with Dane in First Special Forces Group in Iraq, said, "My interactions with MSG Paresi were among the most significant in my life. He was a well-regarded, larger-than-life character. Dane was a very senior operator who made himself accessible, dispensing countless nuggets of advice, covering everything from kit setup to dealing with certain personalities within the company. MSG Paresi really did his best to ensure that we were as prepared as possible. MSG Paresi was 100 percent mission-focused and he did not allow himself to be constrained or limited by the dictates of propriety. I did not know him well, but he played a central role in my initiation as a warrior, and his passing in 2009 left a considerable hole in the community. To me, Dane was the consummate operator and I was fortunate to have encountered him at the beginning of my career. His dedication, intensity, and directness are worthy of emulation and he is sorely missed."

While few details have been made public about Dane's actions that day, even senior agency leaders have said that Dane's actions spared the lives of many others when al-Balawi exited his vehicle and detonated his vest. The agency's director of security, Mary Rose Mccaffrey, spoke at his memorial service. Matt, another officer at Khōst that day, said he "and others owe our lives to the quick thinking and quick reaction of Dane" and two other officers.

Based on my analysis of family comments reported in the press and *Washington Post* articles reconstructing the attack, I believe that Dane and the other two officers recognized in al-Balawi's demeanor, words, and actions as he exited the vehicle that he posed a threat to the post and began to close on that threat in order to mitigate it. While they were unable to stop him from detonating the vest, I believe their actions likely forced al-Balawi to detonate at a less than optimal time and distance from other officers, thereby protecting them from the full force of the blast. Had Dane and the others not taken action, it is quite possible that many others would have died.

Dane was a passionate athlete who stayed in shape in Afghanistan by jogging. Matt described him as a compassionate, strong leader and an inspiration to others. Known for his zest for life and for his smile, Dane left behind a wife and two daughters.

Both Jennifer Matthews and Dane Paresi received stars on the CIA Memorial Wall, and their names are inscribed in the memorial book underneath. Serving as an intelligence officer carries risks, doubly so in a war zone. As then director Leon Panetta said, "The main lesson from this attack is that, like our military, CIA officers are on the front lines against al-Qaeda and its violent allies. They take risks to confront the enemy, gathering information to destroy its networks and disrupt its operations. This is a vicious foe, one that has struck our country before and is determined to do so again."

We all understand the risks when we sign up for the job and we take them on willingly. We do our best to mitigate those risks, but sometimes events happen that are beyond our control and other times we make mistakes. These seven officers died serving their nation as best they knew how, far from home, in incredibly difficult and dangerous circumstances. We thank them for their sacrifice and honor their service.

SIX

Getting Ready for the Future

26

Prince and the Revolution

The Reengineering of Open-Source Intelligence Collection

DOUG NAQUIN

During my thirty-three-year career with the CIA, I was privileged to work with some of the brightest and most dedicated people the agency had to offer. I enjoyed further good fortune because I worked in areas—information technology and open-source intelligence—that experienced substantial change as the twentieth century gave way to the twenty-first. But aside from an eventful three-year stint (1999–2002) as the CIA's deputy chief information officer, the bulk of my career involved learning and managing the art of applying publicly available information to intelligence problems. Specifically, as director of the Foreign Broadcast Information Service (FBIS) from 2002 to 2005 and then of the Director of National Intelligence (DNI) Open Source Center from 2005 to 2012, I spent my last decade at the CIA overseeing an internal overhaul of skills, processes, and business models while striving to educate stakeholders on the growing (and changing) intelligence potential open sources offered—potential that grew year by year.

Over the course of this turbulent decade, I witnessed a number of efforts that were transformational in that they refuted the premise that bureaucracies exist to protect themselves. I also learned that not all intelligence success stories involve spies or sci-fi technology. Some stories, however, remain so below the radar (and not because of secrecy) that they risk going unappreciated, if not being forgotten.

I single out one unheralded but significant intelligence coup spearheaded by a small group of junior engineers who fundamentally altered a key area of intelligence collection. Their efforts bore immediate fruit while setting the stage for a series of innovations that eventually transformed a small—and purportedly obsolete—office into an intelligence community center for open-source collection and analysis. The project was named "Prince," and the office was the FBIS. The year was 1997.

FBIS was a relatively small office with a niche mission that predated the CIA. Created in 1941 to monitor and translate Japanese and German propaganda, FBIS transitioned to the new Central Intelligence Agency in 1947 while retaining its media monitoring and translation missions over the decades. It refocused on new adversaries and consistently provided foreign affairs agencies, the military, and policymakers with invaluable alerts to and analyses of coups, crises, leadership transitions, and armed conflicts. As popular media expanded beyond radio, so did FBIS's remit, but by the mid-1990s several factors conspired to threaten this historically valuable office's existence.

With the Cold War's end, popularization of the internet, and proliferation of global news outlets like CNN, CIA leadership in the 1990s questioned the continued need for an office to collect material widely available to everyone. Facing budget cuts (e.g., the post–Cold War peace dividend) and a growing need to invest in new information technology, the CIA began to regard FBIS—and the Open Source Center in general—as "trade space."

The CIA began the divestment process in 1992 by consolidating its open-source components under FBIS, transferring three offices from the Directorate of Intelligence. The decade following FBIS's fiftieth anniversary saw a steady reduction in staff and dollars to the point that the office's personnel strength in 2002 was approximately half of what it had been in 1992. There were even rumors of FBIS's demise, prompting the *Washington Post*, in a January 31, 1997, editorial and the Federation of American Scientists to rally publicly to the office's defense.

Meanwhile, FBIS and its bureaucratic parent, the Directorate of Science and Technology, acknowledged that the office was overdue for a revamping to address the expanding open-source environment. The office historically had been slow to adopt even basic technology (e.g., computers over typewriters), and workflows had remained largely unchanged since the 1950s. One joke making the rounds was that reengineering in FBIS meant moving from glue to scotch tape in attaching headers to the endless reams of paper that copy editors handled each day.

The Directorate of Science and Technology had addressed this technical aversion as early as the 1980s by seeding an engineering component in FBIS with senior staff from technical offices. Progress was uneven initially but gained traction with the introduction of computer processing (and configuration management) to FBIS headquarters and overseas bureaus. Despite technical progress, however, workflows remained unchanged, and the increasing costs of the "new" technology added to the budgetary strain. By the mid-1990s, with draconian cuts on the horizon, FBIS had no choice but to use technology to realize operational efficiencies. The stage was set for a relatively rare occurrence in government—a bona fide reengineering.

In 1995 FBIS leadership made the bold and controversial decision to cease hard copy publication of its Daily Report—long considered FBIS's flagship product. The pastel-colored compendium organized the day's media translations from around the world and was distributed throughout the government as well as to many university libraries. Yet production of the FBIS Daily Report was labor intensive, requiring forty-plus staffers to put the book together each day as well as a small army of typists and production staff. Electronic production shortened delivery time of a translation from days to seconds, eliminating the headquarters "middle man" and allowing the office to meet its personnel reduction "bogey" for the year. Notably, this soft copy production project, despite its technical and business complexity, was on time and within budget, and FBIS printed its last Daily Report in September 1997. In retrospect, one could consider this achievement—significant itself—as the first phase of FBIS's reengineering effort.

Electronic publication alone was insufficient, however, and FBIS was forced to turn toward its field bureaus—ground that historically had been sacrosanct. For decades FBIS had maintained a global network of bureaus to provide round-the-clock monitoring and production of the world's media. But with the significant reductions to headquarters personnel that electronic production facilitated, few additional efficiencies were to be found at home. Field bureaus could no longer be off limits.

FBIS leadership and its visionary chief of engineering services at the time, Walt Shafer (also the architect of soft copy production), began exploring ways to use information technology to reduce the physical infrastructure (i.e., bricks and mortar) and neutralize geographic constraints on the location of personnel. For example, salaries for FBIS's employees hired overseas sometimes exceeded that of similarly skilled U.S. staff, depending on the country and entitlements. While Shafer and his staff evaluated options for a "bureau of the future," FBIS leadership established a reengineering program office to ensure that whatever technical solutions emerged, the business implications (i.e., efficiencies) could be articulated and evaluated.

In 1996 the bureau-of-the-future effort produced a pilot program called the Latin America-Pilot Demo (LAPD). As its name implies, LAPD was to deploy to a Latin American bureau (given cost and time zone considerations) as a technology-based effort to realize efficiencies. If successful FBIS would expand this technical solution to all of its bureaus. Not uncommonly for leap of faith efforts, discussions—and frustration—abounded around requirements, or lack thereof. As technical staff proposed options, the business (mission) side struggled to see benefits. Nor was the majority of the FBIS staff thrilled about LAPD's intended benefits, the achievement of which entailed reducing further the need for said staff. Despite FBIS leadership's support, LAPD traveled a tough road.

Meanwhile, while the office's attention and hopes centered around LAPD, a first-tour engineer began working with an experienced FBIS bureau chief in Asia to experiment with distributing work in the region to take advantage of time zones. Known as the East Asia Initiative (EAI), this effort emphasized digital collection and subsequent distribution of East Asian media sources via an internet-based network to where they could be "processed" (i.e., reviewed and translated) most efficiently.

As LAPD inched along, EAI gathered steam. Management began to see cost savings—immediate and potential—and despite (or perhaps because of) an apparent lack of technical elegance, mission officers began to champion EAI as a potential enterprise solution. Shifting focus and support from LAPD to EAI, however, was no easy feat. FBIS had invested significant time and effort in LAPD. Changing direction at this stage meant forgoing whatever progress LAPD had made and writing off the investment to date. Moreover, from a contractual standpoint, should FBIS abandon LAPD and pin its hopes on EAI, the government would now assume all technical risk—and blame, should EAI fail.

But change direction FBIS did. Despite the skepticism of experienced technical managers, enthusiastic support for the EAI approach took root in the junior technical ranks, bolstered by a strong endorsement from FBIS's IT architect, Gerry Kowalski. Kowalski's confidence and that of this team of young engineers were important factors in FBIS's decision to adopt EAI as the enterprise approach to field reengineering. More importantly, however, mission (i.e., business) champions stepped forward who were more invested than the technical staff in the success of the reengineering effort. They were willing to work through the inevitable glitches that would arise in a project of this scope and impact. With that kind of support—never evident in LAPD—FBIS placed its money—literally—on the EAI solution.

Not that FBIS had a lot of money to place. Its overseers had given FBIS one-year investment dollars in fiscal year 1997 to fund the reengineering effort, but the quid pro quo was that the CIA's comptroller would subtract twice that amount from FBIS's base budget beginning in fiscal year 1999—in perpetuity. Moreover, a key measure of success was that FBIS was to sustain output (i.e., translations) at 1996 levels in adapting to its lower operating budget. In any context, this was a tall order.

FBIS named the new effort based on the EAI solution called Prince (processing in a collaborative environment). The plan was for small teams to travel to each of FBIS's overseas facilities over the course of fiscal year 1997 to install the needed technical equipment, establish internet/network connectivity, and conduct technical and editorial training for local staff. Interestingly, relatively junior engineers led each of these teams, but the same engineers worked as a team to determine travel schedules and assignments. For its part, management tracked schedules, budget, and dependencies but largely stayed out of the way as these half-dozen employees progressed around the globe, successfully installing Prince—on schedule—at one field site after another. By November 1997 all of FBIS's field sites were on Prince, and the real reengineering work could begin. Furthermore, the books balanced, and the year-long global project ended just under its allotted budget.

With its new networked and processing infrastructure, FBIS's business options grew exponentially. Prince did not in and of itself transform FBIS, but it removed the excuses. No longer tied to bricks and mortar, FBIS managers could now decide whether they needed one bureau or one hundred. And with the ability to deploy people to less-expensive locations (e.g., their homes), a number of cost-effective options for hiring and managing employees came to the fore. To its credit, FBIS management at the time (1997–2000) made tough choices, closed field sites, and reconfigured workflows to stay within its declining budget while, remarkably, exceeding earlier years' production levels many times over. By any measure, FBIS's reengineering was a success, but its success was overshadowed by the fact that many loyal, long-time employees either lost jobs or were encouraged to leave as work changed and personnel ceilings caved.

Nevertheless, the feat of these young engineers—and of FBIS writ large—should not go unnoticed as one considers the evolution of open-source intelligence. In addition to the immediate effects above, Prince had a lasting impact on FBIS's zeitgeist. First, FBIS went from arguably one of the CIA's most technically averse organizations to one of its most technically facile—at least in terms of managing and applying technology to the mission of open-source intelligence. Second, the Prince reengineering experience brought business savvy to FBIS's management culture. Terms like *return on investment*, *opportunity cost*, and *recurring cost* became commonplace in corporate discussions, and managers at all levels were taught and expected to understand and manage their budgets.

Most notably, Prince set the stage for a series of technical investments and strategic decisions in the early 2000s that allowed FBIS to "punch above its weight" as open sources continued their rapid expansion in breadth and scope. Despite the reductions of the 1990s and talk of its demise, FBIS emerged from its Prince-anchored reengineering effort well positioned to face the challenges of twenty-first century intelligence. In fact, FBIS's status changed significantly when it was renamed and repurposed as the DNI Open Source Center in 2005 and given the broader charge of leading intelligence community efforts to develop open-source intelligence capabilities and capacity.

While it may not be possible to attribute this upgrade in responsibility to any one factor, it is doubtful that FBIS would have been capable—or have had the mindset—to take on this much broader assignment without Prince. To that end, it is difficult to talk about the revolution in open sources without giving credit to those—including the half-dozen junior engineers—who took on this massive undertaking and succeeded beyond all expectation.

There are several morals to this story, but the two warranting mention here are (1) that there is no position too junior to have a major and long-lasting impact; and (2) that heroic actions can emerge from anywhere in the organization. Impact is far less about rank and where one works than about recognizing opportunity and having the skill, foresight, and initiative to seize it. That is the indelible lesson of Prince.

Epilogue

The young engineers all left FBIS soon after Prince was completed. Their achievement had made them attractive both to other CIA components and to private sector companies willing to pay handsomely for their talent and experience. While some have remained in or returned to government service, others are well established in the private sector. All still consider the Prince experience a highlight in their careers.

27

Bell Ringers!

ELINOR HOUGHTON KELLY

C an a woman successfully launch and run an innovative start-up in the CIA's Directorate of Operations (DO)? Can a team of thinkers and doers revolutionize DO targeting? In the early 1980s when I joined the DO, it was a dynamic and derring-do place. "Wild Bill" Donovan created the model for it in World War II with his Office of Strategic Services (OSS). The DO was a lean mean machine battling worldwide threats to the United States.

DO field managers had tremendous power and authority. They ran their fiefdoms with minimal headquarters interference. Operations officers (ops officers) achieved glory by recruiting dangerous recalcitrant targets (foreigners with access to important national security information needed by the U.S.). However, the ways in which foreign targets were identified had scarcely changed since the Donovan days. And ops officers viewed many headquarters-based officers as lowly bureaucrats who existed primarily to support heroes risking their lives in the globe's darkest corners.

During the 1980s I ran many successful operations against a variety of targets. I even convinced a terrorist to give up his secrets. Later, I recruited foreign diplomats and other international players. Of course, I spotted my own leads for these operations.

I strongly endorsed the ops officer creed: in the field, we did it all. We spotted targets, we developed them, we recruited them, we obtained foreign intelligence from them. When necessary, we ended our relationships with them.

Eventually, though, I began to question why ops officers spent so much valuable time and effort trolling for good leads. It seemed a rather ad hoc way to conduct business. What if headquarters could develop the methodologies to provide the field with top-quality leads, so the field wouldn't have to find them all? Then ops officers could focus their attention on developing, recruiting, and debriefing those leads. Would that improve the quality and quantity of intelligence? I thought about this for some years before I had an opportunity to test out my theory.

After seven years in the field, I was reassigned to headquarters. My first job was managing Central Eurasia (CE) Division operations in the domestic field. I worked for what later became the National Resources (NR) Division. I experimented with new ways to find leads and new ways to pursue those leads. Daily, I fought fiercely with CE's Russia House officers who opposed anything new. But the CE officers I dealt with were professional. Many gradually warmed up to my newfangled ideas. After a year or so of pitched battles, I was astounded when Russia House invited me to manage their scientific operations.

CE Division was a wonderfully hard-charging place. During my years there, I moved up the operational management chain. These jobs gave me a bird's-eye view of Russian operations worldwide. I also continued to systematically identify some leads for the field. My wonderful boss inspired me. She calmly and capably dealt with worldwide challenges while encouraging her officers to be smart risk takers. I had the good fortune to work for her twice during my career.

Then 9/11 happened. My boss left for a new job. A former career trainee classmate had been trying to convince me to return to the NR Division. When he became division chief, he asked me to manage the intelligence community's Emigre Debriefing Program. He was pivotal in helping me launch the most rewarding phase of my career.

Before the collapse of the Soviet Union, the emigre program had been quite successful. Soviet emigre scientific and academic brainpower provided important insights into Soviet weapons programs and government plans and intentions. But by the time I took over the program, the Soviet Union was history. After a thorough scrub, we concluded that the intelligence obtained did not justify the program's size and expense. The deputy director for operations agreed, and we terminated it.

There were still a few officers and some infrastructure remaining from the program. It seemed to me a readymade platform for a headquarters foreign intelligence targeting shop. We realized, though, that we would have to convince the DO bureaucracy that our leads could produce more successful operations. It turned out to be much more challenging than we expected.

For years, DO reports officers, often in conjunction with the Directorate of Intelligence (DI), had provided excellent leads and substantive info to the field. However, ops officers often viewed this input as background, not worthy of action. And the numbers of leads produced were not large. Reports officers were also overworked. They often did not have the time to reach outside their day-to-day contacts to develop relationships with their intelligence community (IC) intelligence consumers.

In contrast, the ops officers' yardstick was numbers: numbers of assets (targets who have provided vetted, validated foreign intelligence) recruited and numbers of reports disseminated to the IC. That was how ops officers were evaluated, and that was how they got promoted. So ops officers often sought out and recruited targets of opportunity. These were individuals with whom ops officers could establish regular contact during the normal course of their duties. Because they did not usually work in secret facilities, these targets were easier to recruit than some other types of targets. Ops officers spent less time on "harder" targets, which took much more time and effort to recruit.

The 9/11 attacks precipitated a sea change in the directorate, the agency, and the intelligence community. The DO moved heaven and earth to remake itself to address the government's new challenges. Some divisions and ops officers continued their traditional pursuit of foreign intelligence targets. But military targets now took precedence, as did new target types in the counterproliferation, counterterrorism, and information operations arenas.

Reports officers faced the challenge of rapidly building many new IC relationships and developing new requirements to deal with the government's enormous new intelligence gaps. They had to research and send out these new requirements to the field as well as process all of the field reporting.

That was the state of play when I started my targeting shop. We were determined to create a dynamic office that could produce top-quality leads for the domestic field.

We began small, without fanfare. We wanted to create a viable product before trying to market ourselves. First we tapped into numerous reports from officers and DI experts to obtain detailed requirements addressing U.S. intelligence gaps. Initially we focused on hard target country requirements, and then we gradually expanded to include other areas. We designed a database so we could search it by substantive issue and country of interest.

We began to send lead information gleaned from our database to domestic stations. We were disappointed when many stations ignored our leads.

I was surprised that field managers and headquarters thought that the database was unnecessary. But they were experts in their own areas of operation and believed they didn't need outside help. They may also have feared the database would diminish their autonomy and authority. A few progressive chiefs of station tried our leads; when some didn't pan out, they were understandably reluctant to pursue more.

My wonderful deputy and I worked hand in glove for years. She was a terrifically talented officer. We complemented each other's strengths and weaknesses. We worked hard to improve our leads. We also doggedly continued to compile data and develop new ways to find leads.

We began to invent techniques to assist in the counterterrorism fight. For example, we created a unique target mapping methodology. It was the first time that the IC had seen such mapping analysis. The FBI was seized with our invention and immediately began using it.

We learned that the Directorate of Science and Technology (DS&T) wanted the DO to participate in an important interagency counterterrorism program. We volunteered on the spot. The brilliant DS&T visionary directing the program came to believe in what we were doing. He enthusiastically supported our innovations and made it possible for us to advance on multiple fronts for many years.

One early project that we undertook for our mentor was a comprehensive, multilayered weapons mapping project. It took years to research and organize the data. Fortunately, we had plenty of help. The DS&T and the DI provided invaluable input, as did forward-thinking officers in the Department of Homeland Security, Immigration and Customs Enforcement, and the Department of Health and Human Services. When we showed the final version to the FBI, they were impressed. They quickly incorporated it into their nationwide threat matrix.

We obtained new data sets and then invited officers from the National Security Agency's (NSA's) applied mathematics program to visit. When we promised them brand new data to analyze, their extraordinary manager showed up the very next day. He brought along some of his young geniuses. Later he arranged for them and their successors to become long-term members of our team.

With our NSA partners, we pioneered DO and IC use of mathematical modeling for foreign intelligence targeting. The first mathematical model we used to parse the data was the multiattribute utility theory (MAUT) model. I first learned about this methodology from targeting analyses being performed at Las Vegas casinos. In this model, a decision is broken down into independent criteria, the relative importance of each criterion is determined, all options under consideration are listed, and each option on each criterion is rated.

To use this methodology, we asked our DI and DS&T colleagues to provide us with intelligence requirements from both substantive and geographic perspectives. With the experts' help, we boiled those pages-long requirements down into brief, pithy phrases, which we called parameters. Then we developed relative weightings of each of the parameters. At that point we were ready for our mathematicians to apply the MAUT model.

It produced a targeting bonanza! We identified, researched, and sent out dozens of high-quality leads unearthed via the MAUT. Afterward we used the model on every database we could obtain.

Shortly thereafter, we asked our NSAers to develop algorithms to identify individuals with anomalous backgrounds or behaviors. To accomplish that, they developed anomaly-detection linear-regression models. Those models also worked well. Although they did not produce the volume of leads unearthed via the MAUT, the ones we found via this method were important and could not otherwise be located. Domestic stations pursued and recruited many of our MAUT and linear-regression leads.

During the same period, we decided to try to analyze targets' movements from a time series perspective. Our mathematicians developed a methodology that we called "twenty-four-hour clock targeting." It worked very well. For example, we identified a foreigner who regularly crossed the U.S. border on foot in the middle of the night. He turned out to be of high interest. We also used the methodology to analyze the movements of known targets in order to surface new ones.

Suddenly, more offices wanted our help. We needed more people to answer the mail. And we wanted to conduct more targeting experiments. However, NR Division couldn't provide sufficient funds. So we looked farther afield.

We conducted fundraising in the DO. This was new for the directorate. Offices were surprised to be asked. Many were quite willing to contribute once they understood how we could help them. However, one division was insulted when we asked them for money. They even accused us of blackmail! That division had demanded access to one of our databases, but they did not have the necessary approvals to house that data. So we offered to provide in-house targeting training to their officer. We would train her in our techniques and give her access to our data. The division sent a disinterested dullard. After they pulled her back, we suggested they fund a contractor to work for them in our office. That was when the division called the seventh floor and accused us of blackmail. The deputy director for operations was supportive of our position rather than that of the balky division. He asked whether we also held cookie sales to raise funds.

The Director of National Intelligence funded several of our projects, as did many other IC agencies. We hired a brilliant graphic artist when we realized our scientific methodologies were tough to grasp. His graphics were worth a thousand words! Now everyone could actually visualize what we were doing. He also created spiffy unclassified posters to advertise our work. We regularly hung new ones on our vault door. When visitors saw the posters, they realized our office was different. Since I was fundraiser-in-chief, we hung a picture of a tin cup beside my office door.

I was invited to speak at the CIA's 2006 Innovation Summit. Executive Director Dusty Foggo pulled me aside after my presentation. He said our methodologies were groundbreaking and that CIA Director Porter Goss would want to see them asap. Foggo quickly arranged for us to brief the director. But the atmosphere at the briefing was funereal. Goss and Foggo knew their CIA careers were on the rocks. Both departed within the week—unfortunate timing for us.

We experimented with various ways to improve morale and productivity in our office. We expected everyone to work hard and instilled in them a sense of urgency and pride of mission. We encouraged our officers to try new ideas. We looked for and celebrated short-term wins. We rewarded our officers for trying, even when their ideas weren't successful. We shielded them from bureaucratic frustrations, fought hard to get them what they needed.

We fostered formal and informal collaboration among our officers and enjoyed hearing them figure out ways to jointly tackle problems. We told all new employees that they would be mentored by more experienced officers and that they would serve as mentors themselves in the future. We encouraged smiles and laughter, and often held chili cook-offs and other celebrations. For example, we affectionately called our mentor our "godfather" and held a godfather party to celebrate him. A life-sized figure of the godfather from the movie but with our mentor's face on it greeted him when he walked in the door.

Since we couldn't give monetary awards to contractors, we devised a special award. Our graphics artist created a large, colorful foamboard award, tall enough to be seen from everywhere in our vault. Everyone knew who the current awardee was because the current honoree kept the award on their desk until it was awarded to the next person. Staff and contractors alike were delighted to receive this recognition. Contractors also were recognized by their employers for their work for us.

We caught fire! We called ourselves a "think tank with a bottom line: to identify top-notch targets leading to recruitments." We had fun building an enthusiastic, smart team of seasoned experts and young whippersnappers. Our officers included homegrown targeting experts, ops officers, geographers, methodologists, NSA mathematicians, immigration experts, substantive experts, scientists, statisticians, and computer whizzes. Although we had only a few staff positions, we now had officers lining up to fill them. Contractors from many companies clamored to join us, too.

U.S. Senate Select Committee on Intelligence staffers learned of our work. At our suggestion, Congress agreed to fund an interagency targeting center. The Defense Department, Immigration and Customs Enforcement, Department of Homeland Security, and State Department were enthused by the idea. We located CIA office space that housed cutting-edge computer capabilities. We formulated a detailed plan of action and offered all participants access to our unique data and methodologies. We named it the Bright Center—Bridging Gaps in Humint Targeting.

The DO's military liaison office helped set up the center. But the military had only limited data, no methodologies to offer. A retiring military officer unexpectedly announced to us that he was the new center chief. He had no targeting experience and refused to share leadership responsibilities. We did not think the center could be viable under his direction, so we pulled out. The center collapsed. However, Congress decided we could use the already allocated funds for our joint IC projects.

We created the IC's first systematic internet targeting capability. It was our biggest and most productive invention. We regularly obtained hundreds of updated parameters from the DO, the DI, the DS&T, and the IC, and plugged them all into our capability. Now we could find leads around the globe, meeting specific headquarters and field requirements, in multiple languages. Although we focused on counterproliferation, counterterrorism, and information operations leads, we identified hundreds of others as well.

Overseas stations discovered us. Daily, they cabled us for help. Some area divisions initially resented our intrusion into their turf. We invited them to join with us to find good targets. Some did, while others developed targeting methodologies in their own shops.

Domestic stations realized that we could help them. In response to their requests, we produced dozens of tailored targeting packages for them. We also produced twelve comprehensive targeting studies of stations' areas of operation. Each one was packed with more than a hundred pages of detailed targeting information. In addition, we created a wiring diagram project to find and approach targets overseas. All three techniques produced many leads that led to recruitments.

We also developed a project using layered transparencies to assist ops officers in scientific operations. Reports and ops officers successfully used the methodology to locate a critical secret target location overseas.

Our computer whizzes worked for several years to crack the code on a database filled with inaccessible, albeit valuable, information. A defense contractor had created it years earlier, but the company could no longer figure out how to access it. We shared the data with the relevant divisions and later used it to map links to key overseas targets. The database provided dozens of valuable leads, a number of which were later recruited.

We continued to support our DS&T mentor's program with new scientific targeting projects. For example, we dove into an overseas hard target organization of intense interest. The area division had identified only a few high-level targets in an organization with hundreds of thousands of employees. We thought it would be useful to identify lower-level targets more accessible to our officers.

We hired contractors with the relevant area and scientific expertise. Then we researched the organization and conducted intensive analyses of the data we had collected. Our two-hundred-page study identified many viable targets and suggested ways to access them. The DI published our study as an intel report. Then the owning division decided to adopt our methodology to pursue this type of target.

One center requested DO ideas for a global targeting schematic. Fortunately, we were able to collaborate with two retired senior ops officers on this project. Their expertise and willingness to innovate were key to our success. Together we conducted an intensive ninety-day target study. That produced a three-hundred-page blueprint for ops officers worldwide to access the targets. Although the area division for which we had created the project chose not to use our data and methodology, several other offices later employed the methodology.

We launched another project to locate a specific type of elusive target. We discussed our idea with our DS&T mentor. He and a supportive senior National Counterproliferation Center officer then arranged for a Department of Energy national lab grant to detail scientists to our office.

We selected a top Department of Energy scientist for our project. We asked her to analyze and numerically rank certain types of data. Our mathematicians created an algorithm using that data to search scientific dissertation databases for targets. We identified some excellent targets, which the field successfully pursued. The National Counterproliferation Center later adopted this methodology. We also developed similar methodologies to search for other target types in databases worldwide.

We ran many targeting projects for the National Counterterrorism Center using new methodologies that we developed specifically for their types of targets. Our projects produced good counterterrorism leads that led to recruitments.

The deputy director of the FBI's National Security Branch asked me to develop a targeting capability for the FBI. I was intrigued by the offer but regretfully turned it down. I also turned down several other interesting job opportunities. But I continued to believe that I could make a more significant contribution by pushing DO targeting forward.

During the last few years before I retired, DO and IC targeting took off. It was a free-for-all, with no centralized coordination or direction. There was widespread duplication and competition.

We developed an extensive targeting training program in our office. It worked like a charm: we helped the DO grow talented, successful targeters. They obtained field experience and advanced in their careers. Of course, the mothership was there if storm warnings appeared.

In 2009 I was asked to chair the directorate's targeting board. Targeting had become a new profession in the DO, the DI, and the DS&T, and all three directorates collaborated and assisted each other via the agency's targeting board.

There were no meaningful metrics to objectively measure targeting's impact on the quality or quantity of DO operations. Most DO seniors viewed targeting as nice to have but not essential to operations. DO targeting career precepts also needed further development.

As chair, I tackled both of those challenges. I met with fiery DO resistance when I first proposed metrics pegged to recruiting agents and obtaining foreign intelligence. My office had compiled recruitment metrics for some years. Each time one of our leads was recruited, the responsible targeter rang a special bell. Then we all gathered to celebrate! Targeters described how they had identified the lead and then explained the value of the recruitment to the relevant office or center.

We kept a running tally of our recruitments on our wall. It was great for office morale, and the steadily increasing numbers didn't hurt our fundraising efforts either. By the time I retired, our leads had produced a wide variety of recruitments. Those recruitments supported all of the area divisions and nearly all of the centers.

Other targeting officers gradually realized that objective, specific metrics would help convince ops managers of the value of targeting. Targeters also saw these new metrics as a way to enhance their own credentials and perhaps participate in operations themselves. So the board successfully lobbied for directorate-wide implementation of its metrics. During my tenure, the targeting board also wrote new targeter career precepts, which the DO adopted. The DI and the DS&T also developed their own career precepts.

It was tough to launch and run a targeting start-up in the CIA's Directorate of Operations. I met with resistance and even hostility from some quarters. And it took me some time to realize that my efforts were an integral part of much broader changes afoot in the DO and the IC.

Change is inherently threatening. It is particularly threatening to those running successful enterprises in which the parties are wholly invested. The DO prided itself on its ability to get things done very quickly and very well. It didn't see any need to change what had worked extremely well since Donovan was

OSS director. To protect its secrets, it had deliberately insulated itself from outside influences. Had it not been so isolated, officers might have been more flexible in considering change. But the elephant in the room became the new post-9/11 reality.

People need time to understand that change can actually benefit them. They also need to find ways to comfortably incorporate change into their daily work. Ops managers had to adjust to the new role that headquarters began to play in their operations. It was no longer a relatively passive supporter of the field. For the first time, it became an active partner.

Perhaps we should not have tried to push through so many new ideas so quickly. But I was a woman in a hurry! It was exhilarating to invent new ways of doing business and then to see them actually work! We were doing our part for America!

I retired knowing that we had achieved our goal—to invent and implement innovative targeting capabilities leading to DO operational successes. These capabilities produced hundreds of high-quality leads for DO field stations. They were fully researched and immediately actionable. Many would become "bell ringers"!

Ode to New CIA Retirees

(with apologies to *Goodnight, Moon*)

ED MICKOLUS

Goodnight, badge machines.
Goodnight, wave guides.
Goodnight, cables.
Goodnight, *Classification Guide*.
Goodnight, *Style Guide*.
Goodnight, reorganizations.
Goodnight, Kryptos.
Goodnight, SDRs.
Goodnight, PDBs.
Goodnight, walk from West Lot.
Goodnight, promotion panels.
Goodnight, Congressional investigations.
Goodnight, media inquiries.
Goodnight, mandatory training.
Goodnight, Horizons.

Hello, memoirs. (Hello, Publications Review Board.)
Hello, wonderful memories of colleagues, accomplishments,
and service.

WRITING LIFE AFTER THE CIA

Books by CIA Alumni

Memoirs by CIA Directors

George H. W. Bush. *Looking Forward: An Autobiography*. New York: Bantam, 1987.

William Colby and Peter Forbath. *Honorable Men: My Life in the CIA*. New York: Simon and Schuster, 1978.

Allen Dulles. *The Craft of Intelligence*. New York: Harper and Row, 1963.

Robert Gates. *From the Shadows: The Ultimate Insider's Story of Five Presidents and How They Won the Cold War*. New York: Simon and Schuster, 1996.

Michael Vincent Hayden. *Playing to the Edge: American Intelligence in the Age of Terror*. New York: Penguin, 2016.

Richard Helms, with William Hood. *A Look Over My Shoulder: A Life in the Central Intelligence Agency*. New York: Random House, 2003.

Michael Morell, with Bill Harlow. *The Great War of Our Time: The CIA's Fight from Al Qa'ida to ISIS*. New York: Twelve, 2015.

Leon Panetta and Jim Newton. *Worthy Fights: A Memoir of Leadership in War and Peace*. New York: Penguin, 2014.

George J. Tenet, with William Harlow. *At the Center of the Storm: My Years at the CIA*. New York: HarperCollins, 2007.

Stansfield Turner. *Secrecy and Democracy—The CIA in Transition*. Boston: Houghton Mifflin, 1985.

Memoirs by Intelligence Officers

Michele Rigby Assad. *Breaking Cover: My Secret Life in the CIA and What It Taught Me about What's Worth Fighting For*. Carol Stream IL: Tyndale Momentum, 2018.

Fenton Babcock. *CIA Years: A Mercurial Intelligence Career: Between Two Book Ends*. Self-published, Infinity Publishing, 2009.

Fenton Babcock and Evelyn Babcock. *New Lives for Old*. Self-published, Rose Dog Press, 2011.

Robert Baer. *See No Evil: The True Story of a Ground Soldier in the CIA's War on Terrorism*. New York: Crown, 2002.

Robert Baer and Dayna Baer. *The Company We Keep: A Husband-and-Wife True-Life Spy Story*. New York: Crown, 2011.

Nada Bakos, with Davin Coburn. *The Targeter: My Life in the CIA, on the Hunt for the Godfather of ISIS*. New York: Little, Brown, 2019.

Milt Bearden and James Risen. *The Main Enemy: The Inside Story of the CIA's Final Showdown with the KGB*. New York: Random House, 2003.

Glenn Carle. *The Interrogator: An Education*. New York: Nation Books, 2012.

Duane R. Clarridge. *A Spy for All Seasons: My Life in the CIA*. New York: Scribner, 1996.

Miles Copeland. *The Game Player: Confessions of the CIA's Original Political Operative*. London: Aurum Press, 1989.

Henry Crumpton. *The Art of Intelligence: Lessons from a Life in the CIA's Clandestine Service*. New York: Penguin, 2013.

William J. Daugherty. *In the Shadow of the Ayatollah: A CIA Hostage in Iran*. Annapolis: Naval Institute Press, 2001.

Jack Devine, with Vernon Loeb. *Good Hunting: An American Spymaster's Story*. New York: Farrar, Straus and Giroux, 2014.

Lawrence Devlin. *Chief of Station/Congo: Fighting the Cold War in a Hot Zone*. New York: Public Affairs, 2008.

Florence Fitzsimmons Garbler. *CIA Wife: One Woman's Life Inside the CIA*. Santa Barbara: Fifthian Press, 1994.

Tom Gilligan. *CIA Life: 10,000 Days with the Agency*. Guilford CT: Foreign Intelligence Press, 1991.

Austin Goodrich. *Born to Spy: Recollections of a CIA Case Officer*. Self-published, iUniverse, 2004.

Donald Gregg. *Pot Shards: Fragments of a Life Lived in CIA, the White House, and the Two Koreas*. Washington DC: New Academia Publishing/Vellum Books, 2014.

Robert L. Grenier. *88 Days to Kandahar: A CIA Diary*. New York: Simon and Schuster, 2015.

Howard Philips Hart. *A Life for a Life: A Memoir: My Career in Espionage Working for the Central Intelligence Agency*. Lulu Press, 2015.

Richard Holm. *The American Agent: My Life in the CIA*. London: St. Ermin's Press, 2003.

Richard Holm and Timothy Miller. *The Craft We Chose: My Life in the CIA*. Mountain Lake Park MD: Mountain Lake Press, 2011.

E. Howard Hunt. *Undercover: Memoirs of an American Secret Agent*. Berkeley CA: Berkley Publishing, 1974.

———. *American Spy: My Secret History in the* CIA, *Watergate and Beyond*. New York: Wiley, 2007.

Jack Kassinger. *Holding Hands with Heroes*. Self-published, Dorrance Publishing, 2010.

Bina C. Kiyonaga. *My Spy: Memoir of a* CIA *Wife*. New York: Harper Perennial, 2001.

Martha E. Leiker. *From Silence to Secrecy: A Memoir*. Self-published, iUniverse, 2010.

James Lilley, with Jeffrey Lilley. *China Hands: Nine Decades of Adventure, Espionage and Diplomacy*. New York: Public Affairs, 2004.

Chris Lynch. *The* CI *Desk:* FBI *and* CIA *Counterintelligence As Seen From My Cubicle*. Self-published, Dog Ear Publishing, 2010.

Melissa Boyle Mahle. *Denial and Deception: An Insider's View of the* CIA. New York: Nation Books, 2005.

Shelly Mateer. *Single in the* CIA. Self-published, False Buddha, 2015.

Elizabeth P. McIntosh. *Sisterhood of Spies: The Women of the* OSS. Annapolis: Naval Institute Press, 1998.

Stuart Methven. *Laughter in the Shadows: A* CIA *Memoir*. Annapolis: Naval Institute Press, 2014.

Cord Meyer. *Facing Reality: From World Federalism to the* CIA. New York: Harper & Row, 1980.

Edward Mickolus, ed. *Stories from Langley: A Glimpse Inside the* CIA. Washington DC, and Lincoln: Potomac Books/University of Nebraska Press, 2014.

Lindsay Moran. *Blowing My Cover: My Life as a* CIA *Spy*. New York: Putnam, 2005.

Kay Shaw Nelson. *The Cloak and Dagger Cook: A* CIA *Memoir*. Gretna LA: Pelican, 2009.

Floyd L. Paseman. *A Spy's Journey: A* CIA *Memoir*. St. Paul MN: Zenith Press, 2004.

Shirley H. Perry. *After Many Days*. Ashland OR: Hellgate Press, 2010.

Martha Peterson. *The Widow Spy*. Wilmington NC: Red Canary Press, 2012.

David Atlee Phillips. *The Night Watch: 25 Years of Peculiar Service*. New York: Atheneum, 1977.

———. *Secret Wars Diary: My Adventures in Combat, Espionage Operations and Covert Action*. Bethesda MD: Stone Trail Press, 1989.

John Rizzo. *Company Man: 30 Years of Controversy and Crisis in the* CIA. New York: Scribner, 2014.

Jose A. Rodriguez, Jr., with Bill Harlow. *Hard Measures: How Aggressive* CIA *Actions after 9/11 Saved American Lives*. New York: Threshold Editions, 2013.

H. K. Roy. *American Spy: Wry Reflections on My Life in the* CIA. Buffalo: Prometheus Books, 2019.

Steven Ruth. *My Twenty Years as a* CIA *Officer: It's All about the Mission*. Self-published, CreateSpace, 2011.

Ted Shackley, with Richard A. Finney. *Spymaster: My Life in the* CIA. Washington DC: Potomac Books, 2005.

Kevin Michael Shipp. *In From the Cold*: CIA *Secrecy and Operations, A* CIA *Officer's True Story*. Vidalia GA: Ascent Publishing, 2010.

———. *From the Company of Shadows*. Vidalia GA: Ascent Publishing, 2012.

J. Perry Smith. *The Unlikely Priest*. Jacksonville FL: Padre Nuestro, 2011.

Jamie Smith. *Gray Work: Confessions of an American Paramilitary Spy*. New York: William Morrow, 2015.

Joseph Burkholder Smith. *Portrait of a Cold Warrior*. New York: Putnam, 1976.

Russell Jack Smith. *The Unknown* CIA: *My Three Decades with the Agency*. McLean VA: Berkeley Books, 1989.

Alan B. Trabue. *A Life of Lies and Spies: Tales of a* CIA *Covert Ops Polygraph Operator*. New York: Macmillan, 2015.

T. J. Waters. *Class 11: Inside the* CIA*'s First Post-9/11 Spy Class*. New York: Dutton, 2006.

Ralph Weber. *Spymasters: Ten* CIA *Officers in Their Own Words*. Wilmington DE: Scholarly Resources, 1999.

Valerie Plame Wilson. *Fair Game: My Life as a Spy, My Betrayal by the White House*. New York: Simon and Schuster, 2007.

Overviews of Intelligence Culture and Humor

Roger Hall. *You're Stepping on My Cloak and Dagger*. New York: W. W. Norton, 1957.

Charles E. Lathrop. *The Literary Spy: The Ultimate Source for Quotations on Espionage and Intelligence*. New Haven CT: Yale University Press, 2004.

Edward Mickolus. *The Secret Book of CIA Humor*. Gretna LA: Pelican, 2011.

———. "A Guide to Popular Student Books on Intelligence: What Do Students Think They Know about Intelligence before They Walk into the Classroom?" *The Intelligencer: Journal of US Intelligence Studies* 19, 1 (2012): 67–71; reprinted in Peter Oleson, ed. *Guide to the Study of Intelligence* Washington DC: Association of Former Intelligence Officers, 2016.

———. *The Secret Book of Intelligence Community Humor*. Ponte Vedra FL: Wandering Woods Publishing, 2018.

———. *Two Spies Walk into a Bar*. Ponte Vedra FL: Wandering Woods Publishing, 2018.

James Olson. *Fair Play: The Moral Dilemmas of Spying.* Washington DC: Potomac, 2006.

Tom Sileo. *CIA Humor: A Few True Stories from a 31-Year Career.* Alexandria VA: Washington House, 2004.

Covert Action

Gary Berntsen and Ralph Pezzullo. *Jawbreaker: The Attack on Bin Laden and al Qaeda: A Personal Account by the CIA's Key Field Commander.* New York: Crown, 2005.

William J. Daugherty. *Executive Secrets: Covert Action and the Presidency.* Lexington: University Press of Kentucky, 2004.

Gary Schroen. *First In: An Insider's Account of How the CIA Spearheaded the War on Terror in Afghanistan.* New York: Ballantine, 2005.

Science and Technology

Dino Brugioni. *Eyeball to Eyeball: The Inside Story of the Cuban Missile Crisis.* New York: Random House, 1990.

Antonio J. Mendez, with Malcolm McConnell. *The Master of Disguise: My Secret Life in the CIA.* New York: Perennial, 1999.

Antonio Mendez and Jonna Mendez, with Bruce Henderson. *Spy Dust: Two Masters of Disguise Reveal the Tools and Operations That Helped Win the Cold War.* New York: Atria Books, 2002.

Gregory W. Pedlow and Donald E. Welzenbach. *The CIA and the U-2 Program, 1954-1974.* Washington DC: Center for the Study of Intelligence, 1998.

David Robarge. *Archangel.* Washington DC: Center for the Study of Intelligence, 2007.

Kevin Ruffner, ed. *Corona: America's First Satellite Program.* Washington DC: CIA History Staff, 1995.

Robert Wallace and H. Keith Melton, with Henry R. Schlesinger. *Spycraft: The Secret History of the CIA's Spytechs, from Communism to Al-Qaeda* New York: Plume, 2009.

Supporting Operations and Analysis

Richard G. Irwin. *KH601: And Ye Shall Know the Truth and the Truth Shall Make You Free: My Life in the Central Intelligence Agency.* Self-published, Fortis, 2010.

John F. Sullivan. *Of Spies and Lies: A CIA Lie Detector Remembers Vietnam.* Lawrence: University Press of Kansas, 2002.

———. *Gatekeeper: Memoirs of a* CIA *Polygraph Examiner.* Washington DC: Potomac, 2007.

Intelligence Analysis

Sarah Miller Beebe and Randolph H. Pherson. *Cases in Intelligence Analysis: Structured Analytic Techniques in Action.* Thousand Oaks CA: CQ Press, 2011.

Robert M. Clark. *Intelligence Analysis: A Target Centric Approach,* 5th ed. Washington DC: CQ Press, 2016.

Carol Dumaine and L. Sergio Germani, eds. *New Frontiers of Intelligence Analysis: Shared Threats, Diverse Perspectives, New Communities.* Washington DC: Central Intelligence Agency, 2005.

Ben B. Fischer. *At Cold War's End: U.S. Intelligence on the Soviet Union and Eastern Europe, 1989-1991.* Washington DC: Center for the Study of Intelligence, 1999.

Roger Z. George and James Bruce, eds. *Analyzing Intelligence: Origins, Obstacles, and Innovations.* Washington DC: Georgetown University Press, 2008.

Roger Z. George and Robert D. Kline, eds. *Intelligence and the National Security Strategist: Enduring Issues and Challenges.* Washington DC: National Defense University Press, 2004.

Roger Z. George and Harvey Rishikof. *The National Security Enterprise: Navigating the Labyrinth.* Washington DC: Georgetown University Press, 2017.

Gerald K. Haines and Robert E. Leggett, eds. CIA*'s Analysis of the Soviet Union 1947-1991.* Washington DC: Center for the Study of Intelligence, 2001.

John Helgerson. *Getting to Know the President:* CIA *Briefings of Presidential Candidates, 1952-1992.* Washington DC: Center for the Study of Intelligence, 1995.

Richards J. Heuer, Jr. *The Psychology of Intelligence Analysis.* Washington DC: Center for the Study of Intelligence, 2007.

Richards J. Heuer, Jr., ed. *Quantitative Approaches to Political Intelligence: The* CIA *Experience.* Boulder: Westview Press, 1978.

Richards J. Heuer, Jr., and Randolph H. Pherson. *Structured Analytic Techniques for Intelligence Analysis.* Washington DC: CQ Press, 2014.

Philip Houston, Michael Floyd, and Susan Carnicero, with Don Tennant. *Spy the Lie.* New York: St. Martin's, 2013.

———. *Get the Truth: Former* CIA *Officers Teach You How to Persuade Anyone to Tell All.* New York: St. Martin's, 2015.

Morgan Jones. *The Thinker's Toolkit: Fourteen Powerful Techniques in Problem Solving.* New York: Crown Business, 2009.

Louis M. Kaiser and Randolph H. Pherson. *Analytic Writing Guide.* Reston VA: Pherson Associates, 2013.

Sherman Kent. *Strategic Intelligence for American World Policy*. Princeton: Princeton University Press, 1966.

Mark M. Lowenthal and Robert M. Clark. *The Five Disciplines of Intelligence Collection*. Washington DC: CQ Press, 2015.

Edward Mickolus. *Briefing for the Boardroom and the Situation Room*. Washington DC: Daniel Morgan Academy Press, 2016.

Philip Mudd. *The HEAD Game: High-Efficiency Analytic Decision Making and the Art of Solving Complex Problems Quickly*. New York: Liveright, 2015.

John Nixon. *Debriefing the President: The Interrogation of Saddam Hussein*. New York: Random House/Blue Rider Press, 2016.

Bruce Pease. *Leading Intelligence Analysis*. Washington DC: CQ Press, 2019.

Katharine Hibbs Pherson and Randolph H. Pherson. *Critical Thinking for Strategic Intelligence*, 2nd ed. Washington DC: CQ Press, 2016.

Randolph H. Pherson. *Handbook of Analytic Tools and Techniques*, 5th ed. Reston VA: Pherson Associates, 2018.

Randolph H. Pherson and Alysa Gander. *Iraq's Aluminum Tubes Case Study*. Reston VA: Pherson Associates, 2015.

Randolph H. Pherson, Ryan Larson, Joseph Levine, and Zachary Wingate. *Uncharted Territory: Conflict, Competition, or Collaboration in the Arctic?* Reston VA: Pherson Associates, 2015.

Randolph H. Pherson, Laura C. Lenz, Kelly A. Pilka, and Darjan Vujica. *The Murder of JonBenet Ramsey Case Study*. Reston VA: Pherson Associates, 2015.

Randolph H. Pherson and John Pyrik. *Analyst's Guide to Indicators*. Reston VA: Pherson Associates, 2017.

Randolph H. Pherson, Walt Voskian, and Roy A. Sullivan, Jr. *Analytic Briefing Guide*. Reston VA: Pherson Associates, 2017.

David Priess. *The President's Book of Secrets: The Untold Story of Intelligence Briefings to America's Presidents from Kennedy to Obama*. New York: Public Affairs, 2016.

James E. Steiner. *Homeland Security Intelligence*. Washington DC: CQ Press, 2014.

Rebecca Vogel and Randolph H. Pherson. *Iraq WMD: Facts, Fiction and Yellowcake Case Study* Reston VA: Pherson Associates, 2015.

Walter Voskian and Randolph H. Pherson. *Analytic Production Guide for Managers of Intelligence and Business Analysis*. Reston VA: Pherson Associates, 2015.

Tim Walton. *Challenges in Intelligence Analysis: Lessons from 1300 BCE to the Present*. London: Cambridge University Press, 2010.

Intelligence Community

Douglas F. Garthoff. *Directors of Central Intelligence as Leaders of the U.S. Intelligence Community—1946-2005*. Washington DC: Center for the Study of Intelligence, 2005.

Mark M. Lowenthal. *Intelligence: From Secrets to Policy*, 7th ed. Washington DC: CQ Press, 2016.

U.S. Intelligence History

William F. Buckley, Jr. *Spytime: The Undoing of James Jesus Angleton*. San Diego: Harcourt, 2000.

Harold P. Ford. *CIA and the Vietnam Policymakers: Three Episodes 1962-1968*. Washington DC: Center for the Study of Intelligence, 1998.

Bill Harlow. *Rebuttal: The CIA Responds to the Senate Intelligence Committee's Study of Its Detention and Interrogation Program*. Annapolis: U.S. Naval Institute Press, 2015.

H. Keith Melton and Robert Wallace. *The Official CIA Manual of Trickery and Deception*. New York: HarperCollins, 2009.

Antonio Mendez and Jonna Hiestand Mendez, with Matt Baglio. *The Moscow Rules: The Secret CIA Tactics That Helped America Win the Cold War*. New York: PublicAffairs, 2019.

George J. A. O'Toole. *The Encyclopedia of American Intelligence and Espionage: From the Revolutionary War to the Present*. New York: Facts on File, 1988.

———. *Honorable Treachery: A History of U.S. Intelligence, Espionage, and Covert Action from the American Revolution to the CIA*. New York: Atlantic Monthly Press, 1991.

David Robarge. *Intelligence in the War for Independence*. Washington DC: Center for the Study of Intelligence, 1997.

P. K. Rose. *Black Dispatches: Black American Contributions to Union Intelligence during the Civil War*. Washington DC: Center for the Study of Intelligence, 1999.

Richard E. Schroeder. *The Foundation of the CIA: Harry Truman, the Missouri Gang, and the Origins of the Cold War*. Columbia: University of Missouri Press, 2017.

Britt Snider. *The Agency and the Hill: CIA's Relations with Congress, 1946-2004*. Washington DC: CIA Center for the Study of Intelligence, 2008.

Stansfield Turner. *Burn Before Reading: Presidents, CIA Directors, and Secret Intelligence*. New York: Hachette, 2005.

Michael Warner, ed. *The CIA under Harry Truman*. Washington DC: Center for the Study of Intelligence, 1994.

Michael Warner. *The Office of Strategic Services: America's First Intelligence Agency.* Washington DC: Center for the Study of Intelligence, 2000.

Intelligence Overview

Ruben Arcos and Randolph Pherson, eds. *Intelligence Communication in the Digital Era: Transforming Security, Defence, and Business.* Self-published, Palgrave Pivot, 2015.

Bruce D. Berkowitz and Allen E. Goodman. *Best Truth: Intelligence in the Information Age.* New Haven CT: Yale University Press, 2000.

J. Ransom Clark. *Intelligence and National Security: A Reference Handbook.* Westport CT: Praeger, 2007.

———. *American Covert Operations: A Guide to the Issues.* Westport CT: Praeger, 2015.

Ray Cline. *The CIA Under Reagan, Bush and Casey: The Evolution of the Agency from Roosevelt to Reagan.* Washington DC: Acropolis, 1981.

———. *The CIA Reality vs. Myth.* Washington DC: Acropolis, 1982.

Allen Dulles. *Great True Spy Stories.* New York: Harper and Row, 1968.

Howard P. Hart. *Intelligence Thoughts: Afghanistan and Iran.* Self-published, lulu.com, 2011.

Michael Hayden. *The Assault on Intelligence: American National Security in an Age of Lies.* New York: Penguin Random House, 2018.

Frederick P. Hitz. *The Great Game: The Myth and Reality of Espionage.* New York: Knopf, 2004.

Arthur S. Hulnick. *Fixing the Spy Machine.* Westport CT: Praeger, 1999.

———. *Keeping Us Safe: Secret Intelligence and Homeland Security.* Westport CT: Praeger, 2004.

Tony Jordan. *Spies, Assassins, and Such.* Self-published, Amazon Digital Services, 2017.

Hayden B. Peake. *The Reader's Guide to Intelligence Periodicals.* Washington DC: 1992.

Hayden B. Peake and Samuel Halpern. *In the Name of Intelligence: Essays in Honor of Walter Pforzheimer.* Washington DC: NIBC Press, 1994.

Walter Pforzheimer, ed. *Bibliography of Intelligence Literature.* Washington DC: Defense Intelligence College, 1985.

Robert W. Pringle. *Historical Dictionary of Russian and Soviet Intelligence.* Lanham MD: Rowman & Littlefield, 2015.

Fred W. Rustman. *CIA, Inc.: Espionage and the Craft of Business Intelligence.* Washington DC: Brassey's, 2002.

Jennifer Sims and Burton Gerber, eds. *Transforming Intelligence.* Washington DC: Georgetown University Press, 2005.

Thomas F. Troy. *Donovan and the* CIA: *A History of the Establishment of the Central Intelligence Agency.* Frederick MD: University Publications of America, 1981.

Counterintelligence

Tennent H. Bagley. *Spy Wars: Moles, Mysteries and Deadly Games.* New Haven CT: Yale University Press, 2007.

Sandra Grimes and Jeanne Vertefeuille. *Circle of Treason: A* CIA *Account of Traitor Aldrich Ames and the Men He Betrayed.* Annapolis: Naval Institute Press, 2012.

Brian Latell. *Castro's Secrets: Cuban Intelligence, the* CIA, *and the Assassination of John F. Kennedy.* New York: St. Martin's Griffin, 2013.

Edward Mickolus. *The Counterintelligence Chronology: Spying by and Against the United States from the 1700s through 2014.* Jefferson NC: McFarland, 2015.

James Olson. *To Catch a Spy: The Art of Counterintelligence.* Washington DC: Georgetown University, 2019.

Jennifer Sims and Burton Gerber. *Vaults, Mirrors, and Masks: Rediscovering U.S. Counterintelligence.* Washington DC: Georgetown University Press, 2008.

Bob Stephan. *Stalin's Secret War: Soviet Counterintelligence Against the Nazis, 1941–1945.* Lawrence: University Press of Kansas, 2003.

Michael J. Sulick. *Spying in America: Espionage from the Revolutionary War to the Dawn of the Cold War.* Washington DC: Georgetown University Press, 2012.

———. *American Spies: Espionage Against the United States from the Cold War to the Present.* Washington DC: Georgetown University Press, 2013.

Robert Wallace, H. Keith Melton, and Henry R. Schlesinger. *Spy Sites of New York City.* Boca Raton: The Foreign Excellent Trenchcoat Society, 2012, and Washington DC: Georgetown University Press, 2020.

Robert Wallace and H. Keith Melton, with Henry R. Schlesinger. *Spy Sites of Washington, D.C.* Washington DC: Georgetown University Press, 2017.

International Politics

William F. Buckley, Jr. *The Fall of the Berlin Wall.* New York: Wiley, 2004.

Charles G. Cogan. "The New American Intelligence: An Epiphany." Working Paper. Boston: Harvard University Project on the Changing Security Environment and American National Interests, 1993.

———. *Oldest Allies, Guarded Friends: The United States and France since 1940.* Westport CT: Praeger, 1994.

———. *Charles De Gaulle: A Brief Biography with Documents*. New York: Bedford/ St. Martin's, 1995.

———. *Forced to Choose: France, the Atlantic Alliance, and NATO—Then and Now*. Westport CT: Praeger, 1997.

———. *The Third Option: The Emancipation of European Defense, 1989-2000*. Westport CT: Praeger, 2001.

———. *French Negotiating Behavior: Dealing with La Grande Nation*. Washington DC: United States Institute of Peace, 2003.

L. Gray Cowan. *The Economic Development of Morocco*. Santa Monica: The Rand Corporation, 1958.

———. *Local Government in West Africa*. New York: Columbia University Press, 1958.

———. *British and French Education in Africa: A Critical Appraisal*. New York: Columbia University Institute of African Studies, 1964.

———. *Education and Nation-Building in Africa*. New York: Praeger, 1966.

———. *France and the Saar, 1680-1948*. Tucson: AMS Press, 1966.

———. *The Dilemmas of African Independence*. London: Walker, 1968.

———. *Recent Developments in Higher Education in the Francophone African Countries: Three Reports*. Washington DC: Overseas Liaison Committee, American Council on Education, 1969.

———. *The Cost of Learning: The Politics of Primary Education in Kenya*. New York: Teachers College Press, 1970.

———. *Black Africa: The Growing Pains of Independence*. New York: Foreign Policy Association, 1972.

———. *Divestment and Privatization of the Public Sector: Case Studies of Five Countries*. Washington DC, 1983.

———. *Privatization in the Developing World*. Westport CT: Greenwood Press, 1990.

Karl W. Deutsch and William J. Foltz, eds. *Nation Building in the Baltic States: Transforming Governance, Social Welfare, and Security in Northern Europe*. New York: Atherton Press, 1966.

———. *Nation Building in Comparative Contexts*. New York: Routledge, 2010.

Eric Freiwald. *The Building and Training of the 4th Armored Division, 1941-1944*. Ann Arbor MI: UMI Dissertation Services, 2002.

William J. Foltz. *From French West Africa to the Mali Federation*. New Haven CT: Yale University Press, 1965.

———. *Social Structures and Political Behavior of Senegalese Elites*. New Haven CT: Yale University Press, 1971.

William J. Foltz and Henry Bienen. *Arms and the African: Military Influences on Africa's International Relations.* New Haven CT: Yale University Press, 1985.

John B. E. Hittle. *Michael Collins and the Anglo-Irish War.* Washington DC: Potomac Books, 2011.

Michael T. Kindt, Jerrold Post, and Barry R. Schneider, eds. *Know Thy Enemy II: A Look at the World's Most Threatening Terrorist Networks and Criminal Gangs.* Maxwell Air Force Base AL: U.S. Air Force Counterproliferation Center, 2007.

Brian Latell. *After Fidel: The Inside Story of Castro's Regime and Cuba's Next Leader.* New York: Palgrave Macmillan, 2002.

———. *History Will Absolve Me: Fidel Castro: Life and Legacy.* New York: Rosetta Books, 2016.

Richard W. Mansbach. *Dominican Crisis, 1965.* Atlanta: Facts on File, 1971.

———. *Northern Ireland: Half a Century of Partition.* Atlanta: Facts on File, 1973.

———. *Web of World Politics: Non-State Actors in the Global System.* Upper Saddle River NJ: Prentice-Hall, 1976.

———. *In Search of Theory: A New Paradigm for Global Politics.* New York: Columbia University Press, 1981.

———. *The Global Puzzle: Issues and Actors in World Politics.* Boston: Houghton Mifflin College Division, 1994.

Richard W. Mansbach and Kirsten L. Taylor. *Introduction to Global Politics.* New York: Routledge, 2011.

Cord Meyer. *Peace or Anarchy.* Boston: Little, Brown, 1947.

Edward Mickolus. ITERATE: *International Terrorism: Attributes of Terrorist Events, Data Codebook.* Ann Arbor MI: Inter-University Consortium for Political and Social Research, 1976.

———. *Annotated Bibliography on International and Transnational Terrorism.* New York: Practicing Law Institute, 1979.

———. *The Literature of Terrorism: A Selectively Annotated Bibliography.* Westport CT: Greenwood Press, 1980.

———. *Transnational Terrorism: A Chronology of Events, 1968-1979.* Westport CT: Greenwood Press, 1980.

———. *International Terrorism: Attributes of Terrorist Events, 1968-1977,* ITERATE 2 *Data Codebook.* Ann Arbor MI: Inter-University Consortium for Political and Social Research, 1982.

———. *Terrorism, 1988–1991: A Chronology of Events and a Selectively Annotated Bibliography.* Westport CT: Greenwood Press, 1993.

———. *Terrorism, 2005-2007.* Westport CT: Greenwood Press, 2008.

———. *The Terrorist List: The Middle East.* Westport CT: Greenwood Press, 2009.

———. *Terrorism 2008-2012: A Worldwide Chronology*. Jefferson NC: McFarland, 2014.

———. *Terrorism 2013-2015: A Worldwide Chronology*. Jefferson NC: McFarland, 2016.

———. *Terrorism Worldwide 2016*. Jefferson NC: McFarland, 2018.

———. *Terrorism Worldwide 2017*. Jefferson NC: McFarland, 2018.

———. *Terrorism Worldwide 2018*. Jefferson NC: McFarland, 2019.

Edward Mickolus, with Joseph T. Brannan. *Coaching Winning Model United Nations Teams*. Washington DC: Potomac Books/University of Nebraska Press, 2013.

Edward Mickolus, with Peter Flemming. *Terrorism, 1980-1987: A Selectively Annotated Bibliography*. Westport CT: Greenwood Press, 1988.

Edward Mickolus, Todd Sandler, and Jean Murdock. *International Terrorism in the 1980s: A Chronology, Volume 1: 1980-1983*. Ames IA: Iowa State University Press, 1988.

———. *International Terrorism in the 1980s: A Chronology, Volume 2: 1984-1987*. Ames IA: Iowa State University Press, 1989.

Edward Mickolus, with Susan L. Simmons. *Terrorism, 1992-1995: A Chronology of Events and a Selectively Annotated Bibliography*. Westport CT: Greenwood Press, 1997.

———. *Terrorism, 1996-2001: A Chronology of Events and a Selectively Annotated Bibliography*. Westport CT: Greenwood Press, 2002.

———. *Terrorism, 2002-2004: A Chronology*. Westport CT: Greenwood Press, 2006.

———. *The Terrorist List: Asia, Pacific, and Sub-Saharan Africa*. Westport CT: Greenwood Press, 2010.

———. *The Terrorist List: Europe*. Westport CT: Greenwood Press, 2010.

———. *The Terrorist List: Eurasia*. Westport CT: Greenwood Press, 2010.

———. *The Terrorist List: North America*. Westport CT: Greenwood Press, 2010.

———. *The Fifty Worst Terrorist Attacks*. Santa Barbara CA: Praeger/ABC-Clio, 2014.

Philip Mudd. *Black Site: The CIA in the Post-9/11 World*. New York: Liveright, 2018.

———. *Takedown: Inside the Hunt for al Qaeda*. Philadelphia: University of Pennsylvania Press, 2013.

Emile Nakhleh. *A Necessary Engagement: Reinventing America's Relations with the Muslim World*. Princeton NJ: Princeton University Press, 2009.

Phillip F. Nelson, Ronald G. Kukal, Ernest A. Gallo, and Phillip F. Tourney. *Remember the Liberty!* Waterville OR: Trine Day, 2017.

James Earl Parker, Jr. *Codename Mule: Fighting the Secret War in Laos for the CIA*. Annapolis: Naval Institute Press, 1995.

———. *Covert Ops: The CIA's Secret War in Laos*. New York: St. Martin's, 1997.

———. *Last Man Out: A Personal Account of the Vietnam War*. New York: Ballantine, 2000.

———. *The Vietnam War Its Ownself*. Self-published, CreateSpace, 2015.

———. *Battle for Skyline Ridge: The CIA Secret War in Laos*. Havertown PA: Casemate, 2019.

Paul R. Pillar. *Terrorism and U.S. Foreign Policy*. Washington DC: Brookings Institution, 2003.

———. *Intelligence and U.S. Foreign Policy: Iraq, 9/11, and Misguided Reform*. New York: Columbia University Press, 2014.

———. *Why America Misunderstands the World: National Experience and Roots of Misperception*. New York: Columbia University Press, 2016.

Kenneth M. Pollack, Daniel L. Byman, Martin S. Indyk, Suzanne Maloney, Michael E. O'Hanlon, and Bruce Riedel. *Which Path to Persia: Options for a New American Strategy Toward Iran*. Washington DC: Brookings Institution Press, 2009.

Jerrold Post, ed. *Castro's Special Period in a Time of Peace: A Conference by the Cuban American National Foundation*. Cuban American National Foundation, 1990.

Jerrold Post. *Leaders and Their Followers in a Dangerous World: The Psychology of Political Behavior*. Ithaca: Cornell University Press, 2004.

———. *The Psychological Assessment of World Leaders: With Profiles of Saddam Hussein and Bill Clinton*. Ann Arbor: University of Michigan Press, 2005.

———. *The Mind of the Terrorist: The Psychology of Terrorism from the IRA to al-Qaeda*. New York: St. Martin's Griffin, 2008.

———. *Narcissism and Politics: Dreams of Glory*. New York: Cambridge University Press, 2014.

Bruce Riedel. *Truman. American Diplomacy and a Middle Eastern Peace Settlement, 1949–1952*. Providence RI: Brown University, 1975.

———. *The Search for Al Qaeda: Its Leadership, Ideology, and Future*. Washington DC: Brookings Institution Press, 2010.

———. *Deadly Embrace: Pakistan, America, and the Future of the Global Jihad*. Washington DC: Brookings Institution Press, 2011.

———. *Avoiding Armageddon: America, India, and Pakistan to the Brink and Back*. Washington DC: Brookings Institution Press, 2013.

———. *What We Won: America's Secret War in Afghanistan, 1979–89*. Washington DC: Brookings Institution Press, 2014.

———. *JFK's Forgotten Crisis Tibet, the* CIA, *and Sino-Indian War.* Washington DC: Brookings Institution Press, 2015.

———. *Kings and Presidents: Inside the Special Relationship Between Saudi Arabia and America Since FDR.* Washington DC: Brookings Institution Press, 2017.

Juan R. Rivera. *Survived Vietnam: The Story of How I Beat the Odds.* Self-published, 2014.

Robert S. Robins and Jerrold Post. *When Illness Strikes the Leader: The Dilemma of the Captive King.* New Haven CT: Yale University Press, 1993.

———. *Political Paranoia: The Psychopolitics of Hatred.* New Haven CT: Yale University Press, 1997.

Kermit Roosevelt. *Countercoup: The Struggle for the Control of Iran.* New York: McGraw-Hill, 1979.

Michael Scheuer. *Imperial Hubris: Why the West Is Losing the War on Terror.* Washington DC: Potomac Books, 2004.

———. *Through Our Enemies' Eyes: Osama bin Laden, Radical Islam, and the Future of America.* Washington DC: Potomac Books, 2007.

———. *Marching Toward Hell: America and Islam After Iraq.* New York: Free Press, 2009.

———. *Osama bin Laden.* New York: Oxford, 2012.

Barry Schneider and Jerrold Post, eds. *Know Thy Enemy: Profiles of Adversary Leaders and Their Strategic Cultures.* Collingdale PA: Diane Pub. Co., 2004.

Theodore Shackley. *The Third Option: An American View of Counterinsurgency Operations.* New York: McGraw-Hill, 1981.

Devin R. Springer, James L. Regens, and David Edger. *Islamic Radicalism and Global Jihad.* Washington DC: Georgetown University Press, 2009.

Mike Tucker and Charles "Sam" Faddis. *Operation Hotel California: The Clandestine War Inside Iraq.* Guilford CT: The Lyons Press, 2009.

Stansfield Turner. *Terrorism and Democracy.* New York: Houghton Mifflin, 1991.

———. *Caging the Genies: A Workable Solution for Nuclear, Chemical, And Biological Weapons.* Boulder CO: Westview Press, 1999.

Fiction

Scott M. Baker. *Yeitso.* Gilbert AZ: Blood Bound Books, 2014.

———. *Rotter World: Volume One of the Rotter World Saga.* Brentwood TN: Permuted Press, 2012.

———. *Rotter Nation: Volume Two of the Rotter World Saga.* Self-published, Schattenseite Books, 2015.

———. *Rotter Apocalypse: Volume Three of the Rotter World Saga.* Self-published, Schattenseite Books, 2015.

——. *The Vampire Hunters: Book One of The Vampire Hunters Trilogy*. Self-published, Schattenseite Books, 2016.

——. *Vampyrnomicon: Book Two of The Vampire Hunters Trilogy*. Self-published, Schattenseite Books, 2016.

——. *Dominion: Book Three of The Vampire Hunters Trilogy*. Self-published, Schattenseite Books, 2016.

Scott M. Baker (writing as Josh Matthews). *Dead Water*. Gilbert AZ: Keith Publications, 2010.

——. *Nazi Ghouls from Space*. Self-published, Schattenseite Books, 2014.

——. *Cruise of the Living Dead: A Zombie Anthology*. Self-published, Schattenseite Books, 2016.

——. *Hell Gate*. Spartanburg SC: Burning Willow Press, 2016.

——. *Incident on Ironstone Lane and Other Horror Stories*. Self-published, Schattenseite Books, 2016.

Lynn Baughey and Peter Earnest. *Harry Potter and the Art of Spying*. Minneapolis: Wise Ink Creative Publishing, 2017.

Chase Brandon. *The Cryptos Conundrum*. New York: Tor, 2012.

William F. Buckley, Jr. *Saving the Queen*. Nashville: Cumberland House Publishing, 1976.

——. *Stained Glass*. New York: Doubleday, 1978.

——. *Who's on First: A Blackford Oakes Mystery*. New York: Avon Books, 1980.

——. *Marco Polo, If You Can*. New York: Doubleday, 1981.

——. *The Story of Henri Tod*. New York: Doubleday, 1983.

——. *See You Later Alligator*. Nashville: Cumberland House, 1985.

——. *The Temptation of Wilfred Malachey*. New York: Workman, 1985.

——. *High Jinx: A Blackford Oakes Mystery*. Nashville: Cumberland House, 1986.

——. *Mongoose, R.I.P.* New York: Random House, 1987.

——. *Tucker's Last Stand*. New York: Random House, 1990.

——. *A Very Private Plot*. Nashville: Cumberland House, 1993.

——. *Brothers No More*. New York: Doubleday, 1995.

——. *Elvis in the Morning*. New York: Harcourt, 2001.

——. *Last Call for Blackford Oakes*. New York: Harcourt, 2005.

Karen Cleveland. *Need to Know*. New York: Ballantine Books, 2018.

Gene Coyle. *The Dream Merchant of Lisbon: The Game of Espionage*. Self-published, Xlibris, 2004.

——. *Diamonds and Deceit: The Search for the Missing Romanov Dynasty Jewels*. Self-published, AuthorHouse, 2011.

——. *No Game for Amateurs: The Search for a Japanese Mole on the Eve of WWII*. Self-published, AuthorHouse, 2014.

——. *A Spy's Lonely Path*. Self-published, AuthorHouse, 2014.

——. *Nazi Gold, Portuguese Wine, and a Lovely Russian Spy*. Self-published, AuthorHouse, 2016.

——. *If You Can't Trust a Fellow Spy: A Story of Friendships, Betrayal and Revenge*. Self-published, AuthorHouse, 2017.

Michael R. Davidson. *Harry's Rules*. Long Branch NJ: MRD Enterprises, 2013.

——. *Incubus*. Winter Park FL: Legacy Publisher, 2013.

——. *The Inquisitor and the Maiden: Caliphate, Volume 1*. Self-published, CreateSpace, 2013.

——. *The Incubus Vendetta*. Self-published, Amazon Digital Services, 2014.

——. *Krystal*. Long Branch NJ: MRD Enterprises, 2014.

——. *Retribution: Caliphate*. Self-published, Amazon Digital Services, 2014.

——. *Eye for an Eye*. Self-published, Amazon Digital Services, 2015.

——. *The Dove*. Long Branch NJ: MRD Enterprises, 2017.

Michael R. Davidson and Kseniya Kirillova. *In the Shadow of Mordor*. Long Branch NJ: MRD Enterprises, 2016.

——. *Successor*. Long Branch NJ: MRD Enterprises, 2017.

Blanche Dudley. *Siggy's Parade: Helping Kids with Disabilities Find Their Strengths*. Far Hills NJ: New Horizon Press, 2014.

——. *Siggy and the Bullies*. Self-published, Dog Ear Publishing, 2013.

——. *Bumble's Surprise: The Gift of Kindness*. Reston VA: Blanche Dudley Books, 2018.

Jim Farrell. *Brooklyn Boy*. Self-published, iUniverse, 2014.

——. *Kiss Me Kate, and Other Stories*. Self-published, iUniverse, 2014.

——. *The Extraordinary Banana Tree*. Self-published, iUniverse, 2015.

——. *The Barge of Curiosity*. Palm Coast FL: Michael Ray King Publishing, 2016.

——. *Mikey's Quest for Father God*. Self-published, iUniverse, 2016.

——. *The Committee and Other Stories*. Self-published, iUniverse, 2017.

Alex Finley. *Victor in the Rubble: A Satire*. Washington DC: Smiling Hippo Press, 2016.

Andre Le Gallo. *The Caliphate*. New York: Leisure Books, 2010.

——. *The Red Cell*. Mountain Lake Park MD: Mountain Lake Press, 2014.

——. *Satan's Spy*. Mountain Lake Park MD: Mountain Lake Press, 2015.

Bill Harlow. *Circle William*. New York: Scribner, 1999.

Susan Hasler. *Intelligence*. New York: Thomas Dunne Books, 2010.

——. *The Flat Bureaucrat*. Asheville NC: Bear Page Press, 2015.

——. *Project Halfsheep*. Asheville NC: Bear Page Press, 2015.

Courtney Hunt. *Forever a Bridesmaid*. Self-published, KDP, 2015.

——. *The Lost Art of Second Chances*. Self-published, Kindle Press, 2015.

———. *Once a Bridesmaid*. Self-published, KDP, 2015.

———. *Apple Cider*. Self-published, KDP, 2016.

———. *Berries and Cream Chai*. Self-published, KDP, 2016.

———. *Café au Lait*. Self-published, KDP, 2016.

———. *Cherry Blossom Cappuccino*. Self-published, KDP, 2016.

———. *Coconut Iced Coffee*. Self-published, KDP, 2016.

———. *Cup of Joy*. Self-published, KDP, 2016.

———. *Cupid's Kiss*. Self-published, KDP, 2016.

———. *Fireworks Frappe*. Self-published, KDP, 2016.

———. *Java Frost*. Self-published, KDP, 2016.

———. *Lucky Latte*. Self-published, KDP, 2016.

———. *Pumpkin Spice*. Self-published, KDP, 2016.

———. *Thanksgiving Dream*. Self-published, KDP, 2016.

———. *Always a Bridesmaid*. Self-published, IndieWrites, 2017.

———. *Billionaire Babes Club*. Self-published, IndieWrites, 2017.

———. *Kiss a Bridesmaid*. Self-published, IndieWrites, 2017.

———. *Tropical Tryst*. Self-published, Romance Collections, 2017.

E. Howard Hunt. *East of Farewell*. Uncommon Valor Press, 1942.

———. *Limit of Darkness*. New York: Random House, 1944.

———. *Stranger in Town*. New York: Random House, 1947.

———. *The Calculated Risk: A Play*. 1948.

———. *Maelstrom*. New York: Farrar, Straus, 1948.

———. *Bimini Run*. New York: Berkley Medallion, 1949.

———. *The Violent Ones*. Medford OR: Armchair Fiction and Music, 1950.

———. *The House on Q Street*. New York: Dell, 1959.

———. *Murder on Her Mind*. New York: Dell, 1960.

———. *Berlin Ending: A Novel of Discovery*. G. P. Putnam, 1973.

———. *Give Us This Day*. New York: Arlington House, 1973.

———. *The Judas Hour*. New York: Pinnacle, 1973.

———. *Lovers Are Losers*. New York: Pinnacle, 1973.

———. *Whisper Her Name*. New York: Pinnacle, 1973.

———. *From Cuba, With Love*. New York: Pinnacle, 1974.

———. *Washington Payoff*. New York: Pinnacle, 1975.

———. *Hargrave Deception*. New York: Stein and Day, 1979.

———. *Gaza Intercept*. New York: Stein and Day, 1981.

———. *Cinnamon Skin*. 1982.

———. *L'Inganno*. Milan: Arnoldo Mondadori, 1983.

———. *Cozumel*. New York: Stein and Day, 1985.

———. *Kremlin Conspiracy*. New York: Stein and Day, 1985.

———. *Guadalajara*. New York: Stein and Day, 1990.

——. *Murder in State*. New York: St. Martin's, 1990.

——. *Body Count*. New York: St. Martin's, 1992.

——. *Chinese Red*. New York: St. Martin's, 1992.

——. *Mazatlán: A Jack Novak Thriller*. Boston: Dutton, 1993.

——. *Ixtapa*. Boston: Dutton, 1994.

——. *Islamorada*. Boston: Dutton, 1995.

——. *Paris Edge*. New York: St. Martin's, 1995.

——. *Izmir*. Boston: Dutton, 1996.

——. *Dragon Teeth: A Novel*. Boston: Dutton, 1997.

——. *Guilty Knowledge*. New York: Forge Books, 1999.

——. *Sonora*. New York: Forge Books, 2000.

——. *Hotel Omicidi*. Italy: Polillo, 2011.

E. Howard Hunt (writing as John Baxter). *A Foreign Affair*. New York: Avon, 1954.

——. *A Gift for Gomala*. Philadelphia: Lippincott, 1962.

E. Howard Hunt (writing as Gordon Davis). *I Came to Kill*. New York: Pinnacle Books, 1953.

——. *House Dick*. New York: Hard Case Crime, 1961.

——. *Counterfeit Kill*. New York: Pinnacle Books, 1963.

——. *Ring Around Rosy*. Robbinsdale MN: Fawcett, 1964.

——. *Where Murder Waits*. Robbinsdale MN: Fawcett, 1965.

E. Howard Hunt (writing as Robert Dietrich). *The Cheat*. Boynton Beach FL: Pyramid Books, 1954.

——. *Be My Victim*. New York: Dell, 1956.

——. *Murder on the Rocks*. New York: Dell, 1957.

——. *My Body*. New York: Lancer Books, 1962.

E. Howard Hunt (writing as P. S. Donoghue). *Angel Eyes*. Dell, 1961.

——. *Dublin Affair*. Boston: Dutton, 1988.

——. *Sarkov Confession*. New York: Zebra, 1989.

——. *Evil Time*. Boston: Dutton, 1992.

E. Howard Hunt (writing as David St. John). *Return from Vorkula*. New York: Signet, 1965.

——. *Festival for Spies*. New York: Signet Books, 1966.

——. *On Hazardous Duty*. London: Frederick Muller, 1966.

——. *The Towers of Silence*. New York: Signet, 1966.

——. *One of Our Agents Is Missing*. New York: Signet Books, 1967.

——. *Mongol Mask*. New York: Dell, 1968.

——. *The Sorcerers*. Robbinsdale MN: Fawcett Crest, 1969.

——. *Diabolus*. New York: Weybright and Talley, 1971.

——. *The Coven*. Robbinsdale MN: Fawcett Crest, 1973.

Tony Jordan *Flying Blind*. Clinton TN: Spy Hill Publishing, 2016.

———. *The Train*. Clinton TN: Spy Hill Publishing, 2015.

Jack Kassinger. *Noble Cause*. Mesa AZ: Brighton Publishing, 2011.

———. *Storms Over Zimbabwe: The OPCON Finding*. Mesa AZ: Brighton Publishing, 2013.

———. *The Hunt for Njonjo*. Mesa AZ: Brighton Publishing, 2014.

———. *Pursued: The Emir of al-Shabaab*. Mesa AZ: Brighton Publishing, 2015.

Alma Katsu. *The Taker*. New York: Simon and Schuster/Gallery Books, 2011.

———. *The Reckoning*. New York: Simon and Schuster/Gallery Books, 2012.

———. *The Descent*. New York: Simon and Schuster/Gallery Books, 2014.

———. *The Hunger*. New York: GP Putnam, 2018.

Rob Kresge. *Murder for Greenhorns*. Albuquerque: ABQ Press, 2010.

———. *Painted Women*. Albuquerque: ABQ Press, 2011.

———. *Death's Icy Hand*. Albuquerque: ABQ Press, 2013.

———. *Saving Lincoln*. Albuquerque: ABQ Press, 2013.

———. *Warrior Hearts*. Albuquerque: ABQ Press, 2014.

———. *Unearthing the Bones*. Albuquerque: ABQ Press, 2015.

———. *Over the Brink*. Albuquerque: ABQ Press, 2016.

D. J. Mallmann. *Shibboleth*. Self-published, Amazon Digital Services, 2017.

Francine Mathews. *Death in the Off-Season: Nantucket Mystery #1*. New York: William Morrow, 1994.

———. *Death in Rough Water: Nantucket Mystery #2*. New York: William Morrow, 1995.

———. *Death in a Mood Indigo: Nantucket Mystery #3*. New York: Bantam, 1997.

———. *Death in a Cold Hard Light: Nantucket Mystery #4*. New York: Bantam, 1998.

———. *The Cutout*. New York: Bantam, 2001.

———. *The Secret Agent*. New York: Bantam, 2002.

———. *Blown*. New York: Bantam, 2005.

———. *The Alibi Club*. New York: Bantam, 2007.

———. *Jack 1939*. New York: Riverhead Books, 2012.

———. *Too Bad to Die*. New York: Riverhead Books, 2016.

Francine Mathews (writing as Stephanie Barron). *Jane and the Unpleasantness at Scargrave Manor: Being the First Jane Austen Mystery*. New York: Crimeline, 1996.

———. *Jane and the Man of the Cloth*. New York: Crimeline, 1997.

———. *Jane and the Wandering Eye*. New York: Bantam, 1998.

———. *Jane and the Genius of the Place*. New York: Bantam, 1999.

———. *Jane and the Stillroom Maid*. New York: Bantam, 2000.

———. *Jane and the Prisoner of Wool House*. New York: Bantam, 2001.

———. *Jane and the Ghosts of Netley*. New York: Bantam, 2004.

——. *Jane and His Lordship's Legacy.* New York: Bantam, 2005.

——. *Jane and the Barque of Frailty.* New York: Bantam, 2006.

——. *A Flaw in the Blood.* New York: Bantam, 2008.

——. *The White Garden: A Novel of Virginia Woolf.* New York: Random House, 2009.

——. *Jane and the Madness of Lord Byron.* New York: Bantam, 2010.

——. *Jane and the Canterbury Tale.* New York: Bantam, 2011.

——. *Jane and the Twelve Days of Christmas.* New York: Soho Crime, 2014.

——. *Jane and the Waterloo Map.* New York: Soho Crime, 2016.

Jason Matthews. *Red Sparrow.* New York: Scribner, 2013.

——. *Palace of Treason.* New York: Scribner, 2015.

——. *The Kremlin's Candidate.* New York: Scribner, 2017.

George J. A. O'Toole. *An Agent on the Other Side.* Philadelphia: D. McKay, 1973.

——. *Poor Richard's Game.* New York: Delacorte, 1982.

George J. A. O'Toole and Nicholas Cosgrove. *The Cosgrove Report: Being a Private Inquiry of a Pinkerton Detective into the Death of President Lincoln.* New York: Grove Press, 2009.

Valerie Plame and Sarah Lovett. *Blowback.* New York: Berkley, 2013.

——. *Burned.* New York: Blue Rider Press, 2014.

Bill Rapp. *Angel in Black.* Pittsburgh: Pemberton Mysteries, 2006.

——. *A Pale Rain.* Pittsburgh: Pemberton Mysteries, 2007.

——. *Berlin Breakdown.* Pittsburgh: Pero Thrillers, 2008.

——. *Burning Altars.* Pittsburgh: Pemberton Mysteries, 2012.

——. *Tears of Innocence.* Waterville ME: Five Star, 2015.

——. *The Hapsburg Variation.* Kenmore WA: Coffeetown Press, 2017.

William F. Rogers and David Lindgren. *The Penitent Spy.* Conneaut Lake PA: Page Publishing, 2018.

Fred W. Rustman. *The Case Officer.* Double Tap Books, 2012.

——. *Plausible Denial.* Double Tap Books, 2013.

——. *False Flag.* Double Tap Books, 2017.

——. *False Flag.* Washington DC: Regnery, 2018.

Marshall S. Thomas. *The Black March.* St. Petersburg FL: Booklocker, 2006.

——. *Secret of the Legion.* Self-published, Amazon Digital Services, 2009.

——. *March of the Legion.* Self-published, Amazon Digital Services, 2011.

——. *Prophet of ConFree.* St. Petersburg FL: Booklocker, 2012.

——. *Cross of the Legion.* Self-published, CreateSpace, 2013.

——. *Curse of the Legion.* Self-published, Amazon Digital Services, 2013.

——. *Prophet and the Blood March.* St. Petersburg FL: Booklocker, 2013.

——. *Slave of the Legion.* Self-published, CreateSpace, 2013.

——. *Soldier of the Legion.* Self-published, CreateSpace, 2013.

——. *Prophet and the Eye*. St. Petersburg FL: Booklocker, 2014.

——. *Prophet and the Creature from Eternity*. St. Petersburg FL: Booklocker, 2016.

——. *Prophet and Deadman's Dogs*. St. Petersburg FL: Booklocker, 2017.

——. *Prophet and the Fields of Glory*. St. Petersburg FL: Booklocker, 2017.

James Tiptree, Jr. *Ten Thousand Light-Years From Home*. New York: Ace Books, 1973.

——. *Star Songs of an Old Primate*. New York: Del Rey, 1978.

——. *Up Walls of the World*. New York: Berkley, 1979.

——. *Warm Worlds and Otherwise*. New York: Ballantine Books, 1979.

——. *Out of Everywhere and Other Extraordinary Visions*. New York: Ballantine Del Rey, 1981.

——. *Brightness Falls from the Air*. New York: Tor Books, 1985.

——. *Byte Beautiful: Eight Science Fiction Stories*. New York: Doubleday, 1985.

——. *The Starry Rift*. New York: Tor Books, 1986.

——. *Tales of the Quintana Roo*. Sauk City WI: Arkham House, 1986.

——. *Crown of Stars*. New York: Tor Books, 1988.

——. *The Color of Neanderthal Eyes*. New York: Tor, 1989.

——. *The Girl Who Was Plugged In*. New York: Tor, 1989.

——. *Houston, Houston, Do You Read?* New York: Doubleday, 1996.

——. *Meet Me at Infinity*. New York: Tor Books, 2001.

——. *Her Smoke Rose Up Forever*. San Francisco: Tachyon Publications, 2004.

T. L. Williams. *Cooper's Revenge*. Ponte Vedra FL: First Coast Publishers, 2013.

——. *Unit 400: The Assassins*. Ponte Vedra FL: First Coast Publishers, 2014.

——. *Zero Day: China's Cyber Wars*. Ponte Vedra FL: First Coast Publishers, 2017.

——. *The Last Caliph*. Ponte Vedra FL: First Coast Publishers, 2019.

Miscellaneous Topics

Merrily C. Baird. *Symbols of Japan: Thematic Motifs in Art and Design*. New York: Rizzoli, 2001.

William F. Buckley, Jr. *God and Man at Yale: The Superstitions of 'Academic Freedom.'* Washington DC: Gateway Editions, 1951.

——. *Up from Liberalism*. Eastford CT: Martino Fine Books, 1959.

——. *The Committee and Its Critics: A Calm Review of the House Committee on Un-American Activities*. New York: G. P. Putnam's Sons, 1962.

——. *Rumbles Left and Right: A Book About Troublesome People and Ideas*. New York: Putnam, 1963.

——. *The Unmaking of a Mayor*. New York: Encounter Books, 1965.

———. *The Jeweler's Eye: A Book of Irresistible Political Reflections.* New York: Putnam, 1968.

———, ed. *American Conservative Thought in the Twentieth Century: Did You Ever See a Dream Walking?* Indianapolis: Bobbs-Merrill, 1970.

———. *The Governor Listeth: A Book of Inspired Political Revelations.* New York, Putnam, 1970.

———. *Quotations from Chairman Bill.* Arlington House, 1970.

———. *Cruising Speed: A Documentary.* New York: Bantam Books, 1971.

———. *Inveighing We Will Go.* New York: Putnam, 1972.

———. *Four Reforms: A Guide for the Seventies.* New York: G. P. Putnam's Son, 1973.

———. *United Nations Journal: A Delegate's Odyssey.* New York: Putnam, 1974.

———. *Execution Eve and Other Contemporary Ballads.* New York: Putnam, 1975.

———. *Airborne: A Sentimental Journey.* New York: Simon and Schuster, 1978.

———. *A Hymnal: The Controversial Arts.* New York: G. P. Putnam's Son, 1978.

———. *Atlantic High: A Celebration.* New York: Doubleday, 1982.

———. *Overdrive: A Personal Documentary.* New York: Doubleday, 1983.

———. *Right Reason.* New York: Doubleday, 1985.

———. *Racing through Paradise: A Pacific Passage.* Boston: Little, Brown, 1987.

———. *On the Firing Line: The Public Life of Our Public Figures.* New York: Random House, 1989.

———. *Gratitude: Reflections on What We Owe to Our Country.* New York: Random House, 1990.

———. *In Search of Anti-Semitism.* New York: Continuum International Publishing Group, 1992.

———. *Windfall: The End of the Affair.* New York: Random House, 1992.

———. *Happy Days Were Here Again: Reflections of a Libertarian Journalist.* New York: Random House, 1993.

———. *McCarthy and His Enemies.* Washington DC: Regnery, 1995.

———. *Nearer, My God: An Autobiography of Faith.* Eugene OR: Harvest, 1997.

———. *The Lexicon: A Cornucopia of Wonderful Words for the Inquisitive Word Lover.* Eugene OR: Harvest, 1998.

———. *The Right Word.* New York: Harcourt Brace, 1998.

———. *Nuremburg: The Reckoning.* Boston: Houghton Mifflin Harcourt, 2002.

———. *Getting It Right.* Washington DC: Regnery, 2004.

———. *Miles Gone By: A Literary Biography.* Washington DC: Regnery, 2004.

———. *Cancel Your Own Goddamn Subscription: Notes and Asides from National Review.* New York: Basic Books, 2007.

———. *Flying High: Remembering Barry Goldwater.* New York: Basic Books, 2008.

———. *The Reagan I Knew.* New York: Basic Books, 2008.

———. *Let Us Talk of Many Things: The Collected Speeches.* New York: Basic Books, 2008.

———. *A Torch Kept Lit: Great Lives of the Twentieth Century.* New York: Crown Forum, 2016.

Terry Joseph Busch. *Effective Corporate Decision Making: Six Steps to Success.* Self-published, CreateSpace, 2014.

———. *Effective Organizational Leadership: The Essential Ingredients.* Self-published, CreateSpace, 2014.

———. *Habits That Define Poor Managers: A Rogues Gallery.* Self-published, CreateSpace, 2014.

———. *An Executive Trail Guide: Thinking and Behaving for Success.* Self-published, CreateSpace, 2015.

———. *What the Best Managers Know and Do.* Self-published, CreateSpace and Ingram Spark, 2018.

Scott Clevenger and Sheri Zollinger. *Better Living Through Bad Movies.* Self-published, iUniverse, 2006.

Charles G. Cogan. *La Republique de Dieu.* Paris: Jacob Duvernet, 2008.

———. *Digital Is the New Third Age: Adventures in the Blogosphere.* Self-published, Amazon, 2014.

———. *The Good, the Bad, and the Far-Out: Poems and Aphorisms, Part 1.* Self-published, Amazon, 2015.

Charles G. Cogan and Lynn Hunt. *Charles De Gaulle and French Revolution and Human Rights.* New York: Bedford/St. Martin's, 1995.

L. Gray Cowan. *History of the East Asian Institute, Columbia University, 1948–1953.* New York: Columbia University Press, 1954.

———. *A History of the School of International Affairs and Associated Area Institutes, Columbia University.* New York: Columbia University Press, 1954.

———. *A Summary History of the African Studies Association, 1957–1969.* New Brunswick NJ: Rutgers University African Studies Association, 1970.

———. *The Role of the State University in Developing Land Use Planning Information Systems in New York State.* Graduate School of Public Affairs, State University of New York at Albany, 1975.

L. Gray Cowan and Gerold T. Robinson. *History of the Russian Institute, Columbia University 1946–1953.* New York: Columbia University Press, 1954.

Charles Dalgleish. *Recon Marine: An Account of Beirut and Grenada.* Detroit: Grenadier Books, 1995.

Walter Gavenda and Michael Shoemaker. *A Guide to Haunted West Virginia.* Leesburg VA: Gauley Mount Press, 2013.

Pamela Chase Hain. *A Confederate Chronicle: The Life of a Civil War Survivor: Shades of Blue and Gray*. University of Missouri Press, 2005.

——. *Murder in the State Capitol: The Biography of Lieutenant Colonel Robert Augustus Alston, 1832–1879*. Macon GA: Mercer University Press, 2013.

Peter Murray Hain. *Frank K. Hain and the Manhattan Railway Company: The Elevated Railway*. Jefferson NC: McFarland, 2011.

Jason R. Hanson. *Spy Secrets That Can Save Your Life*. New York: TarcherPerigee, 2015.

Courtney Hunt. *The History of Iraq*. Westport CT: Greenwood Press, 2005.

Lois Kelly and Carmen Medina. *Rebels at Work: A Handbook for Leading Change from Within*. Sebastopol CA: O'Reilly Media, 2014.

Victor Marchetti. *The Rope-Dancer*. New York: Grosset Dunlap, 1971.

Edward Mickolus. *Food with Thought: The Wit and Wisdom of Chinese Fortune Cookies*. Self-published, CreateSpace, 2015.

——. *His Words*. Ponte Vedra FL: Wandering Woods Publishing, 2018.

Edward Mickolus, with Joe Rendon. *Take My Weight, Please: Fitness From Head to Toe, the Cowboy Joe Way*. Ponte Vedra FL: Wandering Woods, 2019.

Paul Newman, Robert Wallace and Jack Bick. *Nine From the Ninth*. New York: Writers Club Press, 2002.

George J. A. O'Toole. *The Assassination Tapes*. New York: Zebra Books, 1977.

——. *The Spanish War: An American Epic 1898*. New York: W. W. Norton, 1986.

Lester Paldy. *For an Okay Free Woman: Poems*. Stony Brook NY: Night Heron Press, 1992.

——. *Transits: Poems*. Stony Brook NY: Night Heron Press, 2013.

Nicholas Reynolds. *Writer, Sailor, Soldier, Spy: Ernest Hemingway's Secret Adventures, 1935–1961*. New York: William Morrow, 2017.

David Priess. *How to Get Rid of a President: History's Guide to Removing Unpopular, Unable, or Unfit Chief Executives*. New York: PublicAffairs, 2018.

Juan R. Rivera. *Double Six, Dominoes for the Entire Family!* London: Double Six Publishing, 2009.

John Robert Shaw and Sara Janet Weitzer Shaw. *The New Horizon Ladder Dictionary of the English Language*. New York: Signet, 1970.

——. *Adventures of the Mad Monk Ji Gong: The Drunken Wisdom of China's Famous Chan Buddhist Monk*. North Clarendon VT: Tuttle Publishing, 2014.

——. *Selected Memoirs of a U.S. Marine*. Ashland OR: Hellgate Press, 2017.

Sara Janet Weitzer Shaw. *Spies, Black Ties, and Mango Pies: Stories and Recipes from CIA Families All Over the World*. Washington DC: CIA Family Advisory Board, 1997.

——. *The Jatakas: Birth Stories of the Bodhisatta*. Penguin Classics, 2007.

Opponents, Disaffected, and Defectors

Sam Adams. *War of Numbers: An Intelligence Memoir.* Hanover NH: Steerforth, 1994.

Philip Agee. *Inside the Company: CIA Diary.* New York: Stonehill, 1975.

———. *On the Run.* London: Bloomsbury, 1987.

Joseph Hickman and John Kiriakou. *The Convenient Terrorist: Abu Zubaydah and the Weird Wonderland of America's Secret Wars.* New York: Skyhorse, 2017.

Edwin Lee Howard. *Safe House: The Memoirs of the Only CIA Spy to Seek Asylum in Russia.* Bethesda MD: National Press Books, 1995.

Ishmael Jones. *The Human Factor: Inside the CIA's Dysfunctional Intelligence Culture.* New York: Encounter Broadsides, 2010.

John Kiriakou. *Doing Time Like a Spy: How the CIA Taught Me to Survive and Thrive in Prison.* Los Angeles: Rare Bird Books, 2017.

John Kiriakou, with Michael Ruby. *The Reluctant Spy: My Secret Life in the War on Terror.* New York: Bantam Books, 2010.

Victor Marchetti and John D. Marks. *The CIA and the Cult of Intelligence.* New York: Alfred A. Knopf, 1974.

Melvin A. Goodman. *Failure of Intelligence: The Decline and Fall of the CIA.* Lanham MD: Rowman and Littlefield, 2008.

———. *National Insecurity: The Cost of American Militarism.* San Francisco: City Lights Publishers, 2013.

———. *Whistleblower at the CIA: An Insider's Account of the Politics of Intelligence.* San Francisco: City Lights Publishers, 2017.

Frank Snepp. *Decent Interval* New York: Random House, 1977.

———. *Irreparable Harm: A Firsthand Account of How One Agent Took on The CIA in an Epic Battle Over Free Speech.* Lawrence: University Press of Kansas, 1999.

CONTRIBUTORS

Elizabeth Arens reports that in addition to working, she is a very busy single mom of her ten-year-old daughter. Ms. Arens currently works part-time as an editor. In her free time, she enjoys traveling with her teenage daughter and doing volunteer work.

Chip Beck, at age sixty-nine, is still traveling the world, having returned from a two-month, nine-country tour of European countries from Iceland to Italy and now preparing for another trip to South Africa. After leaving the CIA, he served as a special investigator for POW/MIAs and as director of community affairs in Baghdad (2003–5); worked in Africa as director of the State Department's peacekeeper training program (ACOTA); spent a year in Haiti as a police advisory group manager; earned a doctorate; worked as a security manager in remote parts of East Africa; traveled five times to Cuba, linking American and Cuban political cartoonists to improve bilateral relations and understanding; and learned the basics of Arabic, Swahili, and Creole while advancing his French and Spanish. He is a working artist, writer, photographer, and gentleman farmer in rural Virginia.

Robert Blansfield still takes continuing education classes that keep him in touch with what is happening in the business world as well as security practices.

Kimberley Condas received her bachelor's degree from DePauw University and her master's degree in library science from Indiana University. She retired after a thirty-two-year career with the

CIA, where she held positions in the CIA Library, the National Reconnaissance Office historical declassification program, and the CIA's information review and release program.

Gene Coyle is an adjunct professor at IU Bloomington, teaching courses on the history of espionage. He is the author of the spy novel *The Dream Merchant of Lisbon*. He met his wife, Jan (Waters), at IU, and they were married in Beck Chapel. The couple lives in Bloomington, Indiana.

Hector J. Escobar III received a bachelor's degree in history from the University of Texas at El Paso (UTEP) and a master's degree in intelligence and national security studies at UTEP's National Security Studies Institute, an Intelligence Community-Center of Academic Excellence–accredited institution. Hector also lived in Jordan, where he attended the University of Jordan in Amman and focused on the Arabic language and Middle Eastern studies while working at a nonprofit organization. He is currently working on another master's degree, in defense and strategic studies, at UTEP.

Susan Hasler lives with her husband, her cats, and her parrots in the Shenandoah Valley of Virginia. She has written three novels about the CIA: *Intelligence*, *Project HALFSHEEP*, and *The Flat Bureaucrat*. She appeared in the 2013 documentary *Manhunt: The Search for Bin Laden*.

Elinor Houghton Kelly worked in the Directorate of Operations during her thirty-year career at the CIA. She spent the first twenty years running and managing operations. Then she built a unique government start-up to research and implement innovative targeting methodologies for clandestine operations. Since her retirement, she and her husband have been enjoying their historic house in a charming North Carolina river town, where she manages family real estate. She recently began to write about the CIA, drawing especially upon her experience and expertise in driving innovation in a government bureaucracy.

Jeffrey J. Johnson left the CIA in 2015 but has continued his career in public service. He has worked as a management consultant on change management and reengineering initiatives for several federal agencies, including the Department of Veterans Affairs, the State Department, and the National Archives.

Robert Kresge, a Vietnam veteran, worked for thirty years as an analyst for the CIA on subjects ranging from North Korea to international terrorism and from gray market arms dealers to stopping the genocide in Bosnia. He spent his career writing nonfiction—analyses of intelligence gathered by human collectors or by sophisticated electronic means or photographic evidence of developments of interest to a wide range of consumers and the White House. His thirty years in the active U.S. Army and Army Reserve, where he eventually became a colonel, were concerned mainly with counterintelligence—the identification of foreign intelligence efforts to penetrate U.S. security to learn what we knew or to feed disinformation that would hamper our ability to respond to real threats. In retirement Kresge has published an award-winning Civil War thriller and seven historical mysteries set in Wyoming during the late 1800s.

Ed Mickolus teaches at the University of North Florida and is the Deborah M. Hixon Professor of Intelligence Tradecraft at the Daniel Morgan Graduate School in Washington DC, where he served as acting chair of the department of intelligence studies. (Deborah Hixon gave her life for her country in the 1983 bombing of the U.S. embassy in Beirut; her name is in the Book of Honor in front of the Memorial Wall at CIA headquarters.) He is the author of thirty-six books on intelligence, terrorism, teaching, humor, and other topics.

Douglas Naquin, who was chief of FBIS's Engineering Services Group during the CIA's Prince effort (1997–99), went on to become the CIA's deputy chief information officer. He helped manage the consolidation of agency IT resources and components as the

CIA developed—and realized—its first enterprise IT strategy. In 2002 Naquin returned to FBIS as director and led its evolution into what became the DNI Open Source Center in 2005, following recommendations from post-9/11 studies on improving the intelligence community's use of open sources. Since retiring from CIA in 2012, Naquin has divided his time between independent consulting and coaching and competing in CrossFit. As a consultant, Naquin advises clients on strategic planning and implementation—specifically, how to position themselves for new business opportunities or expand their current scope through disciplined processes. His clients have included U.S. government and private sector organizations with global operations. Naquin coaches CrossFit in Ashburn, Virginia, and finished in the top thirty worldwide (out of eleven hundred) in his age group in the 2015 CrossFit Games.

Mary O'Sullivan is a retired CIA senior executive with extensive experience in strategic planning, operational budgeting, project management, human resource development, instructional design and development, and intelligence analysis and production. Her career included several leadership positions, culminating with deputy director of the Office of Policy Support, with responsibility for senior review of The President's Daily Brief. She has received major awards for the establishment of CIA University and the Directorate of Intelligence's first online daily intelligence publication. Upon retirement she worked for Pherson Associates for ten years, teaching analytic thinking and writing at various intelligence community institutions and in the public and private sector. She received the instructor of the year award from the International Association for Intelligence Education in 2016.

Lester Paldy is distinguished service professor of technology and society and distinguished service professor emeritus of pathology at Stony Brook University, State University of New York.

James Pasqualini, after retiring, moved back to Slippery Rock, Pennsylvania, to a little town north of Pittsburgh. He enjoys spending time with his five children and seven grandchildren. He also enjoys watching the Pittsburgh sports teams, golfing, and hunting. He has been with his girlfriend, Karen, for the last few years. He contracts for the U.S. government part-time and consults with a few government contractors as a subject matter expert. Working part-time allows him to spend more time with his son, Joe, as he slowly recovers from his serious injuries. He misses the people at the agency and working to support its important mission, but retirement has been working out very well for him.

After three overseas tours with the agency, **Doug Patteson** moved to Philadelphia, where he earned a master's degree in business administration from the Wharton School. After grad school he moved to New England, where he has yet to get used to the winters. He has worked in both technology and manufacturing firms and currently serves as the chief financial officer of a manufacturing firm with a global footprint. He writes on intelligence topics and serves as both an actor in and advisor to film and TV productions. Doug and his wife Susan have four children and live on a gentleman's farm in the foothills of the White Mountains.

After one day in retirement, **Robert Phillipson** obtained a position handling international licensing for Cluett, Peabody and Company, a large U.S. corporation that owned Arrow shirts and Arrow clothing as well as Gold Toe socks. The skills developed during his agency time were easily translated into the realm of private industry. Dealing with agencies in other countries for licensing issues was the same as dealing with a foreign liaison service. Working a joint venture deal in China was the same as recruiting good people and putting them together for a project. There is life after the agency.

Paul R. Pillar taught full-time at Georgetown University for several years after retiring from government service. He continues to write and speak on international affairs as a nonresident senior fellow of Georgetown's Center for Security Studies and as a contributing editor for *The National Interest*.

The 9/11 terrorist attacks prompted **Michael Douglas Smith** to join former colleagues and volunteer to return to government service. He served as a contract instructor for seven years in the Career Analyst Program, the training program for new DI analysts, at the CIA's Sherman Kent School for Intelligence Analysis. He had a great time re-engaging with officers whom he had known and worked with in the past, and meeting and teaching new analysts eager to help prevent another 9/11 attack. In 2012 he moved to the Office of the Director of National Intelligence to help develop and deliver a course on intelligence integration. He left that job in 2014, took a short break from working, and returned to Washington in 2016 to head the master's degree program at the Daniel Morgan Graduate School of National Security in the District of Columbia. In 2017 he returned to the intelligence community, where he continues to work as a contractor.

Janet M. Stiegler retired in 2014 in the Wilmington, North Carolina, area. For the next three years she facilitated training in the Washington DC area. She currently volunteers with the Cape Fear Literacy Council, which provides adult literacy and English as a Second Language training for those seeking to improve their reading, writing, and language skills. She is also active in the Cape Fear River Watch, whose mission is to protect and improve the water quality of the Lower Cape Fear River Basin through education, advocacy, and action. When not in the Wilmington area, she and her husband are working through a bucket list of foreign and domestic travel destinations.

Kathy Thomas is still running around the intelligence community as a contractor, which she will likely continue to do for the next twenty years or so. She recently earned a master's degree in communication management from the University of Southern California. She continues to pursue her lifelong passion of stalking eighties rockers and spends what little free time is left with her husband and rescued dogs. Kathy has been the lead singer in a few local bands, but she wants Jon Bon Jovi and Bret Michaels to know that she's available to sing back-up for them anytime.

Peggy Tuten and her husband retired to coastal Georgia. She worked for six years as a part-time reference librarian at Florida State College–Jacksonville. They enjoy seeing the world and spend several months a year traveling in the United States and Canada in their Airstream trailer, along with their two cats. Peggy is active in local community groups, enjoys researching her family roots, and is a volunteer genealogist with her local chapter of the Daughters of the American Revolution.

Terrence L. Williams is a retired CIA operations officer (1980–2009). He now lives in Ponte Vedra Beach, Florida, with his wife, Carol. Writing under the pen name T. L. Williams, he has authored four award-winning novels: *Cooper's Revenge, Unit 400: The Assassins, Zero Day: China's Cyber Wars,* and *The Last Caliph.*

INDEX

AAT. *See* Office of Advanced Analytic Tools
ABM Branch, 48, 52
ACDA. *See* Arms Control and Disarmament Agency
Achille Lauro, hijacking of, 66
Aden, attack in, 154
Advanced Research Projects Agency, 55
Afghanistan, 126, 143, 155, 156, 234, 255; operations in, 233; Soviet invasion of, 17; training camps in, 154
Africa Division, 126, 252
The Agency (television show), 161, 163
Ahern, Chuck, 48
Air Florida Flight 90, crash of, 75
Air Force Combat Command, 112
Air Force One, 4
Alcott, Louisa May, 46
Alec Station, 257
Allen, Charlie, 67–68
al-Qaeda, 256, 258, 260; *Cole* attack and, 154; experts on, 156
Amal, 127
American International School, 238
Ames, Aldrich, 62, 150
Ames, Rick, 120
analysis, 13, 21, 46–56, 77, 83, 140, 144, 181–85, 193, 238, 264; intelligence, 172; leadership, 76; political, 137; reinforcing, 214; research, 82; Soviet, 267; targeting, 275
Analysis Production Staff (APS), 6, 8
analysts, 133, 149, 153, 156, 173, 190; all-source, 171; CTC, 154; DI, 21, 79, 80,

84; economic, 148; media, 171; senior, 153, 155; Soviet, 149
Analytic Culture in the US Intelligence Community (Johnston and Konya), 178–79
Andaman Sea, crash in, 34
Anderson, Gary, 257
Anderson, Terry, 127
Andrews Air Force Base, 40
anthrax, 202, 203
antiballistic missile systems, 48–52
Antideficiency Act, 245, 246
application programs, 181, 195, 247, 248
APS. *See* Analysis Production Staff
Armed Forces Radio, 30
Armitage, Rich, 40
arms control, 76, 137, 138, 203, 206, 207, 208, 219
Arms Control and Disarmament Agency (ACDA), 207, 208
Arms-for-Hostages crowd, 127
Army Security Agency, 63
Army Special Forces, 113, 124, 252, 258
artillery, 201, 237
Arzamas-16 nuclear weapons laboratory, 216
Asia-Pacific Economic Cooperation, 12
assets, 128, 132, 133, 170, 171, 273; commitment to, 131, 133; field, 124; high-value, 169; recruiting, 117; termination of, 131
assignments, 185; interesting/challenging, 184; nontraditional, 227; overseas, 227; substantive, 175–76

321